The Enlargement of the European Union

The Enlargement of the European Union

A Guide for the Entrepreneur

Ine Lejeune

and

Walter Van Denberghe

PricewaterhouseCoopers

John Wiley & Sons, Ltd

Other Wiley Editorial Offices

John Wiley & Sons Inc., 111 River Street, Hoboken, NJ 07030, USA

Jossey-Bass, 989 Market Street, San Francisco, CA 94103-1741, USA

Wiley-VCH Verlag GmbH, Boschstr. 12, D-69469 Weinheim, Germany

John Wiley & Sons Australia Ltd, 33 Park Road, Milton, Queensland 4064, Australia

John Wiley & Sons (Asia) Pte Ltd, 2 Clementi Loop #02-01, Jin Xing Distripark, Singapore 129809

John Wiley & Sons Canada Ltd, 22 Worcester Road, Etobicoke, Ontario, Canada M9W 1L1

Wiley also publishes its books in a variety of electronic formats. Some content that appears in print may not
be available in electronic books.

Library of Congress Cataloging-in-Publication Data

Lejeune, Ine.
     The enlargement of the European Union : a guide for the entrepreneur /
Ine Lejeune and Walter van Denberghe.
          p.   cm.
     Includes bibliographical references and index.
     ISBN 0-470-02253-1 (cloth : alk. paper)
     1. European Union–Europe, Eastern.   2. European Union countries–Commercial policy.   3. Europe,
Eastern–Commercial policy.   4. Industrial policy–European Union countries.   5. Industrial policy–Europe,
Eastern.   6. Labor policy–European Union countries.   7. Labor policy–Europe, Eastern.
8. Corporations–Taxation–European Union countries.   9. Corporations–Taxation–Europe, Eastern.
10. Entrepreneurship–Europe, Eastern.   11. Infrastructure (Economics)–Europe, Eastern.
12. Telecommunication–Europe, Eastern.   13. Information technology–Europe, Eastern.   14. Environmental
policy–Europe, Eastern.   15. Europe–Economic integration.   16. European federation.   I. Denberghe,
Walter van.   II. Title.
     HC240.25.E852L45 2004
     337.1′42–dc22   2004007052

British Library Cataloguing in Publication Data

A catalogue record for this book is available from the British Library

ISBN 0-470-02253-1

Typeset in 10/12pt. Stone Sans by TechBooks, New Delhi, India
Printed and bound in Great Britain by MPG Books Ltd, Bodmin, Cornwall
This book is printed on acid-free paper responsibly manufactured from sustainable forestry
in which at least two trees are planted for each one used for paper production.

Contents

Foreword

1 May 2004 is set to be a historic date. With the accession of 10 new member states the European Union will become the largest historical, social-political realisation achieved without a clash of arms.

What Europe is about to undertake is to extend the stability and prosperity we have achieved in the current EU into the future and over to our neighbours.

Enlargement will bring not only political stability but also economic benefits for the EU as a whole. Of course, the impact at first will not be dramatic. The 10 central European economies account for only 5% of EU GDP. But they do represent significant long-term business opportunities and with a prospect of 4.5% yearly growth over the next decade, the 10 acceding countries provide one of the soundest investment climates in emerging markets. Moreover an impressive integration of the candidate countries into the EU economy has already taken place. Nearly two-thirds of the candidate countries' trade is with the EU. Today, Foreign Direct Investment (FDI) from the EU constitutes over 20% of total investment in the candidate countries.

Business plays an important role in the European Union. The European Union as a market is characterised by the freedom of movement of goods, services, workers and capital, where businesses can compete on fair terms.

Economic barriers between the various national member states are still being broken down. Nearly every day, the European institutions launch initiatives promoting the internal market and measures to enhance the competitiveness of European enterprises.

It is essential that business people know these rules, which shape today's economic reality in the 15 "old" member states and will be shaping tomorrow's reality in a Europe of 25 member states. Beyond any doubt, those who have thoroughly acquainted themselves with Europe's rules and their application in the accession member states will gain a head start. This applies equally to companies in the current and the new member states.

The enlargement process does not end with accession. It is the task of Europe, national governments, professional associations and providers of corporate services to inform business appropriately and show them the way. This book must be seen as a contribution by its authors to this beneficial awareness exercise.

Karel Van Miert
Former Vice-President of the European Commission

Preface

On 1 May 2004, the biggest ever enlargement of the European Union becomes fact. At that moment, 10 countries will join the European Union and we will see the largest single market in the world (66% larger than the United States of America). The candidate member states are Cyprus, the Czech Republic, Estonia, Hungary, Latvia, Lithuania, Malta, Poland, Slovakia and Slovenia. In Athens, on 16 April 2003, these 10 candidate member states and the 15 existing member states signed the Treaty of Accession.

In order to be able to join up to the European Union, the candidate member states have had to meet a series of political and economic criteria. In addition, they have to have incorporated the European Union's *"acquis communautaire"* (over 90,000 pages of rules) into their national legislation and be in a position to implement it.

Firms that do business with or in the candidate member states – or that are planning to do so in the near future – have to prepare today. For that, they have to know the economic framework and expansive impact of the accession.

The fact that the Commission will still be investing 49,520 million euros in transitional assistance in the new member states until 2006 goes to show the importance of what is happening. At the same time, accession is planned for 2007 for Rumania and Bulgaria. And Turkey and Croatia also want to join.

With this in view, we have written this book together with the multi-disciplinary EU Accession Team at PricewaterhouseCoopers. Among the topics we deal with are competition and distribution rules, intellectual property, HR aspects, corporation tax, VAT, customs duties and environmental legislation, together with the impact of enlargement on IT systems and processes within businesses.

We have tried to set out a framework, not only for senior management but also for others with responsibilities within a company.

For this reason, we also mention as many sources as possible, so that the reader him or herself can further delve into the wide-ranging material available. However, the information in this publication is presented in a summarised form and is intended to provide general guidance only. Specific professional advice should be obtained before any action is taken.

In writing this book, we have, more than ever, come to the realisation that enlargement of the European Union is a not-to-be-missed opportunity for every company that does or wants to do business with or in any of the countries concerned. With an expanded market of 450 million people, there can be no dubiety there.

Ine Lejeune
Partner, PricewaterhouseCoopers
Indirect Tax Leader Europe

A view from the accession countries.

From our experience over the last two years of raising the issue of accession with a wide range of businesses, the impact of the introduction of 90,000 pages of legislation can be summarised as falling within two areas: "back office compliance" and "business strategic". It is these two areas within a business that need to be managed from an accession perspective. Whether they are short-term or long-term and are managed independently or together depends upon the structure and culture of a company and their approach to market.

The majority of companies have concentrated on the back office compliance issues pre-accession, however it has not proved to be easy. Legislation is still developing and in some instances the legislation will not exist much before 1 May 2004. A real lack of public information, poor economic trading conditions and the fact that accession may cost business money are not welcoming messages.

There will be both direct and indirect costs that will result from new tax situations on 1 May 2004. Some may be managed and avoided but mostly there will be a bottom line cost resulting from the introduction of EU legislation.

One of the major issues facing businesses is the fact that although EU might technically have harmonized law, there are still areas in which a country can choose to interpret individual legislation. A lot of EU law is an interpretation based on interpretation – that is the reality facing us.

The introduction of EU law is making companies rethink or bring forward their business strategies for particular countries and the region as a whole. Furthermore, the opportunities that "harmonized" legislation brings of having more consistency across the enlarged EU is allowing some companies to simplify their structures and benefit from the opportunities that accession brings. One recent impact of this is that a number of major players in the region have started discussing shared service centres as a way of managing effectively and efficiently the administrative obligations that they will have to manage post accession.

Another area of rationalisation and opportunity in the legislation is within the logistics area. If we look at what happened after the single market was created in 1993 in Western Europe we can expect the same trends to materialise in terms of regional distribution hubs, and fewer in country warehouses enabling shorter supply chains.

One of the other major comments we hear from people involved in management of the accession process is how they are suddenly faced with a new issue, which nobody has considered before. However, as was mentioned, the introduction of legislation has been done before in 1993 when the single market was created and also when the last batch of accession countries joined. There does not have to be a reinventing of the wheel, as most issues are not new.

In conclusion, a range of legislative issues will be late in being passed into law but we do know the boundaries of this legislation. As a result, a company can know what to expect and what it has to do to manage its business to prepare for EU accession.

Antoni Turczynowicz
Partner, PricewaterhouseCoopers
EU accession team

Monika Diekert
Partner, PricewaterhouseCoopers
EU accession team

Acknowledgements

We would like to give special thanks to Erik Stessens, Indirect Tax Manager, Fabricom GTI, Ruud Tusveld, Tax Partner, Customs Group, Netherlands and all our PricewaterhouseCoopers colleagues in the accession countries.

1 Enlargement of the European Union: Facts and Figures

1.1 Enlargement – an historic opportunity[1]*

It all began with the Treaties of Paris in 1951 setting up the European Coal and Steel Community (ECSC). This was then described as an historic event, for, less than ten years after the Second World War, the Coal and Steel Community brought together six countries: Germany, France, Italy, the Netherlands, Belgium and Luxembourg.

The negotiations regarding Coal and Steel were at that time difficult. It was a big step to give up national autonomy for the behoof of a new international institution. More than half a century later, the interests of Europe are fact. Every businessperson, whether within or outside the European Union (EU), has to take account of European decisions, regulations and directives.

At present, European legislation runs to some 90 000 pages. And the volume is growing every day. In other words, there is not a single subject on which Europe does not have, or does not want to have, something meaningful to say.

For a businessperson trading locally, regionally or globally this is a good thing. Europe does not just ensure transparency and comparability in respect of products and services offered within the Union. It also offers legal certainty that the free movement of goods,[2] labour,[3] services[4] and capital[5] and the freedom of establishment[6] apply to all.

On 1 May 2004, the European Union will expand by 10 new member states. The European Union will then have 25 member states. The following states will be acceding to the Union: Cyprus, the Czech Republic, Estonia, Hungary, Latvia, Lithuania, Malta, Poland, Slovakia and Slovenia.

On 1 May 2004, the territory of the European Union will expand by around 20%.[7] Its population will grow by 75 million.[8] The gross national product of the Internal Market will increase by 6%.[9] That day will see a consumer market (in terms of individuals) that is 66% larger than that of the United States of America.[10]

---

* You will find the source references for this chapter on page 14.

In the meantime, a further three countries are itching also to become members of the European Union: Romania, Bulgaria and Turkey. It is expected that the first two countries will join on 1 January 2007.[11] For Turkey, accession negotiations have not yet officially started.

For Europe, 1 May 2004 is an important milestone. It is a challenge brimful of opportunities. In the history of the world, the enlargement will be described as one of the most important events achieved without conflict.

1.2 How did the European Union come about? An historical overview[12]

Table 1.1 Historical time-line.

Date	Historical event
18 April 1951	The Six (Belgium, France, Germany, Italy, Luxembourg and the Netherlands) sign the Treaty of Paris setting up the European Coal and Steel Community (ECSC).[13]
25 March 1957	The Treaties setting up the European Economic Community (EEC) and the European Atomic Energy Community (Euratom) are signed by the Six (Belgium, France, Germany, Italy, Luxembourg and the Netherlands) in Rome. Henceforth they are called the "Treaties of Rome".[14]
3 February 1958	Signing of the Treaty establishing the Benelux (BElgium, the NEtherlands and LUXembourg) in The Hague.[15]
1 July 1967	The Treaty amalgamating the executives of the European Communities (ECSC, EEC, Euratom) comes into force. Henceforth there is just one Commission and one Council, which nonetheless continue to act according to the rules applying to each of the Communities.[16]
1 January 1973	Denmark, Ireland and the United Kingdom accede to the European Communities.[17]
7–10 June 1979	First direct elections to the European Parliament.[18]
1 January 1981	Greece becomes the tenth member state of the European Community.[19]
1 January 1986	Spain and Portugal join the European Community.[20]
9 November 1989	The fall of the Berlin Wall and the German Democratic Republic opens its borders.[21]
7 February 1992	The Treaty on European Union is signed in Maastricht by the foreign and finance ministers of the member states.[22]
1 January 1995	Austria, Finland and Sweden become members of the European Union.[23]

Table 1.1 (*cont.*)

Date	Historical event
16 April 2003	In Athens, Greece, the accession treaty is signed amongst the EU and Cyprus, the Czech Republic, Estonia, Hungary, Latvia, Lithuania Malta, Poland, Slovakia and Slovenia.[24]
1 May 2004	Europe with 25 member states

Nine of the ten accession countries had to organise referenda before they could ratify the treaty in accordance with their internal constitutions. The results of these referenda have overall been positive:

Malta on 8 March 2003

Slovenia on 23 March 2003

Hungary on 12 April 2003

Lithuania on 10–11 May 2003

Slovakia on 16–17 May 2003

Poland on 7–8 June 2003

Czech Republic on 13–14 June 2003

Estonia on 14 September 2003

Latvia on 20 September 2003

Cyprus ratified the accession treaty on 14 July 2003 in accordance with its internal constitutional procedures.

The ratification process in the present 15 member states still no longer require to be done via a referendum. It is under the internal constitutional procedures in each country that enlargement has been ratified. For the states of notification, we refer to http://db.consilium.eu.int/accords/en/details.asp?id=2003007&lang=en.

1.3 How has the enlargement process gone since the fall of the Wall?

The accession process began with the fall of the Berlin Wall in 1989. The European Union was fast to remove trade-restrictive measures against the former Czechoslovakia, Estonia, Hungary, Latvia, Lithuania, Poland and Slovenia.

At the same time, the EU introduced the Phare programme[26] in order to provide financial support to these countries in re-forming their economies into free-market economies.

In the nineties, association agreements were signed with these former Eastern Bloc countries. These formed the legal basis for the bilateral relations between the European Union and the relevant countries. Such association agreements had already been signed with Malta in 1963 and Cyprus in 1972.

1.4   What were the criteria for accession? The council meeting in Copenhagen on 21–22 June 1993

At the European Council Meeting in Copenhagen in 1993, the then member states decided that these associated countries should be able to accede to the European Union as full members. The question thereafter was "when?"

According to the Copenhagen summit, this would only be possible once the candidate member states had fulfilled the right political, economic and legislative conditions.

The *political criterion* was to ensure that the candidate member states had stable political institutions. They had to guarantee democracy, the rule of law, human rights and respect for the protection of minorities.

The *economic criterion* guaranteed that the candidate member states' economies were functioning properly. The economies had to be able to withstand the pressure of competition and free market forces.

The *legislative criterion* or the "acquis communautaire" is the obligation on each candidate member state to endorse the objectives of the Union in political, economic and monetary areas. For this, the candidate member states have to adjust their official structures, thus transposing European rules into their national laws.

At the Helsinki Council Meeting on 10 December 1999, the final decision to enlarge was taken, the Council thereby following the European Commission's recommendation that the 10 candidate member states should be allowed to accede.

The European Commission has the task of following up and reporting.[27] For this, it set up a communication strategy, which resulted in the publication of reports at regular intervals. Six months before accession by the new member states, the European Commission will draw up a monitoring report on the progress made by each accession country in implementing the "acquis communautaire".[28]

Table 1.2 Progress Reporting.

Date	Progress reports
4 November 1998	First Progress Report for each of the candidate countries of Central and Eastern Europe + Cyprus[29]
13 October 1999	Second Progress Report for each of the candidate countries of Central and Eastern Europe, Cyprus + Malta[30]
8 November 2000	Strategy paper on enlargement and reporting for each of the candidate countries[31]
13 November 2001	Strategy Paper and Report of the European Commission on the progress towards accession by each of the candidate countries[32]
9 October 2002	Strategy Paper and Report of the European Commission on the progress towards accession by each of the candidate countries[33]
5 November 2003	Final report by the Commission to the European Council[34]

1.5 What was the enlargement strategy?

The enlargement strategy for all of the candidate member states encompassed:

- the European conference: this was a multilateral forum for discussing joint issues such as foreign affairs, security, justice and internal affairs, regional cooperation and economic matters. The first one was held in London on 12 March 1998. The subsequent ones were in Luxembourg (6 October 1998) and Brussels (19 July 1999);

- the accession process: this embraces an extensive pre-accession strategy, accession negotiations, a screening of the EU legislation to be implemented and a control procedure.

For the accession negotiations and adoption of the "acquis communautaire" by a candidate member state, the issues were divided into 31 chapters.

1.6 What are the 31 chapters of the "acquis communautaire"?[35]

The "acquis communautaire" encompasses 31 chapters. This is existing Community law as interpreted by the European Court of Justice. It contains rules to promote the European internal market and rules on the various policy areas that the EU is active in.

Table 1.3   31 chapters.

Chapter 1 – Free movement of goods	Chapter 17 – Science and research
Chapter 2 – Free movement of persons	Chapter 18 – Education and training
Chapter 3 – Free movement of services	Chapter 19 – Telecommunications
Chapter 4 – Free movement of capital	Chapter 20 – Culture and audio-visual policy
Chapter 5 – Company law	Chapter 21 – Regional policy
Chapter 6 – Competition	Chapter 22 – Environment
Chapter 7 – Agriculture	Chapter 23 – Consumers and health protection
Chapter 8 – Fisheries	Chapter 24 – Justice and home affairs
Chapter 9 – Transport	Chapter 25 – Customs union
Chapter 10 – Taxation	Chapter 26 – External relations
Chapter 11 – Economic and Monetary Union	Chapter 27 – Common foreign and security policy
Chapter 12 – Statistics	Chapter 28 – Financial control
Chapter 13 – Social policy and employment	Chapter 29 – Financial and budgetary provisions
Chapter 14 – Energy	Chapter 30 – Institutions
Chapter 15 – Industrial policy	Chapter 31 – Other
Chapter 16 – Small and medium-sized enterprises	

1.7   Were transitional measures granted prior to accession?

For each chapter, each candidate member state has been dealt with separately. In each case, it was examined whether transitional measures or temporary derogations to the general EU rules were necessary. This was intended to avoid the introduction of certain legislation distorting the market. The starting point in this was that, upon accession on 1 May 2004, the "acquis communautaire" should come into effect in each member state.

Most derogations were granted in the chapters on agriculture, the environment and taxation.

An extensive overview of the transitional measures can be found in the "Report on the results of the negotiations on the accession of the Ten to the European Union".[36]

1.8   Are the candidate member states prepared?[37]

Although the present member states of the European Union are not themselves always the best pupils in the class, many of them are wondering to what extent the candidate countries are prepared for this extensive transposition.

Since 1998, the European Commission has been running a "twinning" programme with Phare funding (see Table 1.4). It helps the candidate countries

Table 1.4 Twinning projects with Phare funding 1998–2002.[38]

Sector	Agriculture (including veterinary and phyto-sanitary projects)	Environment	Government funding (including taxation, customs, internal market and others)	Justice and home affairs	Social policy	Regional development and preparation of structural funds	Others	Total
Cyprus	—	—	1	1	—	—	—	2
Czech Republic	7	10	16	19	15	6	7	80
Estonia	8	4	8	8	7	3	1	39
Hungary	12	11	12	10	8	4	3	60
Latvia	4	3	13	7	2	4	3	36
Lithuania	7	2	12	12	6	3	8	50
Malta	4	1	1	1	1	1	1	10
Poland	27	12	36	16	12	19	12	134
Slovakia	9	9	10	17	6	3	7	61
Slovenia	9	1	11	8	3	5	3	40

in implementing the "acquis communautaire" into their national laws. In the process, they can rely on the support of experts from the European Union. They help in setting up new structures and setting out their personnel and policy strategy. The Commission makes an annual sum of 3.3 billion euros available for this.

The European Commission reports regularly to the European Council on progress in implementation of the "acquis communautaire". Although, according to the Commission's report of 5 November 2003,[39] implementation of the "acquis communautaire" is already at an advanced stage, nevertheless a number of member states are being urged to work faster.

1.9 What economic changes will there be in the accession countries?

The economic changes that the accession countries have already undergone will not come to a stop on 1 May 2004. Two types of reform will be necessary in this regard.[40]

Economic changes in order to continue to meet the Copenhagen criteria:

— the last remnants of a central planned economy have to disappear completely so that each country becomes a fully fledged market economy. This means that a business can freely set its own prices, that it can do business in a market without barriers to access, that there are no longer limits on foreign trade and that capital can move freely;

— once market hurdles are removed, businesses are to be able to access the free market. They also have to withstand the pressure that that brings;

— the legislative, administrative and institutional framework has to be further adapted in order to create a stable business climate;

— macro-economic stability is necessary, supported by a political consensus in order to realise predictability;

— the government must ensure that it has the necessary infrastructure, that the supply of human capital is present in sufficient numbers and diversified in order to meet demand.

A second category of reforms is intended to give a response to the challenges of demographic evolution, the environment and the development of the information society. These are medium-term challenges, but they are also important for the accession countries.

1.10 Through which programmes is the European Union investing in the candidate member states?[41]

In order to avoid a two-speed Europe, the EU has already invested a great deal in projects for eliminating the candidate countries' backlog.

The financial means that Europe is able to make available for this have been set at 1.24%[42] of its GDP. For 2003, the budget amounts to 99 686 million euros in committed funding and 97 503 million euros in paid funding.[43] The amount can only be altered by unanimous decision.

Europe has prepared the accession process strategically and will be supporting it with various programmes until 2006 (see Table 1.5).[44]

— PHARE (Poland Hungary Aid for the Reconstruction of the Economy – the programme was later extended to the other candidate member states) – Council Regulation 3906/89. This subsidises the development of infrastructure and institutions.

   The budget is fixed annually by the Commission according to population and per capita GDP, taking account of work already carried out (see Table 1.6).

— ISPA (Instrument for Structural policies for Pre-Accession) – Council Regulation 1267/99. The fund supports modifications to the environment and transport infrastructure.

Table 1.5 Expenditure by the European Union for the period 1990–2006 (millions of euros).[a][45]

	1990–1999	2000–2003	2004–2006
Pre- and post-accession (for the 10 countries acceding in 2004)			
Phare	6767.16	6 240.00	4 680.00
ISPA		4 160.00	3 120.00
SAPARD		2 800.00	
Subtotal	6767.16	13 200.00	9 360.00
Post-accession (for the 10 countries acceding in 2004)			
Agriculture			9 577.00
Structural operations			25 567.00
Home affairs			3 343.00
Administration			1 673.00
Subtotal			40 160.00
Total European Union expenditure on enlargement			
Total	6767.16	13 200.00	49 520.00
Average annual total	676.72	3 300.00	16 506.67
As a percentage of EU GNP in 1999	0.08	0.16	0.62
Average annual total as a percentage of the 1999 EU GNP	0.008	0.04	0.21

[a] 2000 prices for pre- and 1999 prices for post-accession. 1990–1999 expenditure based on actual payments, post-1999 based on commitments.

Table 1.6 Phare support.

Countries	Allocations for 2001 (millions of euros)
Bulgaria	153.30
Czech Republic	84.4
Estonia	24.40
Hungary	108.8
Latvia	34.0
Lithuania	67.6
Poland	451.0
Romania	298.7
Slovakia	75.5
Slovenia	28.3
Total	1326.0

Table 1.7 ISPA support.

Countries	Band
Bulgaria	8–12%
Czech Republic	5.5–8%
Estonia	2–3.5%
Hungary	7–10%
Latvia	3.5–5.5%
Lithuania	4–6%
Poland	30–37%
Romania	20–26%
Slovakia	3.5–5.5%
Slovenia	1–2%

The total ISPA budget amounts to 1080 million euros a year (at 2001 prices). Funds are allocated according to population numbers, GDP (in purchasing power parities) and territorial area. This means that, in 2000, Poland received the largest grant, 355 million euros, and Slovenia the smallest, with 16 million euros. Funding is usually limited to 75% of the costs and exceptionally can rise to 85%. Co-financing is therefore necessary, which is possible with help from the European Investment Bank, the European Bank for Regional Development, the Nordic Investment Bank, the Nordic Environmental Fund and national funding. Grants are given within a band (see Table 1.7).

—   SAPARD (Special Accession Programme for Agricultural and Rural Development) – Council Regulation 1268/99: for development in the area of agriculture.

The funding for SAPARD amounts to 540 million euros per annum (at 2001 prices). Grants are made on the basis of agricultural area, agricultural population and per capita GDP. Poland receives 160 million euros a year from this source and Slovenia 6.3 million euros (see Table 1.8).

—   Structure and Cohesion Fund: provides the necessary funding for less developed areas in Europe. After accession, the Structure and Cohesion Fund will take over many of the "obligations" of the pre-accession programmes.[46]

—   Not only European institutions but also other, international financial institutions lend support via a variety of programmes.

—   Investments in a Trans-European Transport Network.

In the accession countries, approximately 20 000 km of roads, 30 000 km of railways, ports and airports need to be built or modernised. Only

Table 1.8   SAPARD support.

Countries	Annual grant (at 1999 prices) (millions of euros)
Bulgaria	52.124
Czech Republic	22.063
Estonia	12.137
Hungary	38.054
Latvia	21.848
Lithuania	29.829
Poland	168.683
Romania	150.636
Slovakia	18.289
Slovenia	6.337

then can the criteria for a Trans-European network within the Union be met. The investments for this are estimated at 100 billion euros. This is an enormous sum in comparison with the GDPs of the accession countries.[47]

For 2010,[48] a number of projects are already on the agenda:

- elimination of the bottlenecks on the Rhine–Main–Danube;

- mixed railway line Lyons–Trieste/Koper–Ljubljana–Budapest;

- mixed railway line Greek/Bulgarian border–Sofia–Budapest–Vienna–Prague;

- mixed railway line Paris–Strasbourg–Vienna–Bratislava;

- motorway Greek/Bulgarian border–Sofia–Nadlac (Budapest)/(Constanta);

- motorway Gdansk–Katowiçe–Brno/Zilina–Vienna.

1.11   What is the European Union's budget after accession?

The future contributions of these member states were set in March 1999 at the Berlin European Council meeting.[49,50]

Although it is only on 1 May 2004 that the new member states accede to the Union, in 2003 they have already been able to apply for funding from the European Union for a full year. In addition, they only have to pay two-thirds of their contributions. They thereby save approximately 1.7 billion euros.

For 2004, this means that they will receive approximately one-and-a-half times more net than they will have received in preparation for accession in 2003. In 2005, this will be three times more and in 2006 three-and-a-half times more.[51]

1.12   The European Union of 25 in figures[52]

On 1 May 2004, there will be 28% more inhabitants in the European Union. They will provide a rise of 4.4% in the European GDP. This is roughly the GDP of the Netherlands.

However, the new member states will not immediately be amongst the wealthiest of member states. What is more, it is expected that the income gap between countries and regions will double. Thus, a great deal more money will be needed in order to make up this lost ground. Today the average per capita GDP in the accession countries is in purchasing power terms approximately 35% of the European Union average.

Table 1.9   Core figure.

Member state	Area in km²	Average population 2001 (000)	Unemployment 2002 (%)	Inflation 2002 (%)	Per capita GDP in purchasing power parities	Exports of goods and services as percentage of GDP 2001	Currency 2001	Capital city 2001
Austria	83 858	8 130	4.1	1.7	25 740	52	euro	Vienna
Belgium	30 538	10 825	7.3	1.6	25 260	85	euro	Brussels
Cyprus	9 251	762 (e)	5.3	2.8	17 180	47 (p)	Cypriot pound	Nicosia
Czech Republic	78 866	10 283	7.3	1.4	13 700	71	Czech crown	Prague
Denmark	43 094	5 359	4.5	2.4	26 660	45	Danish crown	Copenhagen
Estonia	45 227	1 364	9.1	3.6	9 240	91	Estonian crown	Tallín
Finland	338 150	5 188	9.1	2.0	24 170	40	euro	Helsinki
France	549 087	59 191	8.7	1.9 (p)	23 870	28	euro	Paris
Germany	357 031	82 350	8.2	1.3	24 000	35	euro	Berlin
Greece	131 957	10 582	10.3	3.9	15 020	23	euro	Athens
Hungary	93 030	10 188 (e)	5.6	5.2	12 250	61	forint	Budapest
Ireland	70 295	3 854 (e)	4.4	4.7	27 360	98	euro	Dublin
Italy	301 338	57 075	9.1	2.6 (p)	23 860	28	euro	Rome
Latvia	64 589	2 365	12.9	2.0	7 750	45	lat	Riga
Lithuania	65 300	3 478	13.1	0.4	8 960	50	litas	Vilnius
Luxembourg	2 586	442	2.4	2.1	44 160 (p)	152	euro	Luxembourg
Malta	316	393	7.5	2.2 (l)	:	88	Maltese pound	Valletta
Netherlands	35 518	16 046	2.6	2.9 (p)	26 670	65	euro	Amsterdam
Poland	312 685	38 638	20.0	1.9	9 410	28	złoty	Warsaw
Portugal	91 916	10 299	5.0	3.7	16 059	31	euro	Lisbon
Slovenia	20 273	1 992	6.0	7.5	16 210	60	tolar	Ljubljana
Slovakia	49 035	5 397	19.4	3.3	11 200	73	Slovak crown	Bratislava
Spain	505 124	40 266	11.4	3.6	19 510	30	euro	Madrid
Sweden	449 974	8 896	4.9	2.0	23 700	45	Swedish crown	Stockholm
United Kingdom	244 101	60 004 (e)	5.1	1.3	23 530 (p)	27	Pound sterling	London

(e) = estimate; (p) = provisional; : = unavailable; (l) Malta's retail price index.

1.13　Are entrepreneurs investing in the new member states?

The most important investors in Estonia, Latvia, Poland, Slovenia, Slovakia and the Czech Republic (at 1999 prices, stocks in million EUR)[53] are:

— the United Kingdom (28%);

— the Netherlands (18%);

— the Belgian–Luxembourg Economic Union (16%);

— Germany (13%);

— France (12%).

It is noteworthy that six out of the 15 member states are making 87% of the foreign investments.

In relation to their large investment share in the Union, Belgium, Luxembourg and the United Kingdom have not really invested in the accession countries.

The Netherlands, Germany, The United States, Austria and France, on the other hand, account for 65% of foreign investment in the accession countries.

Table 1.10　Largest foreign investments (in million euros).

		Estonia	Latvia	Poland	Slovenia	Slovakia	Czech Republic
Austria	Total	26	22	830	1117	538	1772
	Production	23	7	189	236	110	384
	Textile and timber activities	3	2	19	97	7	85
	Trade and repairs	4	1	86	181	169	488
	Financial intermediation	0	2	432	411	106	477
Belgium and	Total	7	1	572	19	42	984
Luxembourg	Production	2	—	285	8	10	235
	Financial intermediation	—	—	144	0	0	655
Germany	Total	58	152	5366	342	560	4651
	Production	19	52	2357	283	403	2574
	Foodstuffs	0	4	524	46	30	119
	Vehicles and other transport equipment	0	1	310	7	79	663
	Metal and mechanical products	2	5	211	55	112	259
	Trade and repairs	9	28	967	49	82	726
	Financial intermediation	5	35	1190	1	55	428
The Netherlands	Total	38	48	6637	105	388	5368
	Production	3	1	2747	49	239	1463
	Foodstuffs	3	1	1124	29	130	676
	Petroleum, chemical, rubber and plastic products	0	0	324	7	40	157

(cont.)

Table 1.10 (*cont.*)

		Estonia	Latvia	Poland	Slovenia	Slovakia	Czech Republic
	Metal and mechanical products	—	0	289	3	27	81
	Trade and repairs	3	18	1729	35	23	1051
	Transport and communications	22	26	740	1	24	1878
	Financial intermediation	1	0	716	0	80	339
Sweden	Total	996	168	654	3	17	257
	Production	135	44	291	1	11	165
	Textile and timber activities	35	26	99	0	8	101
	Transport and communications	262	35	80	1	0	0
	Financial intermediation	529	31	64	0	0	0
United Kingdom	Total	67	107	939	103	277	885
	Production	17	20	465	45	161	175
	Petroleum, chemical, rubber and plastic products	0	5	207	23	0	0
	Mechanical products	0	0	34	0	158	114
	Trade and repairs	26	35	242	29	107	116
United States of America	Total	97	191	2934	106	278	1176
	Production	34	25	1050	25	149	543
	Petroleum, chemical, rubber and plastic products	11	1	401	9	45	239
	Vehicles and other transport equipment	0	0	433	1	0	144
	Trade and repairs	10	98	773	4	55	61
	Financial intermediation	4	27	—	36	44	317

Source references for Chapter 1

1. http://europa.eu.int/comm/enlargement/arguments.
2. Title I to the Consolidated Version of the Treaty Establishing The European Community, Official Journal C325, 24 December 2002, http://europa.eu.int/eur-lex/en/treaties/.
3. Title III, Chapter 1 (arts. 39 et seq.) to the Consolidated Version of the Treaty Establishing The European Community, Official Journal C325, 24 December 2002, http://europa.eu.int/eur-lex/en/treaties/.
4. Title III, Chapter 3 (arts. 49 et seq.) to the Consolidated Version of the Treaty Establishing The European Community, Official Journal C325, 24 December 2002, http://europa.eu.int/eur-lex/en/treaties/.
5. Title III, Chapter 4 (arts. 56 et seq.) to the Consolidated Version of the Treaty Establishing The European Community, Official Journal C325, 24 December 2002, http://europa.eu.int/eur-lex/en/treaties/.

6. Title III, Chapter 2 (arts. 43 et seq.) to the Consolidated Version of the Treaty Establishing The European Community, Official Journal C325, 24 December 2002, http://europa.eu.int/eur-lex/en/treaties/.
7. http://europa.eu.int/comm/enlargement/docs/pdf/eurostatapril2003. pdf.
8. http://europa.eu.int/comm/enlargement/docs/pdf/eurostatapril2003. pdf.
9. http://europa.eu.int/comm/enlargement/arguments/index_en.htm.
10. http://eurunion.org/profile/EUUSStats.htm.
11. For more information on what chapters of community legislation are currently closed and what chapters are still under discussion, we refer to: http://www.euractiv.com/cgi-bin/cgint.exe/885003-813?714&1015= 9&1014=en_nextwave&-tt=ELNW&-s2=y#nego.
12. http://europa.eu.int/abc/history/index_en.htm.
13. http://europa.eu.int/abc/history/1951/index_en.htm.
14. http://europa.eu.int/abc/history/1957/index_en.htm.
15. http://www.belgium.be.
16. http://europa.eu.int/abc/history/1967/index_en.htm.
17. http://europa.eu.int/abc/history/1973/index_en.htm.
18. http://europa.eu.int/abc/history/1979/index_en.htm.
19. http://europa.eu.int/abc/history/1981/index_en.htm.
20. http://europa.eu.int/abc/history/1986/index_en.htm.
21. http://europa.eu.int/abc/history/1989/index_en.htm.
22. http://europa.eu.int/abc/history/1992/index_en.htm.
23. http://europa.eu.int/abc/history/1995/index_en.htm.
24. http://europa.eu.int/abc/history/2003/index_en.htm.
25. http://europa.eu.int/comm/enlargement/pas/phare/intro.htm.
26. http://europa.eu.int/comm/enlargement/communication/pdf/ sec_737_2000_en.pdf.
27. COM(2002) 700 final, Chapter 3.4 Monitoring and protective measures.
28. http://europa.eu.int/comm/enlargement/report_11_98/index.htm.
29. http://europa.eu.int/comm/enlargement/report_10_99/index.htm.
30. http://europa.eu.int/comm/enlargement/report_11_00/index.htm.
31. http://europa.eu.int/comm/enlargement/report2001/index.htm.
32. http://europa.eu.int/comm/enlargement/report2002/index.htm.
33. http://europa.eu.int/comm/enlargement/report_2003/index.htm.
34. http://europa.eu.int/comm/enlargement.
35. http://europa.eu.int/comm/enlargement/negotiations/pdf/ negotiations_report_to_ep.pdf.
36. http://europa.eu.int/comm/enlargement/faq/index.htm.
37. COM(2002) 700 final – Brussels 9 October 2002, On the Way to the Enlarged Union, Annex 4.
38. COM(2002) 700 final.
39. Enlargement Papers, European Commission, Directorate-General for Economic and Financial Affairs, Number 5, September 2001, http://europa.eu.int/comm/economy_finance.
40. http://europa.eu.int/comm/enlargement/faq/index.htm.
41. http://europa.eu.Int/comm/budget/financing/index_en.htm#revenue.
42. http://europa.eu.int/comm/budget/faq/index_en.htm#2.
43. The Enlargement Process and the Three Pre-accession Instruments: Phare, ISPA, Sapard, http://europa.eu.int./comm/enlargement/pas/phare/pdf/bro-phare-ispa-sapard-2.pdf.

44. http://europa.eu.int/comm/enlargement/faq/faq2.htm#22.
45. SEC(2003) 828, Commission Staff Working Paper, Brussels, 16 July 2003, http://europa.eu.int/comm/regional_policy/newsroom/document/ pdf/annex_chapter21_en.pdf.
46. http://europa.eu.int/comm/ten/transport/revision/hlg/2003_report_ kvm_en.pdf.
47. High Level Group on the Trans-European Network, Chapter 6.1.2. Priority projects to start before 2010 (List 1), http://europa.eu.int/comm/ten/transport/revision/hlg/2003_report_ kvm_en.pdf.
48. http://europa.eu.int/comm/enlargement/faq/faq2.htm#costs.
49. SEC(2002) 102 final, Brussels 30.01.2002, Communication From The Commission, Information Note, http://www.europa.eu.int/comm/enlargement/docs/financialpackage/ sec2002-102_en.pdf.
Common Financial Framework 2004–2006 for the Accession Negotiations.
50. http://europa.eu.int/comm/enlargement/faq.
51. Towards an Enlarged European Union, Key Indicators on Member States and Candidate Countries, http://europa.eu.int/comm/enlargement/docs/pdf/eurostatapril2003. pdf.
52. Eurostat: Statistics in Focus, Economy and Finance, Theme 2, 55/2002, http://europa.eu.int/comm/eurostat/Public/datashop/print-product/ EN?catalogue=Eurostat&product=KS-NJ-02-055-_-N-EN&mode= download.

2 Frequently Asked Questions on the Impact of Enlargement of the European Union for Businesses

2.1 What is the impact on the migration of labour?*

Can we expect an influx of workers from the new member states of the European Union? In order to answer this question, we can best go back in time. When Spain and Portugal acceded to the European Union in 1986, there were fears of an influx of workers to the other member states. In order to prevent this, a seven-year transition period was instituted. The strong upturn in both of these economies had a contrary effect, however. Both Spain and Portugal saw an intake of labour. The transition period was accordingly quickly shortened.[2]

It is especially those EU member states that border the candidate countries that fear an influx of workers from the new member states. Workers that, in addition, are prepared to offer their labour more cheaply than the forms of pay applying in those regions. However, major migration streams are not expected. At present less than 2% of Europeans work in a country other than their home country.[3]

Nevertheless, there is a transition period of a maximum of seven years. This period is split into various phases. After two years, the member states can themselves decide to limit the migration of labour from the new member states by a further three years. This period can subsequently be extended by a further two years.

Migration will also be determined by salary cost. In the member states, national rules on *inter alia* the minimum wage and working time also apply to these workers.

In Table 2.1 we give an indication of the differences in salary levels, albeit the figures are incomplete.[4]

It is not just the differences in productivity that go to explain the major differences in nominal salaries between the candidate member states. Exchange rates also explain the distinction. According to the World Bank's purchasing

---

* You will find the source references for this chapter on page 32.

Table 2.1   Salary data.

Candidate member state from central and eastern Europe	Gross annual salary per employee in USD[5]
Czech Republic	3 694
Estonia	2 478
Hungary	3 708
Latvia	2 000
Lithuania	1 437
Poland	3 429
Slovakia	2 883
Slovenia	11 341
15 EU member states	
Austria	38 624
Belgium	45 333
Denmark	39 079
Finland	37 992
France	41 854
Germany	40 999
Greece	38 624
Ireland	not available
Italy	31 577
Luxembourg	39 004
Netherlands	34 542
Portugal	12 224
Spain	28 653
Sweden	36 004
United Kingdom	26 587

power parity comparison,[6] true salaries in the candidate member states are about one-fifth of EU levels.

As from 1 May 2004, all employment rules for the protection of European workers in the accession countries will have to have been implemented. This is intended to avoid an employment imbalance within Europe. In this regard, we might cite rules on working time, health, safety, discrimination and so forth. Eventually, this will result in a certain levelling-out of salary costs.

2.2   What is the impact on the organisation of production and distribution?[7]

The enlargement of the EU's territory (by 34%) and a rise in its population (by 28%) will increase the demand for goods. However, before goods can be sold they have to be manufactured. Where that is done is dependent on a number of factors such as:

- labour: the availability of a trained workforce;

- taxation: the many fiscal stimuli with which member states persuade prospective businesses to establish in their country;

- support measures: not only nationally but also regionally, facilities are sometimes made available to prospective businesses, from reduced municipal, provincial or cantonal taxes to road-building;

- business climate: businesses prefer to invest in a stable country or region. The frequency of strikes, the functioning of the legal apparatus, the presence of suppliers and the functioning of the authorities are but a few of the factors that have to be taken account of;

- location: the location also has to be accessible, since transport costs are high in hard-to-access areas.

Expectations are that the enlargement of the European Union in central and eastern Europe will lead to a reorganisation of production and distribution for a good many undertakings.

Until 30 April 2004, numerous bilateral treaties will apply in this region between candidate member states, governing the place of production for many goods. This is in order to achieve a favourable tariff of origin and, accordingly, to get as low a duty as possible upon importation into the candidate member states.

As from 1 May 2004, these bilateral treaties disappear. Businesses will then have a free choice as to their production location in the European Union. In this way, regional distribution centres can be created (such as in Hungary), serving a number of countries in the surrounding region. Indirect taxes like VAT and customs and excise duties will thus no longer be a decisive factor in the choice of production location in any of the 25 member states of the European Union. Direct taxes, like corporate income tax, do continue to affect the decision of where to set up a business in the EU: low taxation of business profits is an attraction to any company.

2.3 Can I use the service of carriers from the new member states?

Increased transport activity is expected between, from and to the new member states. In this regard, it is particularly road haulage that is expected to increase. Europe is giving infrastructural support in order to extend the road network.

Can I as a business use the services offered by the transport capacity present in central and eastern Europe? Due to lower wage costs and less stringent regulations, this is currently still a cheaper option.

But it is dependent on *cabotage provisions*. These set the rules of the game under which carriers from one member state can collect goods in another member state. A distinction is drawn between:

- national cabotage: the goods picked up are carried to a destination within the member state where the goods were picked up (Regulation (EEC) 3118/93);

- Community cabotage: the goods are picked up in one member state and carried to another member state (Regulation (EEC) 881/92).

Provided they have the necessary permits, carriers can offer both forms of cabotage.

Upon enlargement of the Union, transitional measures apply to *national cabotage* in order to avoid market distortions. Some national transport markets will be accessible only to a limited extent for the new member states. These restrictions apply for an initial two or three years. The transitional period can be extended up to a maximum of five years in total.

In Table 2.2, we show those countries that have applied for a limited transitional period.[8]

For Community cabotage, there will be no restrictions. This means that a Polish haulier will be able to pick up goods in one member state and take them to another member state.

Table 2.2 Transitional provisions: national cabotage.

	No transition	Two-year transition	Three-year transition
Cyprus	×		
Czech Republic		×	
Estonia		×	
Hungary			×
Latvia		×	
Lithuania		×	
Malta	×		
Poland			×
Slovenia	×		
Slovakia		×	

2.4 What about border controls?[9]

In the single market, the principles of the free movement of goods, services and persons apply. However, this does not mean that no further border controls will be exercised. This is changing only gradually by means of the Schengen Agreement.[10]

At all land borders of member states that have signed the Schengen Agreement there are no further systematic controls. Goods and persons can cross unhindered over the national borders of Austria, Belgium, Denmark, Finland, France, Germany, Greece, Italy, Luxembourg, the Netherlands, Portugal, Spain and Sweden. Ireland and the United Kingdom have not signed the Schengen Agreement.

Inhabitants of the 10 new member states will, after accession, freely be able to move within the EU upon production of a valid passport or identity card.[11]

The opening-up of internal borders between the present and the new member states by introduction of the Schengen Agreement will only be possible with the approval of the European Council of Ministers. One of the most important conditions for accession to the Schengen Area is effective control by the new member states of their external borders. Accession to the Schengen Area will technically not be possible before 2005.

2.5 Are these 10 countries joining the eurozone?[12]

One of the conditions for joining up to the European Union is that the economic criterion must be fulfilled and that the "acquis communautaire" has to be transposed into local legislation. Does this then mean that the euro will be implemented as from 1 May 2004?

No.

A member state has to meet three conditions before it can introduce the euro:

- it has to have made irreversible progress in the functioning of the market economy and competitiveness. Lasting macro-economic stability is also required;

- subsequently, the member state has to participate in the single market and demonstrate progress in fulfilling the conditions for introduction of the euro, including participating in the exchange rate mechanism, which allows only limited variation;

- the member state's budgetary deficit must be less than 3% of GDP and its debt ratio has to be lower than 60% of GDP. Moreover, it has to have low inflation and an interest rate that is in keeping with the average rate of interest for the European Union.

2.6 What will the impact of accession by the 10 member states be on major sectors within the European Union?[13]

2.6.1 The steel industry[14]

Just as the European steel industry radically altered in the mid-1980s, so the steel industry in the accession countries is also undergoing major changes. They have to restore the viability of the steel industry and ensure proper functioning of the single market.

Overcapacity, low productivity, production-driven instead of market-oriented sales and high costs of production are inducing the accession countries to restructure their steel industries.

The most important challenge is being able to compete with the European steel market. This is only possible if the new countries modernise their steel production. Furthermore, they have to become more environmentally friendly.

The steel industry in the accession countries currently lives mainly thanks to state support. After accession, this will no longer be permissible. The Czech Republic and Poland, however, have until the end of 2006 to restructure their steel industries.[15] In addition, Slovakia has to terminate the support it gives to firms in the steel industry by the end of 2009 unless a certain sum is exceeded at an earlier point in time.

This restructuring is intended to result in a steel industry with a cost structure comparable to that which currently exists in the European Union. Production will also be more market-oriented. In addition, the steel industry will be concentrated in a number of regions, such as the Silesia triangle (Silesia in Poland to southern Saxony in Germany and northern Bohemia in the Czech Republic). This concentration will result in both regional and social changes.

2.6.2 The automotive industry[16]

The European Union has seen a strong harmonisation in the technical requirements for motor vehicles. In this, the emphasis is placed on safety and environmental protection. On 1 May 2004, the new member states will also have to satisfy these provisions in the acquis. For car makers, this means an even more homogeneous market, since they will no longer have to gear their products to country-specific requirements.

Since the 1990s, major car producers have also been setting up in these countries, with the prospect of the far-reaching liberalisation of these markets. The most important driving force behind this is the growing market potential. Accession to the European Union has a positive effect on the economic climate, as a result of which disposable incomes also rise. Together with a modernised road network, this leads to a rise in car sales. Another reason why auto producers relocate to the candidate member states is the lower cost of production and well trained labour. However, the European Commission still expects that production units there will mainly serve local markets.

2.6.3   The pharmaceutical industry[17]

For the pharmaceutical industry in central and eastern Europe, enlargement means the opening-up of new markets, albeit under the condition that products have to be in accordance with European rules.

Medicines need approval before they can be brought onto the market. There are two sorts of registration for drugs: national, for local sale, and European, for sale within the whole European Union.[18]

The new member states thus have access as from 1 May 2004 to all medicines that can be sold within the European Union. No new prior market permits will be needed. These permits do nevertheless have to comply with European requirements regarding quality, safety and effectiveness.

A majority of the accession countries have already amended their legislation to the "acquis communautaire" so that few drugs will lose their market permits after accession. However, Cyprus, Latvia, Malta, Poland and Slovenia will have till 2008 to bring their laws into line. The other member states can refuse those products for which an "old" market permit has been granted.[19] The transitional period is as shown in Table 2.3.

Table 2.3   Countries with transitional measures for registration.

Cyprus	Until 31 December 2005
Latvia	Until 1 January 2007
Malta	Until 31 December 2006
Poland	Until 31 December 2008
Slovenia	Until 31 December 2008

2.6.4 Telecommunications

Historically, the accession countries are way behind as regards telecommunications, although this lost ground has already been made up to a large extent by the major international telecommunications operators. The mobile telephone market is developing quickly, partly as a result of the constant increases in disposable income.

2.6.5 The financial sector

The financial market, too, was not as developed when the Wall fell as in the Union. However, the larger part of the lost ground has been made up in the meantime. The sector has fairly rapidly found connections with the international financial networks and institutions. As the pace at which businesses find their way into the new member states quickens, corporate banking will further develop accordingly.

2.6.6 The chemical industry[20]

The stringent European rules in the chemical sector will be more of a burden than a delight to the accession countries.

Poland is the largest producer of chemical products, followed by Hungary and the Czech Republic. The chemical sector is seeing ever-larger foreign investments and the introduction of know-how. Nonetheless, the chemical sector will have a difficult time after accession to the European Union. SMEs in particular will struggle to comply with the new European standards in the realm of safety and care for the environment. Added to this is the fact that European rules are to be tightened up in the future. Into the bargain, wages have risen higher than productivity, which is hardly good for the sector's competitiveness.

2.6.7 The textile and clothing industry[21]

Textiles and clothing are an important sector in the candidate member states. A lot of European textile producers have moved their production there.

After enlargement, however, wages will rise, reducing the competitive advantage. Nevertheless, most textile companies want to keep their chain of production in the vicinity of the European Union. Competition from Asia or relocating production plants to the east (the Balkans and the Ukraine) and the Mediterranean rim also cannot be ruled out, however.

2.7   Does Europe stimulate entrepreneurship?[22]

Small and medium-sized enterprises will continue to assume an important place in the enlarged Europe. They create new jobs. They are highly innovative and dynamic. SMEs are central to the "Lisbon Strategy", or the goal of re-forming Europe into a dynamic and competitive knowledge society by 2010.[23]

Ensuring a stable business climate is the best support for SMEs. The European Charter for Small Businesses, from June 2000, called on the member states to support and encourage SMEs in ten subject areas (http://europa.eu.int/comm/enterprise/enterprise_policy/charter/index.htm):

- education and training for entrepreneurship;

- cheaper and faster start-up;

- better legislation and regulation;

- availability of skills;

- improving online access;

- getting more out of the Single Market;

- taxation and financial matters;

- strengthening the technological capacity of small enterprises;

- making use of successful e-business models and developing top-class small business support;

- developing stronger, more effective representation of small enterprises' interests at Union and national level.

In 2001, it was decided by the European Commission that the accession countries should also be included in the "Lisbon Strategy" by means of the so-called "CC Best" report (http://europa.eu.int/comm/enterprise/enlargement/best.htm). This shows not only the current state of play but also the areas where the candidate member states still have to make improvements.

2.8   What are the most important features of the European legislation on industrial production?[24]

The free movement of goods is one of the fundamentals of the European single market. This is only possible if there are standards that are recognised within the whole Union. Thus, it must not be that a different product has to be produced for each market. Thanks to the European certificate of conformity you can, say, buy a car in any member state and register it in your home country. However, if you buy a DVD player, the plug will differ from state to state.

By means of mutual recognition, technical barriers between member states are being eliminated. Goods and services that satisfy the rules of one member state can in theory also be sold in the other member states. This applies to all goods and services that are not subject to European harmonised legislation.

Industrial products with a high degree of product safety fall under the European harmonised legislation. This because for reasons of public safety, health or environmental protection, member states can derogate from the principle of mutual recognition. There are two types of harmonisation:

- product-specific legislation, such as for motor vehicles and foodstuffs;

- legislation that contains only the essential requirements but no detailed technical specifications, such as for toys, gas appliances and radio and telecommunications equipment.

This latter type of harmonisation is hallmarked by a new approach. This is that Europe does not give a prior approval but merely carries out checks once the goods are already on the market. Depending on the risk profile of the product, either the manufacturer itself issues a statement of conformity or an accredited agency issues a certificate of conformity. The system is therefore founded on a great trust in business.

The candidate member states also have to transpose these Community provisions into their national laws. In addition, they also have to create independent, recognised institutions that can certify the conformity of products.

Useful links in this regard are sites of European standardisation organisations, such as
http:/www.cenorm.be, http://www.cenelec.org or http://www.etsi.org.

The candidate member states have already incorporated most of the legislation on industrial standards into their national laws. The European Commission has monitored this transposition process via periodic reports.[25]

2.9   Will diplomas from the new member states automatically be recognised?[26]

The degrees of doctors, dentists, nurses, wet nurses, vets, pharmacists, architects and lawyers issued in the new member states are automatically recognised. The professional experience of artisans, traders and farmers is automatically recognised.

For other occupations and qualifications, the host countries can even now under Community law set compensatory measures. They can require an applicant to undergo a skills test or a period of training if there are substantial differences between the lengths of the training periods in the host and home countries.

2.10 Can I directly invoke European law if a (candidate) member state has failed to implement a provision?

The legal framework in Europe is for the most part determined by regulations and directives. The customs legislation, for instance, is governed by regulations. The VAT legislation is governed via directives.

A *regulation* is a general rule that is binding on member states in all its parts and of direct application in the member states. "Binding in all its parts" means that the member states have no freedom as regards form and means.

Directives are also general rules, but are only binding as regards to the objective to be achieved. Due to the broader policy freedom accorded to member states in transposing directives, there is less clarity about their direct effect. In practice, however, you should not underestimate the direct effect of directives since national rules have to be interpreted in such a way as is most in accordance with the directive in question. Furthermore, the European Court of Justice has determined that the provision of a directive can have direct effect as well as on the directive itself. A directive is of direct effect where the implementation deadline for the directive has passed and the directive has not been transposed into national law, or not in time or not correctly. A provision has direct effect if it is unconditionally and in sufficient detail lays down the rights that a person can assert against the state.[27]

Thus, the Sixth VAT Directive (77/388/EEC) provides for instance the conditions under which an intra-Community supply of goods is zero-rated for VAT by the seller. However, the Directive does not define how a businessperson officially has to demonstrate to the authorities that the goods have been transported outside the member state. This aspect has to be set down in rules and implementing legislation passed by the individual member states.

Transposition of the directives into national legislation and fleshing out the "freedoms" as laid down in the Treaty is probably the most difficult task for the candidate member states.

2.11 How do I prepare my business for enlargement?

Europe is not unknown to a good many businesspeople. They are faced with it on a daily basis. Confidence in Europe and the "acquis communautaire" is great. This perhaps explains why few businesspeople are preparing for enlargement.

Nonetheless, structured preparation is necessary, since the impact of enlargement on companies that do business with or in the new member states is significant.

What is the best approach to take?

EU MAP[29] is a methodology developed by PricewaterhouseCoopers. It comprises a number of different building blocks. It allows businesses to manage the accession process in a structured manner so as to ensure compliance with the (new) rules and benefit from any opportunities resulting from accession.

The approach distinguishes six building blocks:

1. *Impact study*: the first step consists in mapping out the undertaking in order to examine where the "acquis communautaire" will have an impact. Subsequently, the legal framework prior to 1 May 2004 and as from 1 May 2004 is identified. Thus, a gap analysis can be drawn up, by which it can be determined where the acquis affects the undertaking.

   On the basis of this gap analysis, a project plan is drawn up and the actions to be taken within the various departments are defined (purchases, sales, production, environment, logistics, finance, ICT, HR and legal affairs).

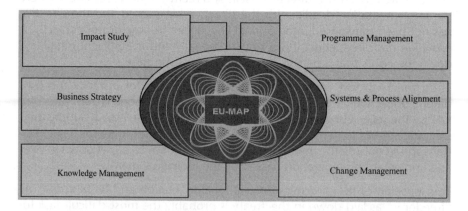

Figure 2.1   EU-MAP.[28]

2. *Programme management*: the efforts needed to bring the undertaking into line with the acquis are reflected in a "programme" respecting all good project management principles including milestones and deliverables. This programme is best managed centrally. The project leader is the pivotal point and manages the programme across the various departments and business units.

3. *Systems and process alignment*: the various changes to systems and processes in the undertaking as a consequence of accession have to be attuned to one another.[30]

4. *Change management*: changes have to be well prepared for and guidance has to be given. The staff, customers and suppliers have to be aware of the changes that occur on 1 May 2004. This can be done by means of information sessions, training and appointing an in-house or external adviser for front-line assistance.

5. *Knowledge management*: knowledge is important. In the run-up to and post 1 May 2004, businesses need reliable information in order to work out developments in the gap that is to be bridged. Businesses can collect this information themselves, use the services of trade associations or advisers.

    To help ensure that the new VAT legislation and the EU Customs Code in the accession countries is implemented in a correct and timely manner, and that it is business-friendly as well as EU-compliant, a number of top investors in the CEE region have joined forces in the EU Accession Forum's Indirect Tax Focus Group. PricewaterhouseCoopers facilitates and project-manages this Group,[31] of which it is also a member. The Group has produced a detailed Analysis Paper identifying and promoting EU VAT best practice, based on the practical experience of its members in the EU. This paper has been the basis for the Group's face-to-face meetings with key Ministry officials in the accession countries. To help its members ensure their own compliance from 1 May 2004, the Group also looks at contingency planning based on identified VAT and customs problem areas.

6. *Business strategy*: in 2007, Romania and Bulgaria are expected to accede to the European Union. Turkey and the Balkan states will also be acceding. Bearing in mind these future changes, it is important for businesses to reflect strategically on their operations in Europe. In which of the 25 (and potentially, as from 1 January 2007, 27) do they want to or need to have operations? Economic, fiscal and legal considerations should not be lost sight of when defining business strategy.

2.12   ICT: status, opportunities and points to note?[32,33]

2.12.1   What are the most important changes in the realm of ICT in the 10 new EU member states?

The "e-Europe" initiative[34] is being extended to the candidate member states via "e-Europe plus". Part of this includes measures for easing access to the ICT market while protecting the rights and privacy of consumers.

Most of the candidate member states have already outlined their policy lines and the legislative framework with regard to ICT. In addition, they are making extensive investments in introducing ICT into government, education and the private sector.

With help from national and international funding, the ICT infrastructure is being further improved. By means of education programmes, the population of the candidate countries are also being made more familiar with ICT. This is also increasing the possibilities for electronic trade.

Since automation is not yet very far advanced, there is little resistance to replacing current systems with new technologies.

2.12.2   What opportunities does this situation offer for western European businesses?

ICT makes communication with suppliers, trade partners and customers easier. Western European businesses can take advantage of existing trading platforms based on the internet and thus conduct electronic trade with partners in the new member states.

The candidate countries are open to new commercial practices. Other countries can get new ways of doing business introduced. They can exercise influence on commercial practices and the underlying application software.

The accession countries are in the course of adapting their quality standards in order to be able to get international certification from institutes such as Carnegie-Mellon University. Low wages and up-to-date technical skills are available within the extended EU. ICT developments can thereby be developed offshore.

2.12.3   What pitfalls do you have to watch out for when choosing your trading partners?

Trade partners are required to adjust their information systems to the EU rules regarding trade obligations (VAT, Intrastat, etc.), security and privacy.

If the business model changes, for example by outsourcing transport, then the internal business processes also have to be adjusted. At the same time, the integrity of and supervision over existing commercial practices and systems have to be maintained, if only to avoid creating hiatuses in switching from the old to the new manner of working.

Looking for a trading partner in an unknown surrounding is not always easy. For advice, one can always consult "interest groupings" or specialist advisers. But be careful that such groupings represent the whole industry sector and not just a limited group of private businesses.

Trade agreements and trade activities are already possible before the governing framework is fully operational. In this, it is important that any transitional provisions are complied with and the final rules become effective as quickly as possible. Only where the rules have been definitively set down in the new member states will the chance of fines or damage to the business's reputation be smaller.

2.13 Are businesses ready for enlargement?

A first survey was conducted by PricewaterhouseCoopers in Belgium. It appeared that the vast majority (90%) of Belgian businesses active in the accession countries still had not thought in November 2002 about the consequences of enlargement. This appears to accord with another survey conducted by PricewaterhouseCoopers[35] in May 2003 and February 2004.

This second survey was carried out by PricewaterhouseCoopers amongst important investors in central and eastern Europe. It appeared that they underestimate not only the impact of enlargement but also the preparatory costs and the time necessary to get their business ready by 1 May 2004.

Of interest in this regard is the fact that businesses that were aware of the impact were thinking more strategically (i.e. beyond 2004) and not only focusing on the impact on their daily operations.

2.14 Where do you find the required information on enlargement of the European Union?

Table 2.4 gives a list of internet addresses that are useful in the quest for information:[36]

Table 2.4 Useful links.

European Info Centres	http://europa.eu.int/comm/enterprise/networks/eic/eic.htm
TAIEX (Technical Assistance Information Exchange Office) of the European Commission for candidate member states. The databases that are administered by this office contain *inter alia* the full texts of the translations of the "acquis communautaire" in the languages of the candidate member states. This database is called CCVista	http://ccvista.taiex.be
LAD (Law Approximation Database) refers to the national legislation of the candidate member states with respect to the "acquis communautaire"	http://lad.taiex.be
CELEX and EUR-Lex of the European Commission, which contains all European legislation in the language of each of the current EU member states	http://europa.eu.int/celex/htm/celex_en.htm http://europa.eu.int/eur-lex/en/index.html
European Commission	http://europa.eu.int/comm/index_en.htm
Cyprus	http://www.cyprus.gov.cy/cyphome/govhome.nsf
Czech Republic	http://www.mfa.cz/missionEU/index.htm
Estonia	http://www.riik.ee/en
Hungary	http://www.magyarorszag.hu/angol/orszaginfo/alapadatok
Latvia	http://www.mk.gov.lv/index.php/en
Lithuania	http://www.lrv.lt/main_en.php
Malta	http://www.gov.mt/index.asp?l=2
Poland	http://www.kprm.gov.pl/english/index.html
Slovakia	http://www.government.gov.sk/english
Slovenia	http://www.sigov.si
Product standards	http://www.cenorm.be http://www.cenelec.org http://www.etsi.org
PricewaterhouseCoopers	http://www.pwc.com/euaccession http://www.euenlargement.be http://www.globalvatonline.com

Source references for Chapter 2

1. http://europa.eu.int/comm/enlargement/faq/index.htm.
2. Free movement for persons – a practical guide for an enlarged European Union, http://europa.eu.int/comm/enlargement/negotiations/chapters/chap2/55260_practica_guide_ including_comments.pdf.

3. http://europa.eu.int/comm/enlargement/faq/#Employment
4. http://europa.eu.int/comm/employment_social/free_movement/index_ en.htm, The Impact of Eastern Enlargement on Employment and Labour Markets in the EU Member States – Final Report: PDF format: Part 1, (22/05/2000), Chapter 3.2, Labour Endowment and Wages.
5. Total workers' remuneration divided by the number of workers.
6. http://europa.eu.int/comm/employment_social/free_movement/index_ en.htm, The Impact of Eastern Enlargement on Employment and Labour Markets in the EU Member States – Final Report: PDF format: Part 1, (22/05/2000), Chapter 3.2, Labour Endowment and Wages.
7. http://europa.eu.int/comm/enlargement/faq/index.htm.
8. http://europa.eu.int/comm/enlargement/negotiations/treaty_of_accession_ 2003/index.htm.
9. http://europa.eu.int/comm/enlargement/faq/index.htm.
10. Since the Treaty of Amsterdam, signed in October 1997, came into force on 1 May 1999, the Schengen acquis (originally signed by the Benelux countries, Germany and France in 1985), integrated into the Treaty on European Union: for the consolidated version of this Treaty see: http://europa.eu.int/eur-lex/en/treaties/dat/EU_consol.pdf.
11. http://europa.eu.int/comm/justice_home/fsj/enlargement/negotiations/ fsj_enlarge_issues_en.htm.
12. http://europa.eu.int/comm/enlargement/faq/index.htm.
13. Enlargement: What can enterprises in the new Member States expect? European Commission, Enterprise Directorate-General, http://europa.eu.int/comm/enterprise/enlargement/doc/questions-answers.pdf.
14. Enlargement: What can enterprises in the new Member States expect? European Commission, Enterprise Directorate-General, http://europa.eu.int/comm/enterprise/enlargement/doc/questions-answers.pdf, Chapter 5.1.
15. Report on the results of the negotiations on the accession of Cyprus, Malta, Hungary, Poland, the Slovak Republic, Latvia, Estonia, Lithuania, the Czech Republic and Slovenia to the European Union, Chapter 6 Competition policy.
16. Enlargement: What can enterprises in the new Member States expect? European Commission, Enterprise Directorate-General, http://europa.eu.int/comm/enterprise/enlargement/doc/questions-answers.pdf, Chapter 5.2.
17. Enlargement: What can enterprises in the new Member States expect? European Commission, Enterprise Directorate-General, http://europa.eu.int/comm/enterprise/enlargement/doc/questions-answers.pdf, Chapter 5.3.
18. With thanks to Beatrijs Van LiedeKerke, Manager, Global Risk Management Service, PricewaterhouseCoopers Belgium.
19. Report on the results of the negotiations on the accession of Cyprus, Malta, Hungary, Poland, the Slovak Republic, Latvia, Estonia, Lithuania, the Czech Republic and Slovenia to the European Union, Chapter 1 Free movement of goods, http://europa.eu.int/comm/enlargement/negotiations/pdf/negotiations_report_ to_ep.pdf.
20. Enlargement: What can enterprises in the new Member States expect? European Commission, Enterprise Directorate-General,

http://europa.eu.int/comm/enterprise/enlargement/doc/questions-answers.pdf, Chapter 5.4.

21. Enlargement: What can enterprises in the new Member States expect? European Commission, Enterprise Directorate-General, http://europa.eu.int/comm/enterprise/enlargement/doc/questions-answers.pdf, Chapter 5.5.

22. Enlargement: What can enterprises in the new Member States expect? European Commission, Enterprise Directorate-General, http://europa. eu.int/comm/enterprise/enlargement/doc/questions-answers.pdf.

23. http://europa.eu.int/comm/lisbon_strategy/index_en.html.

24. Enlargement: What can enterprises in the new Member States expect? European Commission, Enterprise Directorate-General, http://europa.eu.int/comm/enterprise/enlargement/doc/questions-answers.pdf.

25. The acquis of the European Union under the management of the Enterprise DG – List of, http://europa.eu.int/comm/dgs/enterprise/ pdf/acquis_en.pdf.

26. Enlargement Papers, European Commission, Directorate-General for Economic and Financial Affairs, Number 5, September 2001, http://europa.eu.int/comm/economy_finance.

27. European Court of Justice, 5 April 1979, 148/78, Tullio Ratti, Jurispr., 1979, 1629.

28. © 2004 PricewaterhouseCoopers. PricewaterhouseCoopers refers to the network of member firms of PricewaterhouseCoopers International Limited, each of which is a separate and independent legal entity. All rights reserved.

29. Managing the Accession Process©.

30. See also Chapter 2, 2, ICT: Status, Opportunities and Points to Note.

31. More information on the EU Accession Forum ITX Focus Group can be obtained from Antoni Turczynowicz, Partner, TLS EU Accession Leader (Tel: +420 25 115 2900; antoni.turczynowicz@cz.pwc.com).

32. With thanks to Daniel Evrard, Partner, Global Risk Management Service, PricewaterhouseCoopers Belgium.

33. IDC Study, Central and Eastern Europe: Impact of EU Enlargement on ICT Markets, http://europe.eu.int/comm/enlargement.

34. http://europa.eu.int/information_society/eeurope/2002/index_en.htm.

35. EU enlargement surveys, http://www.euenlargement.be.

36. Enlargement Papers, European Commission, Directorate-General for Economic and Financial Affairs, Number 5, September 2001, http://europa.eu.int/comm/economy_finance.

3 Enlargement of the European Union from a Legal Perspective

3.1 What is the "acquis communautaire"?*

The main consequence of the enlargement of the European Union is the implementation and application of the "acquis communautaire" by the accession countries. The "acquis communautaire" is the body of existing Community law which binds the member states together and the European Union. As from 1 May 2004, the present member states will have to treat the accession countries as a part of the European Union. This means that, in some cases, entirely new rules will come into effect with respect to trading relations with these countries.

The "acquis communautaire" embraces the rules in furtherance of a European internal market. It also encompasses rules on the various policy areas in which the EU is involved. One might say that the "acquis communautaire" is the path towards European integration that the present 15 member states have hitherto trodden. In total, it covers some 90 000 or so pages of legislative texts.

The changes to the legislation of the 10 accession countries will not only entail major adjustments for businesses and private citizens in those countries but also for foreign companies holding interests there. That being said, the enlargement does offer new opportunities. On both sides, barriers to market penetration will be gradually eliminated. Social and political cohesion will be made stronger. The implementation of the "acquis communautaire" will furthermore offer greater legal certainty in trade relations with the accession countries.

3.2 The current status of implementation

The European Commission has published voluminous reports on the status of implementation of the "acquis communautaire" in the accession countries.

---

* You will find the source references for this chapter on page 75.

These can be consulted on the European Commission's EU Enlargement web-site at http://europa.eu.int/comm/enlargement.

However, on a legislative and administrative level, there is still a great deal of work to be done. At present, parts of the "acquis communautaire" still have to be transposed. In some cases, rough drafts are under discussion with the parliament of the accession country, no action has been taken whatsoever. Contacts with legal and tax consultancy colleagues in the accession countries also confirm that there is still a long way to go before the entrepreneurs and officials will be conversant with the "acquis communautaire" and apply it correctly. A survey by Burson-Marsteller based on interviews with 30 top officials at the European Commission, reveals that a good many officials at the European Commission have the same opinion.[1]

3.3   What can you as a business do where the "acquis communautaire" has not been or has only partially been implemented?

When directives have not been implemented, or have not been implemented properly, European rules may, under certain conditions, be directly invoked before the national courts. Furthermore, in case there is uncertainty with respect to the application of community law, national courts may request a preliminary ruling from the European Court of Justice in Luxembourg, which ensures consistency in interpretation of Community Law.

In specific cases, a claim may be brought directly before the European Court of Justice.

It is also possible to file a complaint directly with the European Commission.[2] It suffices to send a letter setting out the facts of the case to the European Commission at:

Commission of the European Communities
(for the attention of the Secretary-General)
200 Rue de la Loi
B-1049 Brussels
Belgium

If the Commission is of the opinion that Community law has been breached, it sends the member state in question an official notification of the alleged breach and asks it for its reaction to the findings of the Commission. If the member state does not respond or if its response is unsatisfactory, the Commission then sends a "duly motivated advice" to the member state in question. In this advice, the Commission sets out its opinion and asks the member state to comply with Community law within a given deadline. A good many complaints can be cleared up in this way without any judicial proceedings, albeit court action does in some cases still prove to be necessary.

The European Commission has developed a (non-compulsory) standard complaint form to file complaints. The standard complaint form is enclosed as an appendix to this book.

3.4 What is the importance of regulations and directives?

Regulations and directives are the most important legislative instruments in the European Union.

A *regulation* is a general rule that is binding upon member states in all its parts and directly applicable in all member states. "Binding in all its parts" means that the member states have no choice as to form and method.

Directives are also general rules, but are only binding as to their result. A directive is binding as to the result to be achieved for each member state to which it is directed. The institutions of the member states have a choice as to form and method.[3] Due to the broader policy freedom accorded to member states in transposing directives, there is less clarity about their direct effect.

In practice, however, one should not underestimate the effect of directives. One of the reasons for this is that national rules have to be interpreted in such a manner that is most in accordance with the directive in question.

However, the European Court of Justice has determined that a directive is of direct effect (i.e. that a direct claim can be made under the provisions of a directive) in only a very limited number of cases. For instance, the Court of Justice has decided that, after the expiration of the period fixed for the implementation of a directive a member state may not apply its internal law – even if it is provided with penal sanctions – which has not yet been adapted in compliance with the directive, to a person who has complied with the requirements of the directive.

The following conditions have to be met in this respect:

- the implementation deadline for the directive has passed;
- the relevant provisions of the directive have not, not timely or not correctly been transposed into national law; and
- the relevant provision of the directive unconditionally and in sufficient detail lays down the rights that a person can assert against the state.[4]

Furthermore, wherever provisions of a directive appear to be, from the point of view of their content, unconditional and sufficiently precise, they may be relied on against any national provision which is not in accordance with the directive.[5]

On the other hand, the question as to the effects of an unimplemented directive on legal relations between private persons (also known as horizontal effect) has been clearly defined in the case law of the Court: a directive may not of itself impose obligations on an individual.[6]

3.5 What does the "acquis communautaire" specifically contain?

In the following, we give an overview of the most important legal rules that have an impact on trade with the accession countries as of 1 May 2004.

The overview starts from the four freedoms of the European Union: free movement of goods, free movement of services, free movement of persons and free movement of capital. These freedoms are closely connected.

Free movement of goods, for one, is impossible without free movement of services. Otherwise it would be hard to provide after-sales services. The purpose of these freedoms is the realisation of the internal market. It is this free movement that forms the central cornerstone of the various policy areas within the EU, such as company law, consumer protection, environmental law and free competition.

It concerns rules that form part of the "acquis communautaire", that complement replace or amend the national legislation of the new EU member states. It is often forgotten what a strong influence European law has on our legal systems. This is because European Law is internalised within the national laws of the EU Member States through the transposition of directives, directly applicable regulations and other sources of European Law. As said above, the European Court of Justice ensures the uniform approach and interpretation of European Law.

The "acquis communautaire" and the case law decisions of the European Court of Justice are very extensive. Hence this overview is limited to a selection of rules that are of importance to entrepreneurs, without being exhaustive.

For an overview of the "acquis communautaire" and the case judgments in the areas of social law and indirect and direct taxation, we refer to Chapters 5, 6 and 7. Sectoral policy in respect of agriculture, fishing and nuclear power is omitted because of the highly specialised nature of this legislation.

The overview also looks at the transitional measures accorded to present or future member states. This means that certain parts of the "acquis communautaire" will not yet be implemented upon accession.

3.6 What is the free movement of goods?

One of the objectives of the European Union is realisation of an internal market. For this reason, there must be as few trade barriers between member states as possible. In principle, they are prohibited.

There are two sorts of trade barriers as regards goods: *tariff measures*, such as customs duties and levies of equivalent effect, and *non-tariff measures*, such as quantitative limits and measures of equivalent effect.

For tariff aspects (common customs tariff) and taxes (value-added taxes), we refer to Chapter 6.

In the following, we look only at the non-tariff aspects of the free movement of goods.

The free movement of goods is very important to enlargement. As a matter of principle, a member state may not favour or protect its national businesses, so that companies within the present EU countries can compete on a level playing field within the market in the accession countries.

3.7 What is the prohibition against quantitative import and export restrictions and measures of equivalent effect?

The EC Treaty[7] lays down the principle that quantitative import and export restrictions are prohibited.

Quantitative import or export restrictions are any legal or administrative provisions or official measures that limit the import or export of products according to quantity standards or the value of the goods. In other words, quota restrictions on goods are forbidden.

Not only are pure quotas forbidden but also *measures of equivalent effect*. The European Court of Justice interprets this term broadly. Each measure by a member state that actually does or potentially might directly or indirectly affect intra-Community trade is a measure of equivalent effect.[8]

The classic example of this is national rules that lay down requirements as to the composition or presentation of products but in fact constitute disguised protection for domestic products. It is not, however, necessary that the measure should deliberately set out to disfavour foreign products. Even if this is a coincidental consequence of a national measure, it is incompatible with European law.

Examples of measures of prohibited equivalent effect include:

- reserving the appellations *Sekt* and *Weinbrand* for national products;[9]

- licences that apply only to imports;[10]

- obligatory mention of the country of origin for imported souvenirs;[11]

- a national campaign launched by the government to promote the purchase of national products;[12]

- a compulsory minimum alcohol percentage only for imported vermouth;[13]

- setting such low prices for medicines that the sale of imported products is hampered in favour of domestic products.[14]

There are exceptions, however. The EC Treaty states that prohibitions against or restrictions on imports or exports are justified if they serve the protection of:

- public morality;

- public policy;

- public safety;

- the health and life of humans, animals or plants;

- national treasures possessing artistic, historic or archaeological value; or

- industrial and commercial property.

Such measures must nonetheless be necessary and proportionate as regards their aim, i.e. protection of the interests listed above. This test is known as the "Cassis de Dijon" test. In this case, the European Court of Justice ruled in favour of a french liquor producer who wanted to market the well-know "Cassis de Dijon" liquor on the German market. However, a German statute requiring a minimum concentration of alcohol in liquors, which threshold was not met in the case at hand, prohibited such import. The European Court of Justice recognised that there were no European rules regarding the production and sale of alcoholic drinks, but found that the German measure went too far. Clear labelling was sufficient for the protection of the consumer.[15]

However, a national protective measure is not justified where the aim is already protected by European legislation. The European rules on the safety of toys constitute such a product standard. A national measure that lays down more extensive restrictions on toys[16] is therefore not justified in order to restrict imports.

However, yet another important qualification is introduced, which is to be found in the wording of the EC Treaty itself. The prohibitions or restrictions must not constitute a means of arbitrary discrimination or a disguised restriction on intra-Community trade. An example of this is a prohibition against the advertising of alcoholic drinks for the protection of public health that applies fully for foreign products but only partially for domestic products.

Although the exceptions in principle are exhaustively set out in the EC Treaty and are to be interpreted restrictively according to the European Court of Justice, it would appear in practice that these exceptions are insufficient. Hence, the European Court of Justice has recognised that the list may be expanded upon where there is no European rule and the measure is necessary, proportionate and non-economic in nature.[17]

Some examples: measures to protect consumers, in furtherance of the effectiveness of tax audits, for the protection of working conditions or the environment. Nonetheless, never forget to examine whether or not adequate common European rules exist since, in certain policy areas such as consumer protection, the environment and public health, European initiatives follow close on each other's heels.

3.8 What is the importance of product standards?

The most important European rules that limit the policy competence of the member states are perhaps those on product standards. A large number of directives govern the standards that certain goods have to meet. As of 1 May 2004, these directives will also in principle apply in the new member states. Goods that come onto the market there will then have to satisfy the standards set by these directives.

The most important initiatives at a European level are taken in the following sectors and areas:

- motor vehicles;
- the building industry;
- foodstuffs;
- pharmaceutical products;
- chemical products;
- toys;

- cosmetic products;

- machinery;

- printing machines;

- medical aids;

- electrical and electronic appliances and gas appliances;

- information and telecommunications technologies;

- transport.

General directives on product safety have also been issued.[18]

3.9 How can you know whether a member state has passed domestic measures that limit the free movement of goods?

As regards barriers to the free movement of goods, Decision 3052/95/EC of the European Parliament and of the Council of 13 December 1995 is of importance. It lays down a procedure for the exchange of information with the European Commission. The member states have to follow the Decision if they issue national measures that derogate from the principle of the free movement of goods.

It deals with measures under which products that are lawfully produced or marketed in another member state:

- are directly or indirectly banned;

- are refused such licence as is required;

- have their model or type modified before they can be placed or kept on the market; or

- are withdrawn from the market.

3.10 Are there transitional measures in respect of the free movement of goods?

Table 3.1 Transitional measures: free movement of goods.

Subject-matter	Legislation	Cyprus	Czech Republic	Estonia	Hungary	Latvia	Lithuania	Malta	Poland	Slovakia	Slovenia
Length of the transitional measure regarding the licence for pharmaceutical products (1)	Directive 2001/82/EC and 2001/83/EC	31 Dec. 2005	—	—	—	—	1 Jan. 2007	31 Dec. 2006	31 Dec. 2008	31 Dec. 2008	—

Table 3.1 (*cont.*)

Subject-matter	Legislation	Cyprus	Czech Republic	Estonia	Hungary	Latvia	Lithuania	Malta	Poland	Slovakia	Slovenia
Length of the transitional measure regarding the licence for medical apparatus (2)	Directive 90/385/EC	—	—	—	—	—	—	—	Until lapse of the licence and no later than 31 Dec. 2005	—	—
Maltese derogation for milk chocolate (3)	Directive 2000/36/EC	—	—	—	—	—	—	Unlimited	—	—	—
Length of the transitional measure regarding the maximum level of dioxin in fish (4)	Regulation 466/2001/EC	—	—	31 Dec. 2006	—	—	—	—	—	—	—

— = no transitional measure accorded, i.e. the Regulation/Directive applies as of 1 May 2004.

(1) Medicines for human or veterinary use that were licensed prior to accession continue to be licensed until a certain period after accession in order to allow those having an interest to grant the products a licence in accordance with the "acquis communautaire". Until such time as the licence has been brought into accordance with the "acquis communautaire", the medicine in question can be refused in other member states.

(2) Medical apparatus that was licensed prior to accession continues to be licensed until a certain period after accession in order to allow those having an interest to grant the products a licence in accordance with the "acquis communautaire". Until such time as the licence has been brought into accordance with the "acquis communautaire", the medicine in question can be refused in other member states.

(3) Malta may use the term "milk chocolate" on its territory for the product referred to in point 5 of Directive 2000/36/EC, on condition that the term is at all times accompanied by an indication of the quantity of dry milk solids as laid down by the Directive.

(4) In accordance with transitional measures accorded to the present member states, the Commission may allow Estonia to market fish from the Baltic Sea that exceeds permitted dioxin levels under the following conditions:
- Estonia must show that the average exposure of humans to dioxin in Estonia is no greater than the average level in the present European Union;
- Estonia must show that an information system exists to provide full information to consumers, particularly vulnerable groups of the population. This is in order to avoid health risks;
- Estonia must implement the necessary measures to ensure that such fish or fish products are not brought onto the market in other member states; and
- Estonia must follow up the dioxin levels in fish from the Baltic Sea and report the results annually to the European Commission.

3.11 What is the second freedom: the free movement of persons?

In principle workers, nationals and undertakings can freely choose that member state within the EU where they develop their economic activities. The aim of this is to promote the optimal economic allocation of persons: the terms used are *the free movement of workers* for individuals and *the freedom of establishment* for undertakings.[19]

3.12 What is the free movement of workers?

The "free movement of workers" means that every national of a given member state may work in another member state. A worker from another member state may not be discriminated against by national legislation as regards: employment, pay and other working conditions (particularly dismissal, salary and training).

This means that workers from all EU member states have the right:

- to take up an offer of employment;
- to freely move within the EU for this purpose;

- to reside in the member state in order to carry on an occupation there in accordance with the statutory and administrative provisions that apply to the employment of a national employee;

- to reside on the territory of a member state even after the cessation of employment.

The *prohibition against discrimination* entails inter alia that:

- workers from another member state have to be able to enjoy the same working conditions as national workers;

- a member state may not impose any discriminatory occupational criteria based on nationality;

- workers from other member states have the same social security and tax rights and obligations as domestic workers. This also applies to their dependent children. They are also entitled to student grants, childbirth allowances and unemployment benefit;

- workers can keep the social security rights, including supplementary pensions, that they have built up in their home country;

- workers from another member state do not need to present any visa or similar documents. The employer does have to make a declaration that the worker has been hired or issue a certificate of employment;

- the members of the worker's family also have a right of residence. These persons have to prove their relationship by means of an official document issued by the member state of origin. They also have no visa obligation unless they are not nationals of one of the member states;

- the worker and his family members can remain on the territory of the member state even after having worked there.

The *right of residence* means that the worker and his family are given a residence permit. The documents needed to obtain a residence permit have been harmonised. Moreover, the worker does not have to wait for a residence permit before commencing work. The permit is valid for the whole territory of the issuing state. Its validity is at least five years.

If the worker has worked for more than three months but less than one year, the receiving state issues him with a temporary residence permit. The residence permit cannot be withdrawn on the ground that the worker is no longer employed, is temporarily unable to work or has been made redundant. The costs for issuing the residence documents may not be greater than the costs of issuing an identity card for the state's own nationals.

Frontier workers, seasonal workers and workers that do not work for more than three months in another member state do not need a permit. They only have to register their presence.

The prohibition against discrimination applies not only to rules laid down by the government but also for rules that come from other legal relationships, such as collective labour agreements.

However, the prohibition does not apply for employment in the service of the government.[20] In addition, restrictions on the grounds of public policy, public safety and public health are permitted. The European Court of Justice is attentive to the correct interpretation of these exceptions.

The aforementioned principles are further detailed in European regulations and directives. If you have a problem with recognition of your diploma or the social security of another country, then you can consult the Signpost Service of the Internal Market DG:
http://europa.eu.int/citizensrights/signpost/front_end/signpost_en.htm.

3.13 What is freedom of establishment?

Based on the provisions of the Treaty, the principle of freedom of establishment enables an economic operator (being it a person or a company) to carry on an economic activity in a stable and continuous way in one or more member states without being subject to any discriminatory or restrictive measures which could not be justified by reasons of general interest.

The Commission may request the national authorities to take the measures necessary to respect this principle and/or commence infringement procedure when a national regulation is considered not to be in accordance with the principle of freedom of establishment.

Freedom of establishment also means that one can open a branch in one member state if the undertaking in question is established in another member state. A UK citizen established in France can open a branch in Italy or Belgium.

The freedom of establishment is a right for:

- natural persons and

- companies that have been constituted according to the laws of one of the member states and have their registered office, principal management or main headquarters within the EU. As regards the constitution of subsidiaries or branches, it is required that a company that has only its registered office in the EU has to have an actual, lasting connection with the economy of one of the member states.

3.14   What is the importance of the freedom of establishment?

What does the freedom of establishment mean? Will it be easier after 1 May 2004 to get a "fixed footing" in the accession countries as a business?

The freedom of establishment does not just mean access to the territory of another member state and the right to remain there. Freedom of establishment also means that all restrictions that prevent an independent business from another member state from establishing in a given country are prohibited. For instance, a member state may not accord tax exemptions that apply only to companies that are incorporated according to the national laws of the member state itself.[21]

In order to support the freedom of establishment, there are rules about the reciprocal recognition of diplomas, education and qualifications for regulated occupations such as pharmacists, doctors, vets, dentists, nurses, midwives, architects and lawyers. The freedom of establishment can, however, be limited if this is justified on grounds of public policy, public safety or public health.

The freedom of establishment does not apply to activities in exercise of official authority in a given member state. In addition, the European Court of Justice has set out a number of exceptions, including in the fight against fraud.

3.15   What does this mean for companies?

The ongoing harmonisation of company law has also contributed to the practical realisation of the freedom of establishment. A common market with free competition requires that companies from various member states have more or less the same rights and obligations. Cross-border mergers or divisions of companies may not be encumbered by mutually incompatible national laws.

An overview of the "acquis communautaire" in respect of company law can be found in Chapter 4. As a result of transposition of this part of the "acquis communautaire" into the law of an accession country, a business that has set up a company there could be faced with new rules such as requirements for the publication of notices regarding company dealings and annual reports.

3.16   Will the European Company or Societas Europaea be introduced in the accession countries?

The European Company or Societas Europaea has the abbreviation: SE. The abbreviation SE will also be added after a company's name, like PLC or Ltd.

On 8 October 2004, the European Company Regulation comes into force. The Regulation will therefore be of direct effect in the new member states. The Regulation allows companies established in more than one member state to re-incorporate in the form of a single company within the EU. A European Company is then controlled by one system of rules regarding its functioning and the publication of information. The intention is to greatly reduce the administrative burden in each member state. A recurring criticism of the European Company, however, is that the tax rules have not been harmonised, as a result of which the benefits of the Regulation are limited.

Any limited company (such as, e.g. a UK Ltd, a French SA, a Dutch BV or a German AG) can re-incorporate as a European Company provided its has its registered office and principal management in the EU and:

- it merges with one or more existing public limited companies that have their registered offices and head offices within the EU, provided that at least two of them are governed by the law of different member states; or

- together with one or more companies that have their registered offices and head offices in the EU, it forms a holding SE, provided that each of at least two of the companies

  — are governed by the law of different member states or

  — have had a subsidiary for at least two years that is governed by the law of another member state or a branch that is situated in another member state; or

- together with one or more companies that have their registered offices and head offices in the EU, it forms a subsidiary SE by subscribing for its shares, provided that each of at least two of the companies

  — are governed by the law of a different member state or

  — have had a subsidiary for at least two years that is governed by the law of another member state or a branch that is situated in another member state; or

- it is a public company which has its registered office and head office within the EU and transforms itself as an SE provided that it has had a subsidiary company for at least two years that is governed by the law of another member state.

3.17 Is there also free movement for persons other than businesses or workers?

Private individuals also benefit from the free movement of persons. All nationals of member states have a right of residence (Directive 90/364/EEC of the Council of 28 June 1990 on the right of residence)[22] if they have health care insurance for themselves and the members of their family that covers all risks in the host country and they have sufficient means for their existence.

These conditions were laid down in order to protect the social security system of host countries. A right of residence can be refused on grounds of public policy, public safety or public health.

The right of residence is confirmed by issuance of a "Residence permit for a national of a Member State of the EEC", the validity of which may be limited to five years.

By extending the free movement of persons to persons not in gainful employment, the path has been cleared for so-called "European citizenship". Thus, a number of citizens' rights have been introduced, being European[23] and local council voting rights.[24]

3.18 What about public policy and public safety?

The free movement of persons can be limited on grounds of public policy, public safety or public health. These limitations have to be interpreted restrictively and cannot be founded on economic objectives. For this reason, the European rules provide that restrictive measures are only permitted on the grounds of the personal conduct of the individual. The existence of a criminal conviction or an invalid identity card are not sufficient grounds for such measures. As regards public health, a European list has been drawn up of illnesses that justify restrictive measures.[25]

3.19 Are there any transitional measures regarding the free movement of persons?

In order to avoid present member states being swamped with cheap labour from the east after enlargement, there are transitional measures that may limit the free movement of persons.

3.19.1   Movement from the accession countries to the present member states

With the exception of Malta and Cyprus, there is a general transitional measure for all the other accession countries as regards the free movement of persons.

For two years after accession, the current member states may themselves lay down rules that limit access by workers from the accession countries to their national labour markets. After that period, the European Commission will evaluate the situation. The accession member state can also ask for an evaluation. Depending on the evaluation, a decision will be taken on whether or not the "acquis communautaire" with regard to the free movement of workers has been fully implemented.

The transitional period may not exceed five years. If the labour market in one of the member states is seriously distorted, the transitional period can be extended to seven years.

There is a status quo clause that somewhat softens the transitional measure, since the member states cannot impose any more stringent measures than applied at the time of signature of the accession treaty on 16 April 2003. Furthermore, the member states must give a preference to workers from accession countries as against workers from non-EU countries.

3.19.2   Movement from current member states to the accession countries

Malta is fearful that accession to the EU will entail an influx of labour to the islands. Hence, it can ask for transitional measures that will stay in force until seven years following accession.

3.20   What is the third freedom: the free movement of services?

As from 1 May 2004, the new member states cannot any longer impose restrictions on service providers from other member states. As in the case of the free movement of goods, the opening of these markets in the accession countries will offer service providers in the EU both threats and opportunities. Consumers will be able to enjoy the benefits of competition. The choice will become larger, quality will improve and prices will fall. A fine example of this is the liberalisation of the telephony market.

The EC Treaty[26] states that the provision of services within the EU may not in principle be restricted. This applies to service providers from another member state than that where the recipient of the service is established. A proviso therefore is that the service provider be in another member state. For natural persons, the criterion applied is that of the place of residence. Legal entities can also benefit from this provided they have an economic tie with at least one member state.

The free movement of services has much in common with the free movement of goods. Here, too, as from 1 May 2004, the accession countries will no longer be able to maintain any measures in protection of their national businesses in the market for services.

Activities in exercise of the official authority of a member state are an exception to this. There may also be exceptions for measures inter alia in the areas of:

- public policy;

- public safety;

- culture;

- the fight against fraud;

- consumer protection.

The European Court of Justice also accepts exceptions where they are necessary and proportionate in their aims and no adequate common European rule is available. In this regard, we refer to point 7, "What Is the Prohibition against Quantitative Import and Export Restrictions and Measures of Equivalent Effect?" The lack of any adequate European rules can thus result in distortion of the internal market owing to mutually incompatible national rules. In order to avoid this, a number of initiatives have been taken, such as:

- the European rules on consumer protection;

- the European rules on access to the profession of carrier;

- the European rules on financial service providers.

3.21 What about financial services?

Within the framework of the free movement of services there are a number of European measures regarding banking services, insurance services, investments and trading in securities.

The "acquis communautaire" in this sector deals with the requirements that such institutions have to satisfy. This means that a financial institution that meets all European requirements may conduct business in any member state, even if it is established in another member state. Here, then, there applies the principle of "home country control", whereby the member state where the head office is established exercises supervision over such service providers. The other member states must recognise such supervision. In certain specific cases, however, the host country control principle applies, where the host country may apply or invoke its national laws with respect to financial services (e.g. legislation concerning tax fraud).

The "acquis communautaire" in respect of financial services has been widely extended in the recent years. Alongside the basic Treaty principles, a number of Directives have been issued. An overview follows.

DIRECTIVE: Directive 73/239/EEC of 24 July 1973 (amended on several occasions).
PUBLICATION: Official Journal No. L228 of 16 August 1973, pp. 0003–0019.
SUMMARY: coordination of laws, regulations and administrative provisions relating to the taking up and pursuit of the business of direct insurance other than life assurance.
This Directive institutes a single authorisation in the EU for those insurance undertakings with offices in various member states. For that purpose, the conditions for the issuance of such authorisations are harmonised.
TRANSITIONAL MEASURES: none.

DIRECTIVE: Directive 73/240/EEC of 24 July 1973.
PUBLICATION: Official Journal No. L228 of 16 August 1973, pp. 0020–0022.
SUMMARY: abolition of restrictions on the freedom of establishment in the business of direct insurance other than life assurance.
The member states are obliged to abolish restrictions that, particularly
a. prevent foreign insurance undertakings establishing in the host country under the same conditions and with equal rights as nationals of that country;
b. result from official conduct that has the consequence that foreign insurance undertakings are treated differently in comparison with national ones.
The Directive specifically lists cases for each member state that are to be regarded as restrictions.
TRANSITIONAL MEASURES: none.

DIRECTIVE: Directive 85/611/EEC of 20 December 1985, Directive 88/220/EEC of 22 March 1988.
PUBLICATION: Official Journal No. L375 of 31 December 1985, pp. 0003–0018, Official Journal No. L100 of 19 April 1988, p. 0031–0032.
SUMMARY: coordination of laws, regulations and administrative provisions relating to undertakings for collective investment in transferable securities (UCITS).

This Directive lays down common rules on the conditions for admission of UCITS.
TRANSITIONAL MEASURES: none.

DIRECTIVE: Directive 86/635/EEC of 8 December 1986.
PUBLICATION: Official Journal No. L372 of 31 December 1986, pp. 0001–0017.
SUMMARY: the annual accounts and consolidated accounts of banks and other financial institutions.

This Directive regulates the sub-division and content of the balance sheet and profit and loss account in such annual accounts.
TRANSITIONAL MEASURES: Slovenia: this Directive will not apply up until 31 December 2004 to credit and savings institutions set up before 20 February 1999.

DIRECTIVE: Directive 87/344/EEC of 22 June 1987.
PUBLICATION: Official Journal No. L185 of 4 July 1987, pp. 0077–0080.
SUMMARY: coordination of laws, regulations and administrative provisions relating to legal expenses insurance.
TRANSITIONAL MEASURES: none.

DIRECTIVE: Directive 87/343/EEC of 22 June 1987.
PUBLICATION: Official Journal No. L185 of 4 July 1987, pp. 0072–0076.
SUMMARY: as regards credit insurance and suretyship insurance, coordination of laws, regulations and administrative provisions relating to the taking-up and pursuit of the business of direct insurance other than life assurance.

The objective of this Directive is to institute supplementary financial guarantees for credit insurance and to abolish the German requirement that credit insurance and suretyship insurance may only be provided by specialist undertakings.
TRANSITIONAL MEASURES: none.

DIRECTIVE: Directive 88/357/EEC of 22 June 1988.
PUBLICATION: Official Journal No. L172 of 4 July 1987, pp. 0001–0014.
SUMMARY: coordination of laws, regulations and administrative provisions relating to direct insurance other than life assurance and laying down provisions to facilitate the effective exercise of freedom to provide services.

This Directive lays down further rules with regard to the supervision of insurance companies as regards consumer protection.
TRANSITIONAL MEASURES: none.

DIRECTIVE: Directive 89/117/EEC of 13 February 1989.
PUBLICATION: Official Journal No. L044 of 16 February 1989, pp. 0040–0042.
SUMMARY: obligations of branches established in a member state of credit institutions and financial institutions having their head offices outside that member state regarding the publication of annual accounting documents.

This Directive provides that a branch has to publish the annual accounts, consolidated accounts, annual report, etc. of the institution after audit by the member state where the institution has established its head office. A branch cannot be obliged to publish annual accounts relating to its own business.
TRANSITIONAL MEASURES: none.

DIRECTIVE: Directive 89/298/EEC of 17 April 1989.
PUBLICATION: Official Journal No. L124 of 5 May 1989, pp. 0008–0015.
SUMMARY: coordination of the requirements for the drawing-up, scrutiny and distribution of the prospectus to be published when transferable securities are offered to the public.
TRANSITIONAL MEASURES: none.

DIRECTIVE: Directive 90/232/EEC of 14 May 1990.
PUBLICATION: Official Journal No. L129 of 19 May 1990, pp. 0033–0035.
SUMMARY: approximation of the laws of the member states relating to insurance against civil liability in respect of the use of motor vehicles.
TRANSITIONAL MEASURES: none.

DIRECTIVE: Directive 90/619/EEC of 8 November 1990.
PUBLICATION: Official Journal No. L330 of 29 November 1990, pp. 0050–0061.
SUMMARY: coordination of laws, regulations and administrative provisions relating to direct life assurance, laying down provisions to facilitate the effective exercise of freedom to provide services.
   Directive promoting the free provision of cross-border services in the area of life assurance.
TRANSITIONAL MEASURES: none.

DIRECTIVE: Directive 91/308/EEC of 10 June 1991.
PUBLICATION: Official Journal No. L166 of 28 June 1991, pp. 0077–0083.
SUMMARY: prevention of the use of the financial system for the purpose of money-laundering.
   The Directive prohibits money-laundering and obliges the member states to ensure that credit institutions and financial institutions require identification of their customers by means of supporting evidence when entering into business relations. Furthermore, the Directive governs obligatory cooperation with the authorities in the fight against money-laundering.
TRANSITIONAL MEASURES: none.

DIRECTIVE: Directive 91/674/EEC of 19 December 1991.
PUBLICATION: Official Journal No. L374 of 31 December 1991, pp. 0007–0031.

SUMMARY: annual accounts and consolidated accounts of insurance undertakings.

This Directive principally lays down the content of the balance sheet and profit and loss account under the annual accounts and consolidated accounts of insurance undertakings.

TRANSITIONAL MEASURES: none.

DIRECTIVE: Directive 92/49/EEC of 18 June 1992.

PUBLICATION: Official Journal No. L228 of 11 August 1992, pp. 0001–0023.

SUMMARY: coordination of laws, regulations and administrative provisions relating to direct insurance other than life assurance.

Refinement of the rules on the sole authorisation for such insurance undertakings, instituted by Directive 73/239/EEC of 24 July 1973.

TRANSITIONAL MEASURES: none.

DIRECTIVE: Directive 93/6/EEC of 15 March 1993.

PUBLICATION: Official Journal No. L141 of 11 June 1993, pp. 0001–0026.

SUMMARY: adequacy of investment firms and credit institutions.

This Directive lays down minimum capital requirements for such undertakings taking account of the market risks with which they are faced. Further, rules are imposed regarding supervision and reporting.

TRANSITIONAL MEASURES: none.

DIRECTIVE: Directive 93/22/EEC of 10 May 1993.

PUBLICATION: Official Journal No. L141 of 11 June 1993, pp. 0027–0046.

SUMMARY: investment services in the securities field.

This Directive is aimed at the essential harmonisation necessary and sufficient to secure the mutual recognition of authorisation and of prudential supervision systems, making possible the grant of a single authorisation valid throughout the Community and the application of the principle of home member state supervision; by virtue of mutual recognition, investment firms authorised in their home member states may carry on any or all of the services covered by this Directive for which they have received authorisation throughout the Community by establishing branches or under the freedom to provide services.

TRANSITIONAL MEASURES: none.

DIRECTIVE: Directive 94/19/EC of 30 May 1994.

PUBLICATION: Official Journal No. L135 of 31 May 1994, pp. 0005–0014.

SUMMARY: deposit-guarantee schemes.

A credit institution has various debts that it owes towards the general public, such as funds invested in savings accounts. In order to protect repayment of debts to the public, deposit-guarantee schemes are set up. These schemes ensure repayment in the event that the credit institution is unable to fulfil its obligations in this regard. These schemes are harmonised at a European level to a certain degree by means of this Directive. Thus, the Directive stipulates that deposit-guarantee schemes have to provide that the total deposits from one and the same depositor are covered up to an amount of EUR 20 000 when the deposits are unavailable.

TRANSITIONAL MEASURES:

Estonia
The minimum guarantee level in Estonia is not applicable up until 31 December 2007. Estonia ensures that its deposit-guarantee scheme offers cover to the extent of no less than EUR 6391 up until 31 December 2005 and of no less than EUR 12 782 from 1 January 2006 until 31 December 2007.

Lithuania
Ditto, but here the respective amounts are EUR 14 481 and EUR 17 377. During the transitional period, the other member states retain the right to prevent branches of Lithuanian credit institutions from carrying on business on their territory, unless and until the branch accedes to an officially recognised deposit-guarantee scheme on the territory of the relevant member state in order to cover the difference between the level of guarantee in the accession state and the European level of guarantee.

Latvia
Ditto, but here the amounts are EUR 10 000 and EUR 15 000, respectively.

Slovenia
The Directive does not apply in Slovenia up until 31 December 2004 for credit and savings institutions set up prior to 20 February 1999. Neither the amount nor the scope of the cover offered by a credit institution from another member state in Slovenia may be greater up until 31 December 2005 than the minimum amount and scope of the cover that is offered by the corresponding guarantee scheme in Slovenia.

DIRECTIVE: Directive 97/5/EC of 27 January 1997.
PUBLICATION: Official Journal No. L043 of 14 February 1997, pp. 0025–0030.
SUMMARY: cross-border credit transfers.
This Directive sets down rules that have to be observed by financial institutions in relations with customers in the case of cross-border credit transfers.
TRANSITIONAL MEASURES: none.

DIRECTIVE: Directive 97/9/EC of 3 March 1997.
PUBLICATION: Official Journal No. L084 of 26 March 1997, pp. 0022–0031.
SUMMARY: Directive on investor-compensation schemes.
This Directive obliges the member states to introduce and officially recognise one or more investor-compensation schemes and to ensure that all investment firms that offer investment services belong to that scheme. The

compensation scheme provides investors with cover:

- where the competent authorities have determined that in their view an investment firm appears, for the time being, for reasons directly related to its financial circumstances, to be unable to meet its obligations arising out of investors' claims and has no early prospect of being able to do so, or
- where a judicial authority has made a ruling, for reasons directly related to an investment firm's financial circumstances, which has the effect of suspending investors' ability to make claims against it.

Cover has to be provided for claims arising out of an investment firm's inability to:

- repay money owed to or belonging to investors and held on their behalf in connection with investment business, or
- return to investors any instruments belonging to them and held, administered or managed on their behalf in connection with investment business, in accordance with the legal and contractual conditions applicable.

Cover must extend to EUR 20 000 per investor.

TRANSITIONAL MEASURES

Estonia

The minimum amount of compensation does not apply in Estonia up until 31 December 2007. Estonia will provide that its investor-compensation scheme provides cover of no less than EUR 6391 up until 31 December 2005 and of no less than EUR 12 782 from 1 January 2006 until 31 December 2007.

Hungary

The minimum amount of compensation does not apply in Hungary up until 31 December 2007. Hungary will provide that its investor-compensation scheme provides cover of no less than EUR 3783 up until 31 December 2004 and of no less than EUR 7565 from 1 January 2005 until 31 December 2007.

During the transitional period, other member states retain the right to prevent a branch of a Hungarian investment undertaking established on their territory from carrying on business unless and until the branch has acceded to an officially recognised investor-compensation scheme on the territory of the relevant member state in order to cover the difference between the Hungarian level of compensation and EUR 20 000. Up until 31 December 2007, the amount of cover offered by an investment undertaking from another member state in Hungary may not be greater than the minimum amount of EUR 20 000. During that period, the extent of the cover provided by an investment undertaking from another member state in Hungary may not be more extensive than the cover of the corresponding compensation scheme in Hungary.

Latvia
The minimum amount of compensation does not apply in Latvia up until 31 December 2007. Latvia will provide that its investor-compensation scheme provides cover of no less than EUR 10 000 up until 31 December 2005 and of no less than EUR 15 000 from 1 January 2006 until 31 December 2007.

During the transitional period, other member states retain the right to prevent a branch of a Latvian investment undertaking established on their territory from carrying on business unless and until the branch has acceded to an officially recognised investor-compensation scheme on the territory of the relevant member state in order to cover the difference between the Latvian level of compensation and EUR 20 000.

Lithuania
The minimum amount of compensation does not apply in Lithuania up until 31 December 2007. Lithuania will provide that its investor-compensation scheme provides cover of no less than EUR 5792 up until 31 December 2005 and of no less than EUR 11 585 from 1 January 2006 until 31 December 2007.

During the transitional period, other member states retain the right to prevent a branch of a Lithuanian investment undertaking established on their territory from carrying on business unless and until the branch has acceded to an officially recognised investor-compensation scheme on the territory of the relevant member state in order to cover the difference between the Lithuanian level of compensation and EUR 20 000.

Poland
The minimum amount of compensation does not apply in Poland up until 31 December 2007. Poland will provide that its investor-compensation scheme provides cover of no less than EUR 7000 up until 31 December 2004, of no less than EUR 11 000 from 1 January 2005 until 31 December 2005, of no less than EUR 15 000 from 1 January 2006 until 31 December 2006 and of no less than EUR 19 000 from 1 January 2007 until 31 December 2007.

During the transitional period, other member states retain the right to prevent a branch of a Polish investment undertaking established on their territory from carrying on business unless and until the branch has acceded to an officially recognised investor-compensation scheme on the territory of the relevant member state in order to cover the difference between the Polish level of compensation and EUR 20 000.

Slovakia
The minimum amount of compensation does not apply in Slovakia up until 31 December 2006. Slovakia will provide that its investor-compensation scheme provides cover of no less than EUR 10 000 up until 31 December 2004, of no less than EUR 13 000 from 1 January 2005 until

31 December 2005, and of no less than EUR 16 000 from 1 January 2006 until 31 December 2006.

Slovenia

Slovenia may derogate from the Directive up until 31 December 2005 but neither the amount nor the scope of the cover offered by an investment undertaking from another member state in Slovenia may be greater than the minimum amount and scope of the compensation that is offered by the corresponding compensation scheme in Slovenia.

DIRECTIVE: Directive 98/29/EC of 7 May 1998.
PUBLICATION: Official Journal No. L148 of 19 May 1998, pp. 0022–0032.
SUMMARY: harmonisation of the main provisions concerning export credit insurance for transactions with medium and long-term cover.

This Directive applies to cover for transactions relating to the export of goods and/or services originating in a member state, in so far as this support is provided directly or indirectly for the account of, or with the support of, one or more member states, involving a total risk period of two years or more, that is to say, the repayment period including the manufacturing period. The Annex to this Directive contains the common principles for export credit insurance. It concerns rules concerning the extent of the cover, causes of loss and exclusion of liability, indemnification for claims, premiums, country cover policy (difference between countries with high and low risks) and notification procedures to the European Commission.

TRANSITIONAL MEASURES: none.

DIRECTIVE: Directive 98/26/EC of 19 May 1998.
PUBLICATION: Official Journal No. L166 of 11 June 1998, pp. 0045–0050.
SUMMARY: settlement finality in payment and securities settlement systems.

This Directive is aimed at reducing the systemic risks at a common level that are associated with participation in payment and settlement systems, especially in connection with the insolvency of a participant in such a system.

TRANSITIONAL MEASURES: none.

DIRECTIVE: Directive 98/78/EC of 27 October 1998.
PUBLICATION: Official Journal No. L330 of 5 December 1998, pp. 0001–0012.
SUMMARY: supplementary supervision of insurance undertakings in an insurance group.

This Directive obliges the member states to extend their supervision of insurance undertakings to all other undertakings that might have an influence on the financial situation and activities of regulated insurance undertakings, in order to form a more soundly based judgment of the actual solvency of the insurance undertaking in question.

TRANSITIONAL MEASURES: none.

DIRECTIVE: Directive 2000/46/EC of 18 September 2000.
PUBLICATION: Official Journal No. L275 of 27 October 2000, pp. 0039–0043.
SUMMARY: the taking-up, pursuit of and prudential supervision of the business of electronic money institutions.
TRANSITIONAL MEASURES: none.

DIRECTIVE: Directive 2000/12/EC of 18 March 2000.
PUBLICATION: Official Journal No. L126 of 26 May 2000, pp. 0001–0059.
SUMMARY: the taking-up and pursuit of the business of credit institutions.

This Directive ensures that credit institutions only have to obtain one licence in the EU, which is recognised by all the member states (the so-called single passport). A further principle under the Directive is that, fundamentally, the member state of origin exercises supervision over the financial institution (so-called home country control). Of course, the principles of the single passport and home country control offer broad opportunities for credit institutions in the current and the new member states. Harmonisation of the market in financial services in the accession countries will naturally also offer benefits to customers for such services. A credit institution is defined in the Directive as an undertaking whose business is to receive deposits or other repayable funds from the public and to grant credits for its own account. The Directive lays down the conditions for taking up and pursuing the business of a credit institution, cooperation between the member states within the framework of home country control and the principles of supervision.

TRANSITIONAL MEASURES:

Cyprus
Up until 31 December 2007, this Directive does not apply to Cooperative Credit and Savings Companies in Cyprus in so far as they do not fulfil the Directive's requirements.

Poland
Up until 31 December 2007, this Directive does not apply to cooperative credit institutions that were already established in Poland on the date of accession. Poland shall ensure that the start-up capital required for such cooperative credit institutions is until 31 December 2005 not less than EUR 300 000 and from 1 January 2006 until 31 December 2007 not less than EUR 500 000. During the transitional period, the equity of such undertakings shall not be less than the greatest amount it has achieved since the date of accession.

DIRECTIVE: Directive 2001/17/EC of 19 March 2001.
PUBLICATION: Official Journal No. L110 of 20 April 2001, pp. 0028–0039.
SUMMARY: reorganisation and winding-up of insurance undertakings.

This Directive applies the principle of home country control and states that only the official or judicial authorities of the member state of origin are competent to impose reorganisation measures on an insurance undertaking, including its branches established in other member states together with opening liquidation procedures regarding such undertakings.
TRANSITIONAL MEASURES: none.

DIRECTIVE: Directive 2001/24/EC of 4 April 2001.
PUBLICATION: Official Journal No. L125 of 5 May 2001, pp. 0015–0023.
SUMMARY: reorganisation and winding up of credit institutions.

This Directive advances the principle of home country control and states that only the official or judicial authorities of the member state of origin are competent to impose reorganisation measures on a credit institution, including its branches established in other member states together with opening liquidation procedures regarding such institutions.
TRANSITIONAL MEASURES: none.

DIRECTIVE: Directive 2001/34/EC of 28 May 2001.
PUBLICATION: Official Journal No. L184 of 6 July 2001, pp. 0001–0066.
SUMMARY: admission of securities to official stock exchange listing and information to be published on those securities.

The aim of this Directive is to coordinate the conditions for admission of securities to official listing at stock exchanges situated or active in the member states. This is intended to equalise investor protection at a Community level. They must also make it easier for securities originating from other member states to be admitted to official listing in each of the member states and listing of one and the same security at various stock exchanges in the Community
TRANSITIONAL MEASURES: none.

DIRECTIVE: Directive 2002/65/EC of 23 September 2002.
PUBLICATION: Official Journal No. L271 of 9 October 2002, pp. 0016–0024.
SUMMARY: distance marketing of consumer financial services.

This Directive is aimed at further approximating the statutory and administrative provisions of the member states regarding the distance marketing of consumer financial services. As a result of this coordination, the consumer-protection rules do not vary so widely from member state to member state, which promotes cross-border trade in this regard.
TRANSITIONAL MEASURES: none.

DIRECTIVE: Directive 2002/83/EC of 5 November 2002.
PUBLICATION: Official Journal No. L345 of 19 December 2002, pp. 0001–0051.

SUMMARY: life assurance.

Directive regarding access to and pursuit of the business of direct insurance with regard to life assurance. Harmonisation of admission conditions and principle of single passport.

TRANSITIONAL MEASURES: none.

DIRECTIVE: Directive 2002/92/EC of 9 December 2002.
PUBLICATION: Official Journal No. L009 of 15 January 2003, pp. 0003–0010.
SUMMARY: insurance mediation.

Common rules regarding the registration of intermediaries. Information obligations between member states. Information obligations on intermediaries vis-à-vis their clients.

TRANSITIONAL MEASURES: none.

3.22 Is adoption of the "acquis communautaire" in respect of financial services by the accession countries only of interest to financial service providers?

No. In the first instance, the rules and regulations with respect to financial services have been made in order to protect investors and savers. In principle, investors and savers can now have the same reliance on the soundness of the products and the service providers throughout the European Union, just as with all European rules.

3.23 What about public contracts?

Public contracts have a particular impact on the economy due to the large sums that are involved in such deals. Because only 2% of all public contracts are awarded to firms from other member states, the EU has decided to coordinate the national tender procedures of the member states.

The tender procedure for public contracts for supplies of goods and services and the selection of suppliers is laid down in directives. The Directive on the award of services makes a distinction between priority and residual services. For priority services, stricter rules apply.

Awards with a minor impact on the internal market fall outside the scope of application of the directives. The Directive therefore contains very detailed thresholds.

Adoption of the "acquis communautaire" in respect of public contracts in the accession countries is intended to make it easier for firms in the present member states to compete for public contracts.

DIRECTIVE: Directive 89/665/EEC of 21 December 1989.

PUBLICATION: Official Journal No. L395 of 30 December 1989, pp. 0033–0035.

SUMMARY: coordination of the laws, regulations and administrative provisions relating to the application of review procedures to the award of public supply and public works contracts.

This Directive ensures effective application of the European rules on public contracts by obliging the member states to provide an appeal authority where parties having an interest can review award decisions on grounds of an infringement of Community law. The appeal must include the necessary powers to:

(a) take, at the earliest opportunity and by way of interlocutory procedures, interim measures with the aim of correcting the alleged infringement or preventing further damage to the interests concerned, including measures to suspend or to ensure the suspension of the procedure for the award of a public contract or the implementation of any decision taken by the contracting authority;

(b) either set aside or ensure the setting aside of decisions taken unlawfully, including the removal of discriminatory technical, economic or financial specifications in the invitation to tender, the contract documents or in any other document relating to the contract award procedure;

(c) award damages to persons harmed by an infringement.

TRANSITIONAL MEASURES: none.

DIRECTIVE: Directive 92/13/EEC of 25 February 1992.

PUBLICATION: Official Journal No. L076 of 23 March 1992, pp. 0014–0020.

SUMMARY: coordination of the laws, regulations and administrative provisions relating to the application of Community rules on the procurement procedures of entities operating in the water, energy, transport and telecommunications sectors.

This Directive is a similar directive regarding tender procedures to the preceding one, but is specifically applied to contracts awarded by departments operating in the water, energy, transport and telecommunications sectors.

TRANSITIONAL MEASURES: none.

DIRECTIVE: Directive 92/50/EEC of 18 June 1992.

PUBLICATION: Official Journal No. L209 of 24 July 1992, pp. 0001–0024.

SUMMARY: coordination of procedures for the award of public service contracts.

This Directive governs the procedure to be followed in awarding service contracts with an estimated value of at least EUR 200 000 excluding VAT, including the estimated total remuneration of the service provider. In order to draw a distinction with public supply contracts, this Directive states that what are involved are services where the supplies that are made under the contract are of a lesser value than the services.

The Directive expressly excludes the provision of certain services from its scope of application in a manner similar to the Directive on the supply of goods (see below).

The Directive splits services up into priority and residual services. Stricter rules apply to priority services.

TRANSITIONAL MEASURES: none.

DIRECTIVE: Directive 93/36/EEC of 14 June 1993.
PUBLICATION: Official Journal No. L199 of 9 August 1993, pp. 0001–0053.
SUMMARY: coordination of the procedures for the award of public supply contracts.

This Directive governs the procedure to be followed in the award of public contracts for supplies, including the selection of suppliers.

According to the Directive, public supply contracts are contracts for pecuniary interest concluded in writing involving the purchase, lease, rental or hire purchase, with or without option to buy, of products entered into between a supplier and the "contracting authorities". The "contracting authorities" are the state, regional or local authorities, bodies governed by public law, associations formed by one or several of such authorities or bodies governed by public law. The delivery of such products may in addition include siting and installation operations. Certain contracts are expressly excluded from the scope of application of the Directive. These are contracts:

- awarded in the fields referred to in Articles 2, 7, 8 and 9 of Directive 90/531/EEC or fulfilling the conditions in article 6 (2) of that Directive;
- for supplies that are declared secret;
- supplies execution of which must be accompanied by special security measures in accordance with the legislation in the member state concerned or when the protection of the basic interests of the member state's security so requires;
- for which other procedural rules apply under certain international agreements or according to the particular procedure of an international organisation.

Contracts with a minor impact on the internal market are also excluded from the scope of application of the Directive. Therefore, certain thresholds are detailed in the Directive and it is set out how these thresholds are to be calculated.

TRANSITIONAL MEASURES: none.

DIRECTIVE: Directive 93/37/EEC of 14 June 1993.
PUBLICATION: Official Journal No. L199 of 9 August 1993, pp. 0054–0083.
SUMMARY: coordination of procedures for the award of public works contracts.

This Directive governs the procedure to be followed in awarding contracts for the execution or design of works whereby one of the following services is involved: building works, road-building works, installation, construction and finishing or realisation of works in accordance with the requirements laid down by the contracting authority regardless of how this occurs. Certain works are excluded from the scope of application of the Directive for the same reasons as the immediately preceding Directive with regard to supplies of goods. The value of the works must be estimated at a minimum of BEF 5 000 000 excluding VAT. The rules on procedure and selection are the same as those for awards of goods contracts.
TRANSITIONAL MEASURES: none.

DIRECTIVE: Directive 93/38/EEC of 14 June 1993.
PUBLICATION: Official Journal No. L199 of 9 August 1993, pp. 0084–0138.
SUMMARY: coordination of the procurement procedures of entities operating in the water, energy, transport and telecommunications sectors.
This Directive specifically governs the procedure for awarding contracts in the water, energy, transport and telecommunications sectors.
TRANSITIONAL MEASURES: none.

3.24 What other legislation is relevant for the free movement of services?

The following initiatives are worthy of note:

- the directives on transport services, which are looked at separately in Chapter 4;

- the directives on liberalisation of the energy sector, which are looked at separately in Chapter 4;

- Council Directive 86/653/EEC on the coordination of the laws of the member states relating to self-employed commercial agents;

- Directive 96/71/EC of the European Parliament and of the Council of 16 December 1996 concerning the posting of workers in the framework of the provision of services;

- Directive 97/67/EC of the European Parliament and of the Council of 15 December 1997 on common rules for the development of the internal market of Community postal services and the improvement of quality of service;

- the rules on the protection of personal data and the free movement of such data;

- Information Society Directives on the provision of information in the field of technical standards and rules regarding the legal protection of services under conditional access. In this connection, we mention the European rules on electronic signatures and the protection of personal data.[27] The implementation of these rules in the accession countries will create the same legal framework for the digitisation of business processes, as we now are familiar with in the EU.

3.25 What is the fourth freedom: free movement of capital and payments?

The creation of the internal market requires that businesses should be free to enter into financial transactions. At the same time, investors have to be able to invest where they see fit. This is the free movement of capital. In addition, free movement of payments is also essential for a common market, since payments are inseparably bound up with the movement of goods, services and capital. They are the consideration for the movement of goods, persons and services or the movement of capital itself, such as payments of interest, dividends or profits.

Hence, restrictive measures regarding the movement of capital and payments between member states are prohibited. Moreover, restrictions between member states and third countries are also prohibited.

Examples of prohibited restrictions include:

- a requirement for an official permit for the export of coins, banknotes or bearer cheques;[28]

- a prohibition against taking out mortgages in the currency of another member state;[29] or

- a cumbersome authorisation procedure that makes it difficult for foreigners to purchase real estate[30] (N.B. see section 3.26 "Are there transitional measures for the free movement of capital and payments?").

Exceptions to the aforementioned principle are only justified on grounds of public policy and security, tax or business control measures and for statistical purposes. However, the proportionality requirement does apply. This means that the measure may only restrict the freedom of movement to such an extent as is necessary to achieve the goal. Moreover, other, less harmful measures must not be available.

The accession countries also have to allow the free movement of capital and payments as from 1 May 2004, unless there are transitional measures.

3.26 Are there transitional measures for the free movement of capital and payments?

Table 3.2 Transitional measures: free movement of capital and payments.

Subject-matter	Legal text	Cyprus	Czech Republic	Estonia	Hungary	Latvia	Lithuania	Malta	Poland	Slovakia	Slovenia
Maintenance of restrictions regarding the purchase of second residences except citizens of accession countries. Date of end of transitional measure	Title III, Chapter 4 of the consolidated EC Treaty	31 Apr. 2009	31 Apr. 2009	—	31 Apr. 2009	—	—	Particular (1)	—	—	Particular (2)
Maintenance of restrictions regarding the purchase of agricultural and forestry land. nationals of member states that are self-employed farmers in the accession country in question are excluded from the scope of application of the transitional measure. The Commission may extend the duration of this transitional measure by three years if the market for agricultural land is seriously affected	Title III, Chapter 4 of the consolidated EC Treaty	—	31 Apr. 2011	31 Apr. 2011	31 Apr. 2011	31 Apr. 2011	31 Apr. 2011	—	—	31 Apr. 2011	Particular (2)

— = no transitional measures accorded, i.e. the EU rules apply as of 1 May 2004.

(1)   There are particular rules for the purchase of second residences in Malta whereby EU citizens are prohibited from purchasing such residences unless they have been established for five years on the islands. Malta will be able to maintain these rules on a permanent basis.

(2)   Slovenia may continue for seven years after accession to pass general protectionist economic measures in the real estate sector.

3.27 What is free competition?

Free competition is regarded in the European Union as a condition for economic efficiency. Free competition is monitored by means of the competition policy, which rests on three pillars:

- the rules on cooperation between undertakings;

- the rules for combating abuse of a dominant position; and

- control of concentrations.

Furthermore, competition rules are important for public corporations, state aid and awards of public contracts.

Thus, a European business has to examine whether the contracts it enters into in the new member states comply with the competition legislation. In particular, in this regard we would mention arrangements with competitors, distribution agreements with wide-ranging restrictions on distributors and tying arrangements.

Undertakings that currently receive government support from the accession countries have to examine whether this is still legal after 1 May 2004. If it is not, then the support must stop or will later have to be repaid. Tax break schemes also lapse after 1 May 2004.

3.28 What forms of cooperation between undertakings are permissible?

After 1 May 2004, all contracts entered into in the accession countries have to meet European competition requirements. As a matter of principle, European law prohibits agreements between undertakings and all concerted practices which may affect trade between member states and which have as their object or effect the prevention, restriction or distortion of competition within the common market.

A number of examples of agreements that are automatically void:

- directly or indirectly fixing purchase or selling prices or any other trading conditions;

- limiting or controlling production, markets, technical development, or investment;

- sharing markets or sources of supply;

- applying dissimilar conditions to equivalent transactions with other trading parties;

- making the conclusion of contracts subject to supplementary obligations which have no connection with the subject of such contracts.[31]

Both vertical and horizontal contracts are targeted. It is not necessary that an agreement actually has a negative effect. An indirect or even a potential negative effect is enough for the agreement to be held to be void.

Citizens and businesses can directly invoke these competition rules before national courts, which may make a reference for a preliminary ruling to the European Court of Justice.

3.29 Are there exceptions to free competition?

The prohibition is a matter of principle. This means that there are exceptions for which the prohibition does not apply. These exception rules change throughout the EU on 1 May 2004, for on that date the new Regulation 1/2003[32] comes into force and supersedes the current Regulation 17/62. In this new system, it is no longer possible to apply to the European Commission for exemptions. Undertakings will then themselves have to examine whether their agreements are in conflict with the European prohibition against cartels. The competence of the national competition authorities is also extended.

3.29.1   Old rules

Up until 30 April 2004, the rule is that the prohibition against anti-competitive behaviour can be ignored if the European Commission grants an exemption. There are two types: *individual exemptions* for a given contract or *block exemptions* for a category of contracts.

An exemption is accorded if it can be shown that:

- the contract contributes to improvements in production, distribution or technical or economic progress;

- a fair share of the resulting benefit is enjoyed by consumers;

- no less restrictive alternatives exist for achieving the same goal; and

- competition is not completely circumvented.

Exemptions are always time-limited. The European Commission can also impose particular conditions and obligations.

An exemption has to be applied for with the European Commission. The Commission can take three decisions:

- a *negative clearance*, a decision in which it determines that the agreement falls outside the scope of application of the prohibition;

- a *prohibition*: a determination that there is an infringement and an obligation on the undertakings to end it;

- an *exemption*: a decision whereby the Commission declares that the prohibition does not apply.

One important block exemption is the *exemption for agreements of minor importance* (the "de minimis rule").

3.29.2   New rules

Under the new rules it is no longer possible to ask the European Commission for an individual exemption. In principle, undertakings themselves have to examine whether or not their agreements infringe the European competition rules.

In addition, the new Regulation gives more supervisory competence to national competition authorities and judicial bodies. The Regulation governs the cooperation between the European Commission and the national authorities and also covers procedures and sanctions in order to guarantee the uniform application of the competition rules in the EU.

For example, where a UK undertaking cooperates with a business established in the Czech Republic, after 1 May 2004 it will itself have to examine whether or not the cooperation infringes the European competition rules. If the cooperation does infringe the competition rules, as from 1 May 2004, the national competition authorities will exercise supervisory powers and take the requisite measures.[33] However, the European Commission does retain competence to get involved in the case. If the UK firm considers it is eligible for an exemption on the basis of Article 81(3) of the EC Treaty, then, under the new rules, it need no longer apply for an exemption from the European Commission but has itself to evaluate whether Article 81(3) of the EC Treaty is applicable.

3.30 What is abuse of a dominant position?

An undertaking has a dominant position if it is able to exercise an important and predictable influence on market behaviour. In order to examine whether an undertaking occupies such a position, it is first necessary to delineate the relevant market. This is the market for the products of the undertaking and those that are substitutable for them. In addition, account also has to be taken of the geographical territory within which the undertaking carries on its activities. This market has to extend to the whole common market or a significant part thereof.

Possessing a dominant position[34] is not in itself prohibited, but abusing a dominant position is. However, one or more undertakings may have no dominant position on the common market or a significant part thereof. Furthermore, a dominant position also may not be abused to affect trade between member states. This also applies to the accession countries as from 1 May 2004.

Examples of abuse include:

- directly or indirectly imposing unfair purchase or sales prices or other unfair contractual terms;[35]

- limiting production, sales or technical development to the disadvantage of users;[36]

- applying unequal conditions to trade partners for like contractual performance;

- making entering into a contract conditional on additional performance that has no connection with the subject-matter of the agreement.

The message for businesses is, again, that they must test their relations with firms in the accession countries against this new aspect of the "acquis communautaire".

3.31 Will there be checks on concentrations of undertakings in the accession countries?

As from 1 May 2004, the accession countries also have to take account of the European control rules on concentrations of undertakings. In this connection, we refer to Council Regulation (EEC) no. 139/2004 of 20 January 2004 on the control of concentrations between undertakings.[37]

3.32 What about public corporations?

The aforementioned rules on cooperation between undertakings, abuse of a dominant position and the control of concentrations are also applicable to undertakings controlled by the State and to undertakings which the State endows with special or exclusive rights.

However, there is an exception for undertakings charged with the administration of services of general economic importance or that bear the character of a fiscal monopoly. The exception also applies where a derogation from the competition rules is necessary for them to carry out their assigned purpose. Thus, for example, it is permissible to set aside the competition rules for postal services or rail transport. These companies have a duty to provide a universal service or a minimum service provision duty. If the derogation from the competition rules (as a rule, constitution of a monopoly) is not justified by the special role of general economic importance played by the company, the derogation is proscribed.

Many government agencies that are in a monopoly position are corporations with a network, such as railways, telecommunications, gas or electricity.

In order to enable competition in this sector, a distinction has to be drawn between the infrastructure on the one hand and the services that are offered on the other hand, for it is not economically practicable to lay down a new infrastructure, such as parallel gas networks. Hence, the network administrator has to grant access to its infrastructure to companies willing to supply gas, even its network. In the framework of this principle, reference has to be made to the directives on telecommunications services, transport, postal services, gas and electricity.[38]

3.33 Will state aids still be permitted in the accession countries?

Subsidies that are funded by the government and that distort competition are prohibited where they affect trade between member states. Government measures that reduce certain charges on business, such as favourable loans, exemptions or reductions in social security or tax burdens and capital contributions are likewise not permitted.

The following forms of aid are nonetheless permitted:

- aid having a social character, granted to individual consumers, provided that such aid is granted without discrimination related to the origin of the products concerned;

- aid to make good the damage caused by natural disasters or exceptional occurrences.

The following forms of aid can be allowed by the European Commission or the Council:

- aid to promote the economic development of areas where the standard of living is abnormally low or where there is serious underemployment;

- aid to promote the execution of an important project of common European interest or to remedy a serious disruption in the economy of a member state;

- aid to facilitate the development of certain economic activities or of certain economic areas, where such aid does not adversely affect trading conditions to an extent contrary to the common interest;

- aid to promote culture and heritage conservation where such aid does not affect trading conditions and competition in the Community to an extent that is contrary to the common interest;

- such other categories of aid as may be specified by decision of the Council acting by a qualified majority on a proposal from the Commission.

The European Commission stringently ensures that the state aids rules are duly complied with. If a member state fails to heed a warning to abolish a proscribed form of aid, the European Commission can apply directly to the European Court of Justice.

Where member states want to accord aid to businesses, they must first notify the European Commission, which will then verify that the aid is permissible in terms of the EC Treaty. Regulation (EC) no. 659/1999 of the Council of 22 March 1999 governs this supervisory procedure.[39]

If a business is currently in receipt of aid from an accession country, it certainly must be examined whether this can still continue after accession, since unlawful state aids can be reclaimed with interest.[40]

3.34 Are there transitional measures that temporarily permit certain forms of state aid after accession?

The accession treaty lays down the general rules that state aids and individual subsidies in force in the accession countries and still applying after accession are regarded as existing aid within the meaning of Article 88(1) of the EC Treaty:

- state aids in force prior to 10 December 1994; or

- state aids referred to in the Annex to the Accession Treaty (transitional measures); or

- state aid that was regarded by the relevant authority in the accession country prior to accession as in accordance with the "acquis communautaire" and against which the European Commission has not expressed any objection.

Other aid is regarded as new for the application of Article 88(3) of the EC Treaty. Table 3.3 gives an overview of the other transitional measures. Since the transitional measures in the field of competition are fairly detailed, we also advise you to consult the accession treaty.

Table 3.3 Transitional measures: competition.

Subject-matter	Legal text	Cyprus	Czech Republic	Estonia	Hungary	Latvia	Lithuania	Malta	Poland	Slovakia	Slovenia
Elimination of proscribed fiscal aids for offshore companies	Title VI, Chapter I, second section of the EC Treaty	31 Dec. 2005	—	—	—	—	—	—	—	—	—
Elimination of proscribed fiscal aids for SMEs	Title VI, Chapter I, second section of the EC Treaty	—	—	—	31 Dec. 2011	—	—	31 Dec. 2011	31 Dec. 2011	—	—
Conversion of proscribed fiscal aids for certain large firms into regional investment aid	Title VI, Chapter I, second section of the EC Treaty	—	—	—	The aid is terminated when the ceiling is reached	—	—	The aid is terminated when the ceiling is reached	The aid is terminated when the ceiling is reached	The aid is terminated when the ceiling is reached	—
Elimination of proscribed fiscal aids accorded by local authorities	Title VI, Chapter I, second section of the EC Treaty	—	—	—	31 Dec. 2007	—	—	—	—	—	—
Aid for the restructuring of a sector	Title VI, Chapter I, second section of the EC Treaty	—	Steel industry 31 Dec. 2006	—	—	—	—	Ship-building 31 Dec. 2008	Steel industry 31 Dec. 2006	Favoured steel sector until 31 Dec. 2009 or end of ceiling	—

(cont.)

Table 3.3 (*cont.*)

Subject-matter	Legal text	Cyprus	Czech Republic	Estonia	Hungary	Latvia	Lithuania	Malta	Poland	Slovakia	Slovenia
Elimination of operational subsidies	Title VI, Chapter I, second section of the EC Treaty	—	—	—	—	—	—	31 Dec. 2008	—	—	—
Adjustment of the market for the importation, storage and wholesale of oil products under Article 31 of the EC Treaty	Title VI, Chapter I, second section of the EC Treaty	—	—	—	—	—	—	31 Dec. 2005	—	—	—
Elimination of state aids for protection of the environment	Title VI, Chapter I, second section of the EC Treaty	—	—	—	—	—	—	—	31 Dec. 2010	—	—

— = no transitional measure accorded, i.e. the EU rules are applicable as of 1 May 2004.

Source references for Chapter 3

1. Burson-Marsteller, Enlargement 2004. Big Bang and Aftershocks, http://www.bmbrussels.be/files/news_2.pdf.
2. http://europa.eu.int.
3. Art. 249 of the Consolidated version of the Treaty Establishing the European Community, Official Journal No. C325 of 24 December 2002, http://europa.eu.int/eur-lex/en/treaties/dat/EC_consol.html.
4. Court of Justice, 5 April 1979, 148/78, Tullio Ratti, Jur. H.v.J., 1979, 1629.
5. Court of Justice, 19 January 1982, Case 8/81 Becker [1982] ECR 53; Court of Justice, 19 November 1991, Cases C-6/90 and C-9/90 Francovich and Others [1991] ECR I-5357.
6. Court of Justice, 14 July 1994, C-91/92, Paolo Faccini Dori v Recreb Srl, [1994] ECR, I, 3325.
7. Title I, Chapter 2 (articles 28 *et seq.*) of the Consolidated version of the Treaty Establishing the European Community, Official Journal No. C325 of 24 December 2002, http://europa.eu.int/eur-lex/en/treaties/dat/EC_consol.html.
8. Court of Justice, 11 July 1974, 8/74, Dassonville, Jur. H.v.J., 1974, 837.
9. Court of Justice, 20 February 1975, Commission of the European Communities v. Federal Republic of Germany, 12/74, Jur. H.v.J., 1975, 181.
10. Court of Justice, 8 July 1975, Rewe Zentralfinanz EGmbH v. Landwirtschaftskammer, Jur. H.v.J., 1975, 843.
11. Court of Justice, 17 June 1981, 113/80, Commission of the European Communities v. Ireland, Jur. H.v.J., 1981, 1625.
12. Court of Justice, 24 November 1982, 249/81, Commission of the European Communities Ireland, Jur. H.v.J., 1982, 4005.
13. Court of Justice, 20 April 1983, 59/82, Schutzverband gegen Unwesen in der Wirtschaft v. Weinvertriebs GmbH, Jur. H.v.J., 1983, 1217.
14. Court of Justice, 29 November 1983, 181/82, Roussel Laboratoria BV and others v. State of the Netherlands, Jur. H.v.J., 1983, 3849.
15. Council Directive 88/378/EEC of 3 May 1988 on the approximation of the laws of the member states concerning the safety of toys, Official Journal No. L187 of 16 July 1988, pp. 0001–0013.
16. Court of Justice, 20 February 1979, 120/79, Rewe-Zentral AG v. Bundesmonopolverwaltung für Branntwein, Jur. H.v.J., 1979, 649.
17. This reasoning is also inferred from the Cassis de Dijon case and has been further refined in subsequent decisions by the European Court of Justice.
18. An overview of the general and specific directives regarding product standards can be found on the European Union website: http://europa.eu.int.
19. Title III, Chapters 1 and 2 (arts. 39 *et seq.* of the Consolidated version of the Treaty Establishing the European Community, Official Journal No. C325 of 24 December 2002, http://europa.eu.int/eur-lex/en/treaties/dat/EC_consol.html.
20. Art. 39(4) of the Consolidated version of the Treaty Establishing the European Community, Official Journal No. C325 of 24 December 2002, http://europa.eu.int/eur-lex/en/treaties/dat/EC_consol.html.
21. Court of Justice, 12 April 1994, 1/93, Halliburton Services BV v. Secretary of State for Finance, Jur. H.v.J., 1994, I, 1137.
22. Council Directive 90/364/EEC of 28 June 1990 on the right of residence. Official Journal No. L180 of 13 July 1990, pp. 0026–0027.

23. Council Directive 93/109/EC of 6 December 1993 laying down detailed arrangements for the exercise of the right to vote and stand as a candidate in elections
to the European Parliament for citizens of the Union residing in a member state
of which they are not nationals, Official Journal No. L329 of 30 December 1993,
pp. 0034–0038.
24. Council Directive 94/80/EC of 19 December 1994 laying down detailed arrangements for the exercise of the right to vote and to stand as a candidate in municipal
elections by citizens of the Union residing in a member state of which they are
not nationals, Official Journal No. L368 of 31 December 1994.
25. Council Directive 64/221/EEC of 25 February 1964 on the coordination of special
measures concerning the movement and residence of foreign nationals which
are justified on grounds of public policy, public security or public health, Official
Journal No. P056 of 4 April 1964, pp. 0850–0857.
26. Title III, Chapter 3 (arts. 49 *et seq.* of the Consolidated version of the Treaty
Establishing the European Community, Official Journal No. C325 of 24 December
2002,
http://europa.eu.int/eur-lex/en/treaties/dat/EC_consol.html.
27. Directive 95/46/EC of the European Parliament and of the Council of 24 October
1995 on the protection of individuals with regard to the processing of personal data and on the free movement of such data, Official Journal No. L281 of
23 November 1995, pp. 0031–0050; Directive 2002/58/EC of the European Parliament and of the Council of 12 July 2002 concerning the processing of personal
data and the protection of privacy in the electronic communications sector (Directive on privacy and electronic communications), Official Journal No. L201 of
31 July 2002, pp. 0037–00477; Regulation (EC) No 45/2001 of the European Parliament and of the Council of 18 December 2000 on the protection of individuals
with regard to the processing of personal data by the Community institutions
and bodies and on the free movement of such data, Official Journal No. L008 of
12 January 2001, pp. 0001–0022; Directive 97/66/EC of the European Parliament
and of the Council of 15 December 1997 concerning the processing of personal
data and the protection of privacy in the telecommunications sector, Official Journal No. L024 of 30 January 1998, pp. 0001–0008; Directive 1999/93/EC of the
European Parliament and of the Council of 13 December 1999 on a Community
framework for electronic signatures, Official Journal No. L013 of 19 January 2000,
pp. 0012–0020.
28. Court of Justice, 14 December 1995, C-163/94, C-165/94 and C-250/94, criminal case against Lucas Emilio Sanz de Lera, Raimundo Díaz Jiménez and Figen
Kapanolglu, Jur. H.v.J., 1995, I-4821.
29. Court of Justice, 16 March 1999, C-222/97, Manfred Trummer and Peter Mayer,
Jur. H.v.J., 1999, I-1661.
30. Court of Justice, 1 June 1999, C-302/97, Klaus Konle v. Republic of Austria, Jur.
H.v.J., 1999, I-3099.
31. Article 81 of the Consolidated version of the Treaty Establishing the European
Community, Official Journal No. C325 of 24 December 2002,
http://europa.eu.int/eur-lex/en/treaties/dat/EC_consol.html.
32. Council Regulation (EC) No 1/2003 of 16 December 2002 on the implementation
of the rules on competition laid down in Articles 81 and 82 of the Treaty, Official
Journal No. I, L1 of 4 January 2003.
33. Article 5 of Council Regulation (EC) No 1/2003 of 16 December 2002 on the
implementation of the rules on competition laid down in Articles 81 and 82 of
the Treaty, Official Journal No. I, L001 of 4 January 2003, pp. 0001–0025.

34. An undertaking possesses a dominant position where it is able to act independently in such a way that it is able to carry on business without significantly having to take account of competitors, consumers or suppliers (Decision, 9 December 1971, Continental Can, Official Journal, 1972, No. L7/25.
35. For instance: too high a price, a price not reasonably in proportion to the economic value of the service provided (Court of Justice, 14 February 1978, 27/76, United Brands Company and United Brands Continental BV v. Commission of the European Communities, Jur. H.v.J., 1978, 207.
36. In this regard, we would cite purchase quotas, a far-reaching form of customer relations and preventing the sale of other manufacturers.
37. Council Regulation (EEC) No 139/2004 of 20 January 2004 on the control of concentrations between undertakings, Official Journal No. L24/1 of 29 January 2004, pp. 0001–0022.
38. For an overview of the liberalisation initiatives: http://europa.eu.int/comm/competition/liberalization/legislation.
39. Council Regulation (EC) No 659/1999 of 22 March 1999 laying down detailed rules for the application of Article 93 of the EC Treaty, Official Journal No. L083 of 27 March 1999, pp. 0001–0009.
40. Article 14 of Council Regulation (EC) No 659/1999 of 22 March 1999 laying down detailed rules for the application of Article 93 of the EC Treaty, Official Journal No. L083 of 27 March 1999, pp. 0001–0009.

4 Frequently Asked Questions about the Legal Impact of the Enlargement of the European Union

4.1 Company law: I have a company in an accession country. Will there be any changes in my reporting or other company law obligations?

When you look at the list of directives on company law, it is noticeable that large parts of national company law of the EU's member states are a translation of European directives.

That the European Union concerns itself with this field is only logical. A common market with free competition requires that companies from various member states have more or less the same rights and obligations, so that foreign companies are not at a disadvantage in relation to domestic companies because they are not faced with new company law rules when crossing borders. Nonetheless, a sufficient degree of supervision is ensured over companies. Nor may cross-border mergers and divisions be hampered by unharmonised national laws.

Transposition of the "acquis communautaire" in the accession countries holds both risks and opportunities for businesses familiar with European company law. Introducing European law can affect existing rights and duties in the accession countries. Moreover, the new company law in the accession countries will no longer be unknown to those entrepreneurs, thus facilitating the constitution of companies and branches and merger activity in those countries.

In the following, we give a short overview of the most important European legislation in the field of company law. Note that, here, there are no transitional measures.

DIRECTIVE: First Directive 68/151/EEC of 9 March 1968.
PUBLICATION: Official Journal No. L065 of 14 March 1968, pp. 0008–0012.
SUMMARY: coordination of safeguards which, for the protection of the interests of members and others, are required by member states of companies within the meaning of the second paragraph of Article 58 of the Treaty, with a view to making such safeguards equivalent throughout the community

Aim and scope of application:

In 1968, a directive was issued regarding the obligations of companies for the protection of shareholders and third parties. This Directive only applies to companies that issue shares.

Publication obligations:

Where?

The Directive says that certain information has to be published by creating an official register, with each company having its own file, and notices published in an official national gazette.

What?

The information in question is the following:

- the instrument of incorporation, together with the statutes, where these are set down in a separate instrument;
- changes to these instruments, including any extension of the duration of the company;
- after every amendment to the instrument of constitution or of the statutes, the complete text of the instrument or statutes as amended to date;
- the appointment, termination of office and particulars or persons who, either as a body constituted pursuant to law or as members of any such body
  — are authorised to represent the company in dealings with third parties and in legal proceedings, or
  — take part in the administration, supervision or control of the company.

  It must appear from the disclosure whether the persons authorised to represent the company may do so alone or must act jointly;
- at least once a year, the amount of the capital subscribed where the instrument of constitution or the statutes mention an authorised capital, unless any increase in the capital subscribed necessitates an amendment of the statutes;
- the balance sheet and profit and loss account for each financial year. The document containing the balance sheet shall give particulars of the persons who are required by law to certify it;
- any transfer of the seat of the company;
- the winding up of the company;
- any declaration of nullity of the company by the courts;
- the appointment of liquidators, particulars concerning them and their respective powers, unless such powers are expressly and exclusively derived from law or from the statutes of the company;
- the termination of the liquidation and, in member states where striking off the register entails legal consequences, the fact of any such striking off.

Commercial documents
A further publication obligation concerns on the disclosure of a company's commercial documents of its legal form, the place in which it has its registered office and the location of the register in which and the number under which the company is entered.

Enforceability
Published information is binding towards third parties after a period of two weeks has elapsed from publication. During the two-week period, the information is in principle binding, but it is open to third parties to release themselves therefrom by evidencing that they could not have been aware of the information. In principle, unpublished or improperly published information cannot be enforced against third parties unless it is shown that the third party in question knew of the information.

Legal validity of obligations:
The right to bind a company must be universal, meaning that the persons who, as an organ of the company, are authorised to represent the company have to have this authority vis-à-vis third parties for all aspects of the company. Hence, a company is in principle always bound vis-à-vis third parties by legal dealings undertaken by its organs. There are, however, two exceptions. Dealings in which the organs exceed their legal authority are unenforceable as also dealings that are *ultra vires* in relation to the objects of the company where the company evidences that the third party in question ought, in the circumstances, to have been aware thereof.

Other important points in the rules:
- the organs of companies that are not registered are liable for dealings entered into by such companies regardless of whether or not they have made an error;
- persons that enter into dealings for a company in the course of incorporation are jointly and severally liable therefor if the company does not subsequently assume the dealings;
- the invalidity of the appointment of organs such as directors or members of the management committee cannot be invoked against third parties.

Nullity:
Nullity must always be declared by a court and is a sanction that can only be applied in the exhaustively listed cases under the Directive. One such case is incorporating a company without observing the formal requirements upon incorporation, viz. the requirement of official or judicial oversight upon incorporation or the requirement of a solemn deed where such oversight is not present.

TRANSITIONAL MEASURES: none.

DIRECTIVE: Second Directive 77/91/EEC of 13 December 1976.
PUBLICATION: Official Journal No. L026 of 31 January 1977, pp. 0001–0013.

SUMMARY: the coordination of safeguards which, for the protection of the interests of members and others, are required by member states of companies within the meaning of the second paragraph of Article 58 of the Treaty, in respect of the formation of public limited liability companies and the maintenance and alteration of their capital, with a view to making such safeguards equivalent.

On 13 December 1976, a directive was issued with rules for limited liability companies. The rules concern the following matters:

- required statements in the statutes and the instrument of incorporation;
- a prohibition against the automatic winding-up of companies that fall below the statutorily fixed minimum number of shareholders. Only judicial winding-up is possible where the company does not restore the minimum number of participants;
- controls on the valuation of contributions in kind;
- minimum share capital (25 000 euros): the Directive stipulates that the contribution of work or services cannot be valued. Furthermore, a number of rules are laid down as regards paying up the capital;
- no distribution of profits if, at the last accounting reference date, the net assets were lower than the subscribed capital (there is an exception for variable-capital investment companies);
- interim dividends are permitted if defensible on the basis of interim annual accounts;
- a general meeting of shareholders has to be called where there has been a loss of capital of 50% or more;
- a prohibition in principle against grants of loans by the company to third parties to promote the acquisition of its shares;
- rules regarding increases and reductions in capital and the pre-emption rights of existing shareholders; and
- rules regarding subscription of own shares, cross-holdings and the redemption of own shares.

TRANSITIONAL MEASURES: none.

DIRECTIVE: Third Directive 78/855/EEC of 9 October 1978.
PUBLICATION: Official Journal No. L295 of 20 October 1978, pp. 0036–0043.
SUMMARY: domestic mergers of public limited liability companies.

This Directive governs the procedure that has to be followed where public limited liability companies merge by takeover or through the incorporation of a new company. The procedure has to offer sufficient guarantees to shareholders (e.g. the exchange ratio for shares) and third parties.

TRANSITIONAL MEASURES: none.

DIRECTIVE: Fourth Directive 78/660/EEC of 25 July 1978.
PUBLICATION: Official Journal No. L222 of 14 August 1978, pp. 0011–0031.

SUMMARY: annual accounts of capital companies.

This (often amended) Directive lays down:

- a number of basic principles that the annual accounts and annual reports of capital companies have to fulfil;
- a number of rules regarding the publication of such documents;
- the term medium-sized undertaking.

TRANSITIONAL MEASURES: none.

DIRECTIVE: Sixth Directive 82/891/EEC of 17 December 1982.

PUBLICATION: Official Journal No. L378 of 31 December 1982, pp. 0047–0054.

SUMMARY: division of public limited liability companies.

This Directive governs the procedure to be followed upon the division or divisions of a public limited liability company. The procedure has to offer sufficient guarantees to shareholders (e.g. the exchange ratio for shares) and third parties.

TRANSITIONAL MEASURES: none.

DIRECTIVE: Seventh Directive 83/349/EEC of 13 June 1983.

PUBLICATION: Official Journal No. L193 of 18 July 1983, pp. 0001–0017.

SUMMARY: consolidated accounts of capital companies.

This Directive lays down when and how consolidated annual accounts and a consolidated annual report have to be drawn up.

TRANSITIONAL MEASURES: none.

DIRECTIVE: Eighth Directive 84/253/EEC of 10 April 1984.

PUBLICATION: Official Journal No. L126 of 12 May 1984, pp. 0020–0026.

SUMMARY: approval of persons responsible for carrying out the statutory audits of accounting documents.

This Directive contains specific provisions requiring to be met by company auditors. It deals with diploma requirements and rules regarding the substance of theory training and practical training.

TRANSITIONAL MEASURES: none.

DIRECTIVE: Eleventh Directive 89/666/EEC of 21 December 1989.

PUBLICATION: Official Journal No. L395 of 30 December 1989, pp. 0036–0039.

SUMMARY: disclosure requirements in respect of branches opened in a member state by certain types of company governed by the law of another state.

Scope of application

This Directive is applicable to establishments of public limited liability companies and private limited liability companies that are established in another member state than that in which the parent undertaking is established.

Disclosure requirements

The establishment has to publish documents that contain:

- the address of the branch;
- the activities of the branch;
- the register in which the company file mentioned in the First Directive (see page •••) is kept, together with the registration number in that register;
- the name and legal form of the company and the name of the branch if that is different from the name of the company;
- the winding-up of the company, the appointment of (voluntary) liquidators, particulars concerning them and their powers and the termination of the liquidation;
- insolvency proceedings, arrangements, compositions, or any analogous proceedings to which the company is subject;
- the accounting documents of the company, drawn up, audited and disclosed in accordance with the law of the company's member state;
- details concerning the persons who are authorised to represent the company in dealings with third parties and in legal proceedings;
- as a company organ constituted pursuant to law or as a member of any such organ, in accordance with the disclosure by the company as provided for by the First Directive;
- as permanent representative of the company for the activities of the branch, with an indication of the extent of their powers;
- the closure of the branch.

Commercial documents

Further, it is required that letters and order forms used by the branch must, in addition to the information laid down in the First Directive, mention the register where the branch's company file is kept and the number under which the branch is entered in that register.

Additional disclosure requirements

The member state of the branch can require that the following information is additionally disclosed:

- the signatures of the directors or liquidators;
- the instrument of incorporation and the statutes of the company, together with amendments to those documents;
- a certificate from the register referred to in the First Directive regarding the existence of the company;
- a notice regarding the securities granted over property of the company that are located in the branch's member state in so far as such disclosure is a condition for the validity of those securities.

European branches of non-EU companies

European branches of non-EU companies are under the same minimum disclosure requirements but must also publish the following:

- the law of which state the undertaking falls under;
- the statutes and instrument of incorporation of the company;
- the legal form of the company, its principal place of business and its objects and at least annually, the amount of the subscribed capital if these particulars are not given in the statutes or instruments of incorporation or such documents as amend the statutes or instrument of incorporation.

TRANSITIONAL MEASURES: none.

DIRECTIVE: Twelfth Directive 89/667/EEC of 21 December 1989.
PUBLICATION: Official Journal No. L395 of 30 December 1989, pp. 0040–0042.
SUMMARY: single-member private limited liability companies.

This Directive provides that single-member companies can be incorporated in the member states and governs the disclosure obligations where a company's shares all come to be held by a single person.
TRANSITIONAL MEASURES: none.

DIRECTIVE: Directive 2003/51/EC of 18 June 2003.
REGULATION: Regulation (EC) No. 1606/2002 of 19 July 2002.
PUBLICATION: Official Journal No. L178 of 17 July 2003, pp. 0016–0022; Official Journal No. L243 of 11 September 2002, pp. 0001–0004.
SUMMARY: introduction of the International Accounting Standards (IAS).

Directive amending Directives 78/660/EEC, 83/349/EEC, 86/635/EEC and 91/674/EEC of the Council regarding annual accounts and consolidated annual accounts of certain forms of companies, banks and other financial institutions and insurance undertakings, of application as from 1 January 2005.
TRANSITIONAL MEASURES: none.

REGULATION: Regulation (EC) No. 2137 of 25 July 1985.
PUBLICATION: Official Journal No. L199 of 31 July 1985, pp. 0001–0009.
SUMMARY: European Economic Interest Groupings (EEIGs).

This Regulation institutes a legal person under European law with the aim of facilitating or developing the economic activity of its members or improving or increasing the results therefrom, but not the achievement of profit for itself. The activity of an EEIG has to be in context with the economic activity of its members and may only be ancillary thereto.
TRANSITIONAL MEASURES: none.

REGULATION: Regulation (EC) No. 1346/2000 of 29 May 2000.
PUBLICATION: Official Journal No. L160 of 30 June 2000, pp. 0001–0018.
SUMMARY: insolvency procedures.

This Regulation creates a uniform insolvency procedure in the member states. This was necessary for the proper functioning of the Internal Market.

Without a uniform insolvency procedure, parties would be able to opt for the most favourable national insolvency laws by shipping goods to those countries or by trying by means of certain conduct to lend jurisdiction to the courts in those countries.

The scope of application of the Regulation is limited to collective procedures that, based on the debtor's insolvency, result in the debtor's partially or fully losing control and power of disposal over its assets and a trustee being appointed. Insolvency procedures affecting insurance undertakings and credit institutions, investment undertakings providing services that encompass custody of third parties' money or securities and collective investment undertakings are excluded from its scope of application.

TRANSITIONAL MEASURES: none.

REGULATION: Regulation (EC) No. 2157/2001 of 8 October 2001.
PUBLICATION: Official Journal No. L294 of 10 November 2001, pp. 0001–0021.
SUMMARY: Statute for a European Company (SE).

Finally, we dwell awhile on the Regulation on the Statute for a European Company, or Societas Europaea (SE). SE will be the abbreviation that follows the company name. The Regulation comes into force on 8 October 2004 and allows companies established in more than one member state of the European Union to re-incorporate as a single company within the EU that is governed by an integrated system of rules on how they function and the disclosure of information. This integrated system is intended greatly to reduce the administrative burdens associated with a traditional member state-by-member state approach. A frequent criticism of the SE is that the tax rules have not been harmonised, which erodes the benefits of the Regulation.

A public limited liability company can re-incorporate as a European Company if it has its registered office and principal management in the EU and:

- it merges with one or more companies that have their registered offices and head offices within the EU, provided that at least two of them are governed by the law of different member states; or
- together with one or more companies that have their registered offices and head offices in the EU, it sets up a holding SE provided that each of at least two of the companies:
  — are governed by the law of different member states, or
  — have had a subsidiary for at least two years governed by the law of another member state, or a branch that is situated in another member state; or
- together with one or more companies that have their registered offices and head offices in the EU, it forms a subsidiary SE by subscribing for its shares, provided that each of at least two of those companies:

- — are governed by the law of different member states, or
- — have had a subsidiary for at least two years governed by the law of another member state, or a branch that is situated in another member state; *or*
- — it is a public limited liability company which has its registered office and head office within the EU and transforms into an SE provided it has had for at least two years a subsidiary company governed by the law of another member state;
- — A member state may provide that a company the head office of which is not in the EU may participate in the formation of an SE provided that company is formed under the law of a member state, has its registered office in that member state and has a real and continuous link with a member state's economy.

TRANSITIONAL MEASURES: none.

REGULATION: Regulation (EC) No. 1435/2003 of 22 July 2003.
PUBLICATION: Official Journal No. L207 of 18 August 2003, pp. 0001–0024.
SUMMARY: Statute for a European Cooperative Society (SCE).
TRANSITIONAL MEASURES: none.

4.2 What about intellectual property rights in the enlarged European Union?

4.2.1 The impact of enlargement for holders of intellectual property rights

Under certain conditions, intellectual property rights protect the products of the mind. These are industrial property rights (trade marks, patents, know-how) and copyright, including related rights.

The European intellectual property rights policy is based on two cornerstones. Via Directives, the European legislator tries to approximate national rules on intellectual property rights as much as possible. Furthermore, there is a parallel, autonomous European legislative framework for the protection of certain intellectual property rights within the territory of the Union. With regard to trade marks (Community trade mark) and designs (Community design), the requisite legislative initiatives have already been taken. We will here go more deeply into the latter.

The enlargement of the Union will therefore also have an impact at both levels for the accession countries:

- on the one hand, they have to bring their national legislation on intellectual property rights in line with the relevant European Directives;

- on the other hand, predominantly the expansion of the Community trade mark and the Community design will mean a significant evolution for undertakings that wish to conduct trade in the new member states.

4.2.2   The Community trade mark and the Community design

The Community trade mark and design offer the applicant the opportunity to acquire trade mark or design protection that applies throughout the Union with one single application or registration. This contrasts with the "previous" – but still to a lesser degree existing – practice in which a national application or registration of a trade mark or design enjoys protection only within that territory and has to be dealt with separately by the national or regional offices for industrial property. The Office for Harmonisation in the Internal Market (OHIM) in Alicante deals with applications for Community trade marks and designs.

All applications for Community trade marks and designs that are being filed before the enlargement, will automatically be extended as from 1 May 2004 to the ten new member states. To this end, no additional formalities need to be fulfilled nor additional fees to be paid by the applicant or holder.

A Community trade mark or design whose territorial protection has been extended to the accession member states cannot be declared null and void on the basis of grounds for refusal that become applicable by the accession of candidate member states. There are nonetheless exceptions to this rule. For example, a holder of a Community trade mark cannot prevent the use of its sign when it is used in a purely descriptive manner.

This does not mean that conflicts might exist between Community trade marks and national trade mark rights that already exist in the accession countries. Hence, a holder of existing (national) trade mark rights can start opposition proceedings in one or more accession countries. The opposition procedure is only possible for applications for Community trade marks filed between 1 November 2003 and 30 April 2004 (taking into account potential priority rights).

In practice, however, cases are known of where individuals or undertakings have in bad faith filed trade marks in the candidate member states that are identical or similar to existing Community trade marks. In principle they should thus be entitled to initiate opposition proceedings against the holder of the identical or similar Community trade mark. The OHIM has been informed of these practices and has taken the necessary steps to provide holders of existing Community trade marks with adequate information about the legal steps they have to take to counter such practices.

4.2.3   The "acquis communautaire" in the field of intellectual property rights

In the following, we give a brief summary of the most important European rules dealing with the most current intellectual property rights.

DIRECTIVE: Directive 87/54/EEC of 16 December 1986.

PUBLICATION: Official Journal No. L024 of 27 October 1987, pp. 0036–0040.

SUMMARY: the legal protection of topographies of semiconductor products.

Under this Directive, the member states shall protect topographies of semiconductor products by adopting legislative provisions conferring exclusive rights in accordance with the provisions of the Directive. The topography of a semiconductor product shall be protected in so far as it satisfies the conditions that it is the result of its creator's own intellectual effort and is not commonplace in the semiconductor industry. Where the topography of a semiconductor product consists of elements that are commonplace in the semiconductor industry, it shall be protected only to the extent that the combination of such elements, taken as a whole, fulfils the abovementioned conditions.

TRANSITIONAL MEASURES: none.

DIRECTIVE: Directive 89/104/EEC of 21 December 1988.

PUBLICATION: Official Journal No. L040 of 11 February 1989, pp. 0001–0007.

SUMMARY: the approximation of the laws of the member states relating to trade marks.

This first directive on European trade mark law was instituted with the aim of harmonising the national trade mark laws of the member states in certain respects.

The Directive applies to every trade mark in respect of goods or services which is the subject of registration or of an application in a member state for registration as an individual trade mark, a collective mark or a guarantee or certification mark, or which is the subject of a registration or an application for registration in the Benelux Trade Mark Office or of an international registration having effect in a member state. Below, we give a brief overview of the rules laid down in the Directive.

A trade mark may consist of any sign capable of being represented graphically, particularly words, including personal names, designs, letters, numerals, the shape of goods or of their packaging, provided that such signs are capable of distinguishing the goods or services of one undertaking from those of other undertakings.

The member state in question may refuse to register certain trade mark applications. This will be the case where:

- the signs referred to in the application cannot constitute a trade mark;
- the trade mark applied for is devoid of any distinctive character;
- the trade mark applied for consists exclusively of signs or indications which may serve, in trade, to designate the kind, quality, quantity, intended purpose, value, geographical origin or time of production of the goods or of rendering of the service, or other characteristics of the goods or services;
- the trade mark applied for consists exclusively of signs or indications which have become customary in the current language or in the bona fide and established practices of the trade;
- the application involves signs which consist exclusively of the shape which results from the nature of the goods themselves, or the shape of goods which is necessary to obtain a technical result, or the shape which gives substantial value to the goods;
- the trade marks applied for are contrary to public policy or to accepted principles of morality;
- they are of such a nature as to deceive the public, for instance as to the nature, quality or geographical origin of the goods or services;
- they are identical with an earlier trade mark that is registered for the same goods or services;
- the trade marks applied for are such that because of their identity with, or similarity to, the earlier trade mark and the identity or similarity of the goods or services covered by the trade marks, there exists a likelihood of confusion on the part of the public, which includes the likelihood of association with the earlier trade mark;
- they are identical or similar to an earlier trade mark and do not relate to similar goods, where the older trade mark is known in the European Community and where the use of the more recent trade mark would, without valid reasons, unjustifiably draw benefit from or cause harm to the distinctive power or reputation of the earlier trade mark.

Member states may additionally prohibit registrations such as registrations made in bad faith, the registration of signs of high symbolic or religious value or signs of public interest (such as coats of arms), registrations on the basis of a right to a name, a right of personal portrayal, a copyright or an industrial property right, etc.

The holder of the trade mark right has the exclusive right to use the trade mark and to take action against its use for similar goods or services if this would cause confusion amongst the public or for non-similar goods or services where the trade mark is well known in the member state in question and, as a result of use of the sign without valid reasons, unjustifiable benefit would be drawn from or harm caused to the distinctive power or reputation of the trade mark.

The holder of a trade mark right can transfer the trade mark or license it. Under the Directive, a licence can be issued for all or some of the goods or services for which it is registered and for all or part of the territory of a member state. Licences may be exclusive or non-exclusive.

TRANSITIONAL MEASURES: none.

DIRECTIVE: Directive 91/250/EEC of 14 May 1991.
PUBLICATION: Official Journal No. L024 of 17 May 1991, pp. 0042–0046.
SUMMARY: the legal protection of computer programs.

This Directive lays down an obligation on the member states to protect computer programs and their preparatory design material, by copyright, as literary works within the meaning of the Berne Convention for the Protection of Literary and Artistic Works.

The protection under this Directive is granted to the expression, in any form, of a computer program. The ideas and principles which underlie any element of a computer program including those which underlie its interfaces, are not protected by copyright under this Directive.

In order to be eligible for protection, the computer program must be original or, in other words, be the result of an intellectual creation by the author.

The author has the exclusive right to carry out the following acts:
(a) reproduction of the computer program;
(b) translation, adaptation, arrangement or any other alteration of the computer program;
(c) distribution of the computer program, including the rental right of the computer program.

All the foregoing acts are subject to consent by the author of the program (or his legal successor, e.g. the employer of the programmer). The lawful acquirer of the computer program does nevertheless not need consent for the acts under (a) and (b) where they are necessary for the use of the computer program, including error corrections. Under clearly defined circumstances, a computer program may also be decompiled if this is necessary in order to ensure interoperability with other computer programs.

Copyright is protected during the life of the author and for 70 years after his death or the death of the last surviving author if two or more people have worked on the same computer program. The member states have been given the possibility to provide in their legislation that employees are deemed to transfer their rights to their employer unless otherwise agreed upon.

TRANSITIONAL MEASURES: none.

DIRECTIVE: Directive 93/98/EEC of 29 October 1993.
PUBLICATION: Official Journal No. L290 of 24 November 1993, pp. 0009–0013.
SUMMARY: the harmonisation of the term of protection of copyright and certain related rights.

This Directive states that the protection of copyright over a literary or artistic work shall run for the life of the author and for 70 years after the calendar year of the death of the author of the work or 70 years after the calendar year during which the work is lawfully made accessible to the public in the case of anonymous or pseudonymous works.

For cinematographic or audiovisual works, the Directive states that protection expires 70 years after the calendar year of the death of the last of the following persons to survive: the principal director, the author of the screenplay, the author of the dialogue and the composer of music specifically created for use in the cinematographic or audiovisual work.

The period for which protection is granted for related rights is 50 years after the calendar year of performance, publication, communication to the public, fixation or transmission.

TRANSITIONAL MEASURES: none.

DIRECTIVE: Directive 96/9/EEC of 11 March 1996.
PUBLICATION: Official Journal No. L077 of 27 March 1996, pp. 0020–0028.
SUMMARY: the legal protection of databases.

This Directive defines a database as "a collection of independent works, data or other materials arranged in a systematic or methodical way and individually accessible by electronic or other means" and accords copyright protection to databases which, by reason of the selection or arrangement of their contents, constitute the author's own intellectual creation. Protection under the Directive does not apply to computer programs used in the making or operation of a databases accessible by electronic means.

In addition, the Directive provides for a right for the maker of a database which shows that there has been qualitatively and/or quantitatively a substantial investment in either the obtaining, verification or presentation of the contents to prevent extraction and/or re-utilisation of the whole or of a substantial part, evaluated qualitatively and/or quantitatively, of the contents of that database. This right is called the "sui generis" database right.

The author of a database that is protectable by copyright, as stated above, has the exclusive right to carry out or to authorise:
(a)   temporary or permanent reproduction by any means and in any form, in whole or in part;

(b) translation, adaptation, arrangement and any other alteration;
(c) any form of distribution to the public of the database or of copies thereof. The first sale in the Community of a copy of the database by the rightholder or with his consent shall exhaust the right to control resale of that copy within the Community;
(d) any communication, display or performance to the public;
(e) any reproduction, distribution, communication, display or performance to the public of the results of the acts referred to in (b).

The term of protection accorded to the author of a database in principle expires 15 years from 1 January of the year following the date of completion of the database or the date when the database was first made available to the public before its completion.
TRANSITIONAL MEASURES: none.

REGULATION: Regulation (EC) No. 40/94 of 20 December 1993.
PUBLICATION: Official Journal No. L011 of 14 January 1994, pp. 0001–0036.
SUMMARY: the Community trade mark.

This Regulation lays down an autonomous European framework for the protection of trade marks within the Union, parallel to national trade mark laws. Prior to this Regulation coming into force an undertaking that wished to have its trade mark recognised in the entire EU had to file its trade mark separately in each of the member states or by means of an international registration. The Regulation accords legal protection throughout the Union with one single registration of the trade mark.

There is a separate Regulation that implements Regulation 40/94: Commission Regulation (EC) No. 2868/95 of 13 December 1995 implementing Council Regulation (EC) No. 40/94 on the Community trade mark (Official Journal No. L303 of 15 December 1995, pp. 0001–0032).
TRANSITIONAL MEASURES: none.

DIRECTIVE: Directive 98/44/EC of 6 July 1998.
PUBLICATION: Official Journal No. L213 of 30 July 1998, pp. 0013–0021.
SUMMARY: the legal protection of biotechnological inventions.

The aim of this Directive is to approximate the national patent laws of the member states so as to grant effective protection to biotechnological inventions in order to maintain and promote investment in this field. The Directive obliges the member states to protect biotechnological inventions under national patent law, as set out in the Directive. Such inventions need to meet the requirements of novelty, inventive step and industrial application. In order to qualify as a biotechnological invention, it has to relate to a product consisting of or containing biological material or a process by means of which biological material is produced, processed or used.
TRANSITIONAL MEASURES: none.

DIRECTIVE: Directive 98/71/EC of 13 October 1998.
PUBLICATION: Official Journal No. L289 of 28 October 1998, pp. 0028–0035.
SUMMARY: the legal protection of designs.

This Directive to a large extent harmonises the national design laws of the member states. The Directive applies to designs that are registered

- with the central industrial property offices of the member states;
- at the Benelux Design Office;
- under international arrangements which have effect in a member state and to applications for design rights for such designs.

In order to be able to enjoy legal protection, a design has to be new and have individual character. Legal protection entails a prohibition against third parties using the design. The rightholder has an exclusive right in that regard and can also assign it or license it to third parties.

The term of protection shall before one or more periods of five years up to a maximum of 25 years as from the date of filing the application.

TRANSITIONAL MEASURES: none.

DIRECTIVE: Directive 2001/84/EC of 27 September 2001.
PUBLICATION: Official Journal No. L272 of 13 October 2001, pp. 0032–0036.
SUMMARY: the resale right for the benefit of the author of an original work of art.

This Directive lays down that the member states have to provide a resale right for the benefit of the author of an original work of art, which is defined as an inalienable right, which cannot be waived, even in advance, to receive a royalty based on the sale price obtained for any resale of the work, subsequent to the first transfer of the work by the author.

Furthermore the Directive sets out a number of exceptions that the member states may make to the resale right of authors, determines which works of art are subject to the resale right, the rates, successors in title to a resale right and the term of protection of a resale right.

TRANSITIONAL MEASURES: none.

REGULATION: Regulation 6/2002 of 12 December 2001.
PUBLICATION: Official Journal No. L003 of 5 January 2002, pp. 0001–0024.
SUMMARY: Community designs.

This Regulation creates a separate legislative framework for the protection of designs, parallel to the existing national trade mark laws in the member states of the Union. On the basis of this Regulation and the conditions laid down therein, legal protection of a design can be applied for by filing one single registration, which is then processed by the Office for Harmonisation in the Internal Market (OHIM).

TRANSITIONAL MEASURES: none.

DIRECTIVE: Directive 2001/29/EC of 22 May 2001.
PUBLICATION: Official Journal No. L167 of 22 June 2001, pp. 0010–0019.
SUMMARY: the harmonisation of certain aspects of copyright and related
   rights in the information society.
   This Directive respects the existing European rules on copyright (see
   above), but supplements them, taking into consideration the specific char-
   acteristics of the information society (and particularly the internet).
TRANSITIONAL MEASURES: none.

4.3   What is the impact of enlargement of the EU on the transport sector?

The "acquis communautaire" contains numerous rules regarding transport.
Transport is a very important sector, which has also traditionally seen a great
deal of government intervention. Good, efficient transport is furthermore
essential for the practical realisation of the free movement of goods and
persons.

The functioning of the sector is more or less governed by European rules on
transport. The impact for transport undertakings in the accession countries
is therefore great. As from 1 May 2004, competition within international
transport will be guaranteed. For cabotage transport or domestic transport,
however, there are important exceptions.

The core of EU transport policy is Article 71 of the EC Treaty. It governs:

*   international transport between member states (intra-Community
    transport);

*   the conditions under which transport undertakings are allowed to
    carry out national transportation in a member state in which they are
    resident;

*   the measures that improve the safety of transport;

*   all other appropriate provisions.

The common European rules relate to the operational, technical and social
aspects of transport. Involved are several hundred regulations, directives and
decisions. Where no European rules have been laid down, the statutory and
administrative provisions of the member state of receipt apply. The member state of receipt does, however, have to take account of the principle of
proportionality.

4.4 Will the transport market be liberalised as from 1 May 2004?

By means of a number of transitional measures, the transport market will not yet be fully liberalised on 1 May 2004. In this respect, a distinction has to be drawn between the intra-Community transport of goods and domestic transport of goods or cabotage.

4.4.1 Intra-Community transport of goods

Intra-Community transport of goods will be fully liberalised in all 25 member states as from 1 May 2004. All quantitative restrictions will then be abolished. In order to be granted a Community transport licence, only the qualitative criteria will have to be met. This licence is issued by the member state where the business is established and is valid for five years. This period can, however, be extended. A Community transport licence means harmonisation of the national conditions before transport services can be provided.

4.4.2 Domestic transport or cabotage

Since 1 July 1998, a carrier with a Community licence has also been permitted to carry out cabotage transport services in other member states. Here as well, there are no longer any quantitative restrictions. For the accession countries, however, important transitional measures have been laid down (see section 4.7, "What transitional measures are there in the transport sector?").

4.5 What rules on taxes and technical specifications in the transport sector fall within the "acquis communautaire"?

The "acquis communautaire" regarding transport is very extensive. Hence, we shall only discuss it briefly. For full overviews of the legislation, you can best consult the European Union's website (http://europa.eu.int).

In order to enable competition in the transport sector, it was necessary for member states to harmonise the taxes on road haulage. In this connection, we would mention Directive 1993/89/EEC of the Council of 25 October 1993 on the application by Member States of taxes on certain vehicles used for the carriage of goods by road and tolls and charges for the use of certain infrastructure. In addition, Directive 1999/62/EC of the European Parliament and of the Council of 17 June 1999 on the charging of heavy goods vehicles for the use of certain infrastructure is also of importance.

The harmonised technical rules relate to safety, comfort and the emission of exhaust gases. A few examples:

- reciprocal acceptance of technical vehicle checks;

- the weights, measurements and certain other technical features of certain road vehicles;

- the carriage of dangerous goods by road and controls thereof.

4.6 What social law rules from the transport sector form part of the "acquis communautaire"?

Social harmonisation comprises regulations that lay down common rules regarding work conditions in domestic and cross-border transport. These rules apply to all drivers in the EU, regardless of whether they are employees or self-employed.

The best-known rules are those regarding rest periods. In this connection, we refer to Directive 2002/15/EC of the European Parliament and of the Council of 11 March 2002 on the organisation of the working time of persons performing mobile road transport activities. This Directive applies to all road haulage drivers that are employed by an undertaking established in the EU and to self-employed drivers. The Directive will be applicable as from 23 March 2005.

The average weekly working time is 48 hours, but can be increased to 60 hours provided the average of 48 hours a week is not exceeded in a four-month period. The working time is the sum of the hours worked in various undertakings. An employee is obliged to inform his or her employers about time worked for another employer.

Council Regulation (EEC) No 3820/85 of 20 December 1985 on the harmonisation of certain social legislation relating to road transport also harmonises the social law provisions regarding rest breaks and driving times in the transport sector. Thus, drivers must take a break after six hours' work. Furthermore, drivers that do not fall within the scope of application of the Regulation are obliged to rest for an uninterrupted period of at least 11 hours after the day's shift. The rest period can be reduced by a maximum of one hour if this reduction is offset within the subsequent four weeks. In addition, night-workers may not work more than eight hours per 24-hour period. This can be extended to 10 hours if, over a period of two months, the eight-hour average is not exceeded. However, the member states can derogate from this provided compensatory rest time is required. Other directives state how the driving and rest time is verified.

The aforementioned Directives and Regulations affect the road haulage of goods. In addition, the carriage of persons by road, rail transport, sea transport and air transport are also subject to common European rules.

4.7 What transitional measures are there in the transport sector?

Table 4.1 Transitional measures: transport.

Subject-matter	Legal text	Cyprus	Czech Republic	Estonia	Hungary	Latvia	Lithuania	Malta	Poland	Slovakia	Slovenia
Latest date for liberalisation of national cabotage transport	Regulation (EC) No. 3118//93	—	1 May 2006 (1)	1 May 2006 (1)	1 May 2007 (1)	1 May 2006 (1)	1 May 2006 (1)	—	1 May 2007 (1)	1 May 2006 (1)	—
Date as from which tachographs become compulsory	Regulation (EC) No. 3821/85	1 Jan 2006 (2)	—	—	—	1 Jan. 2006 (3)	1 Jan. 2006 (4)	31 Dec. 2011	31 Dec. 2011	—	—
Extension for national transport businesses to meet certain financial criteria. This transitional measure means that the available capital and reserves only gradually have to reach the minimum set by Directive 96/26/EC up until ...	Directive 96/26/EC	—	—	—	—	31 Dec. 2006	31 Dec. 2006	—	—	—	—
Gradual increase in the restrictions on axle loadings for the national road network up until ...	Directive 96/53/EC	—	—	—	31 Dec. 2007	—	—	—	31 Dec. 2009	—	—
Extension for introduction of vehicle tests for some vehicles used for local transport up until ...	Directive 96/96/EC	—	—	—	—	—	—	31 Dec. 2004	—	—	—

Table 4.1 (*cont.*)

Subject-matter	Legal text	Cyprus	Czech Republic	Estonia	Hungary	Latvia	Lithuania	Malta	Poland	Slovakia	Slovenia
Gradual increase of road tax on some vehicles. Lower tax than the European minimum is allowed up until …	Directive 1999/62/EC	—	—	—	—	—	—	31 Dec. 2005	—	—	—
Some vehicles used for local transport only need to be equipped with speed-limiters as from …	Directive 92/6/EEC	—	—	—	—	—	—	1 Jan. 2006	—	—	—
Access to the market for rail freight transport can be restricted until …	Directive 91/440/EEC	—	—	—	31 Dec. 2006	—	—	—	31 Dec. 2006	—	—
Noisy aircraft from third countries may continue to land until …	Directive 92/14/EEC	—	—	—	31 Dec. 2004 (5)	—	31 Dec. 2004 (6)	—	—	—	—

— = no transitional measures accorded, i.e. the Directive/Regulation applies as from 1 May 2004.

(1) During this period, member states may accord cabotage licences to these carriers on the basis of quotas agreed bilaterally with other member states. Each member state (current and new) can extend this period up to five years. Member states that do not implement an extension can take protective measures and, in times of crisis, re-close their national transport market for so long as a member state continues to make use of the transitional measure. Furthermore, carriers from member states whose market remains closed cannot provide any cabotage transport services in member states that have already opened their markets after two or three years.

(2) Vehicles registered before 1 January 2002 and used in national transport. Drivers must record their driving and rest periods in a personal logbook.

(3) Vehicles registered before 1 January 2001 and used in national transport. Drivers must record their driving and rest periods in a personal logbook.

(4) Vehicles produced before 1 January 1987 and used in national transport. Drivers must record their driving and rest periods in a personal logbook.

(5) For Hungary, the transitional measure applies only for certain third countries.

(6) For Lithuania, the transitional measure applies only for Kaunus International Airport.

4.8 What is the impact of enlargement of the EU on the energy sector?

The European competition rules, including those on state aids or the exercise of a monopoly, also apply to government corporations. Only if it is necessary for their designated task are exceptions possible. This has a great impact on the energy market. Most energy companies are after all public or undertakings to which the national government has accorded a monopoly or exclusive rights.

Businesses of this order may not abuse their dominant positions or monopolies by, for instance, refusing third parties access to an essential facility. An essential facility is an institution or infrastructure that is necessary in order to sell goods or services, such as an electricity or natural gas network.

However, application of the EC Treaty alone is not sufficient to bring the European energy market into accordance with the principles of the internal market. Hence, additional rules have been issued. In the following, the most important of these are discussed.

4.9   What is the "acquis communautaire" in the energy sector?

DIRECTIVE: Directive 68/414/EEC of 20 December 1968.

PUBLICATION: Official Journal No. L308 of 23 December 1968, pp. 0014–0016.

SUMMARY: obligation on member states of the EEC to maintain minimum stocks of crude oil and/or petroleum products.

The aim of the Directive is to safeguard energy supplies in the EEC.

TRANSITIONAL MEASURES: some accession countries get more time to satisfy the obligation of holding a 90-day stock of oil: the Czech Republic and Slovenia until 31 December 2005, Malta until 31 December 2006, Cyprus until 31 December 2007, Poland and Slovakia until 31 December 2008 and Estonia, Latvia and Lithuania until 31 December 2009.

DIRECTIVE: Directive 94/22/EC of 30 May 1994.

PUBLICATION: Official Journal No. L164 of 30 June 1994, pp. 0003–0008.

SUMMARY: the conditions for granting and using authorisations for prospecting and exploring for and the production of hydrocarbons.

This Directive prohibits the member states from discriminating against (foreign) businesses as regards prospecting and exploring for and the production of hydrocarbons in the area released by the member state for such purposes. However, the member states can, on grounds of national security, refuse access to exploitation of such activities for a subject over which third countries or nationals of a third country have *de facto* control.

TRANSITIONAL MEASURES: none.

DIRECTIVE: Directive 96/92/EC of 19 December 1996; Directive 98/30/EC of 22 June 1998.

PUBLICATION: Official Journal No. L027 of 30 January 1997, pp. 0020–0029; Official Journal No. L204 of 21 July 1998, pp. 0001–0012.

SUMMARY: common rules for the internal market in electricity and natural gas.

This Directive lays down the common rules for the production, transmission and distribution of electricity. The Directive governs the manner in which the electricity sector is organised and operates, access to the market, the criteria and procedures that apply for awards of tenders, the grant of permits and exploitation of the networks.

The most important aim of this Directive is to organise free competition up to a certain level within the electricity market by according certain categories of customers the right to enter into supply contracts with producers of their choice.

A similar Directive has been issued for natural gas: Directive 98/30/EC of the European Parliament and of the Council of 22 June 1998 concerning common rules for the internal market in natural gas.

TRANSITIONAL MEASURES: Estonia has time until 31 December 2008 to open up its electricity market. The Czech Republic has time until 31 December 2004 to open up its natural gas market.

4.10 Do the European rules for the protection of consumers and public health apply in the accession countries as from 1 May 2004?

This question is important if you supply products or services to consumers in the accession countries. Are the details stated on the products still legal after enlargement of the European Union? Are the sales techniques deployed still legal after enlargement?

There have been a variety of European initiatives to harmonise the rules on consumer protection and public health. These rules will be applicable without exception in the new member states upon accession. Therefore *no* transitional measures have been laid down.

For a business, it is thus important to know whether it can still bring its goods or services onto the market in the accession countries after enlargement. By contrast, on 1 May 2004, some national restrictions are withdrawn owing to their hindering trade between member states, for in the free movement of goods and services, a restrictive measure cannot be justified if adequate European rules are already in force.

In EC law, a consumer is defined as a natural person acting for a use that cannot be regarded as business or occupational in nature. In principle, the scope of application of directives on consumer protection can also be restricted for this purpose. However, if the directives are wider in their scope of application, we indicate this below.

An overview of the most important relevant European rules follows.

DIRECTIVE: Directive 84/450/EEC of 10 September 1984.
PUBLICATION: Official Journal No. L250 of 19 September 1984, pp. 0017–0020.
SUMMARY: approximation of the laws, regulations and administrative provisions of the member states concerning misleading advertising.

The aim of the Directive is to protect consumers and persons carrying on a trade or business or practising a craft or profession and the interests of the public in general against misleading advertising and the unfair consequences thereof.

Under this Directive, misleading advertising is advertising that in any way deceives or is likely to deceive the persons to whom it is addressed and that, by reason of its deceptive nature, is likely to affect their economic behaviour or that, for those reasons, injures or is likely to injure a competitor.

TRANSITIONAL MEASURES: none.

DIRECTIVE: Directive 85/577/EEC of 20 December 1985.
PUBLICATION: Official Journal No. L372 of 31 December 1985, pp. 0031–0033.
SUMMARY: protection of the consumer in respect of contracts negotiated away from business premises.

In 1985, a Directive was passed in respect of door-to-door sales and other sales off business premises. It is also, inter alia, applicable to sales during excursions organised by the trader. This Directive gives consumers seven days' thinking time and states that the trader must inform the consumer of this right in writing.

TRANSITIONAL MEASURES: none.

DIRECTIVE: Directive 87/102/EEC of 22 December 1986.
PUBLICATION: Official Journal No. L042 of 12 February 1987, pp. 0048–0053.
SUMMARY: approximation of the laws, regulations and administrative provisions of the member states concerning consumer credit.

This Directive is applicable to credit agreements entered into with consumers. This is an agreement whereby a creditor grants or promises to grant to a consumer a credit in the form of a deferred payment, a loan or other, similar financial accommodation.

The Directive does *not* apply to:
- credit agreements or agreements promising to grant credit:
  - intended primarily for the purpose of acquiring or retaining property rights in land or in an existing or projected building,
  - intended for the purpose of renovating or improving a building as such;
- hiring agreements except where these provide that the title will pass ultimately to the hirer;
- credit granted or made available without payment of interest or any other charge;
- credit agreements under which no interest is charged provided the consumer agrees to repay the credit in a single payment;
- credit in the form of advances on a current account granted by a credit institution or financial institution other than on credit card accounts;
- credit agreements involving amounts less than 200 or more than 20 000 euros;

- credit agreements under which the consumer is required to repay the credit:
  - either, within a period not exceeding three months,
  - or, by a maximum number of four payments within a period not exceeding 12 months.

Credit agreements entered into by consumers have to be in writing, and the consumer must receive a copy thereof. The agreement must contain:
- a statement of the annual percentage rate of charge;
- a statement of the conditions under which the annual percentage rate of charge may be amended.

For further details, we refer to the text of the Directive.
TRANSITIONAL MEASURES: none.

DIRECTIVE: Directive 85/374/EEC of 25 July 1985.
PUBLICATION: Official Journal No. L210 of 7 August 1985, pp. 0029–0033.
SUMMARY: approximation of the laws, regulations and administrative provisions of the member states concerning liability for defective products.

This Directive introduces risk liability for producers, which means that a producer is liable for the harm caused by a defect in its product, regardless of whether any blame attaches to the producer. Proof that the product is defective and that there is a causal connection between the loss and the defect is thus sufficient to get compensation.

A product is defined as a movable even though incorporated into another movable or into an immovable. The Directive does not apply to nuclear accidents or services. It is logical that services do not qualify as products, but note that electricity and gas are regarded as goods. In principle, only the producer is liable within the framework of this Directive, but a supplier that presents himself as a producer, the importer of products into the EU and a conditional bearer of product liability are deemed to be producers. A conditional bearer of product liability can be any supplier of the product until it can be established who the producer is. The supplier can release himself from such liability by informing the damaged party within a reasonable period of his supplier, the importer into the EU or the producer.

The Directive provides that a product is defective when it does not provide the safety which a person is entitled to expect, taking all circumstances into account, including the time when the product was put into circulation. The revealed "damage" means that caused by death or by personal injuries and that to any item of private property other than the defective product itself, with a lower threshold of 500 euros. The national legislation of the member states governs any economic loss. Furthermore, the Directive allows the member states to limit liability for death or personal injury to a minimum of 70 million euros.
TRANSITIONAL MEASURES: none.

DIRECTIVE: Directive 97/7/EC of 17 February 1997.
PUBLICATION: Official Journal No. L144 of 4 June 1997, pp. 0019–0027.
SUMMARY: protection of consumers in respect of distance contracts.

This Directive provides that, before a distance contract is entered into, the consumer has to be in possession of the following information, which has to be provided clearly and understandably:
- the identity of the supplier and, in some cases, his address;
- the main characteristics of the goods or services, together with price;
- the delivery costs;
- the arrangements for payment, delivery or performance;
- the existence of a right of withdrawal and the means of exercising that right;
- the time for which the offer is valid, the price and any minimum duration of the contract;
- the cost of using the means of distance communication;
- the place where complaints can be lodged;
- information regarding the service;
- the conditions for cancelling the agreement.

The withdrawal period is seven days if the requisite information is provided and three months if it is not.

Furthermore, the Directive states that public bodies, consumer organisations and professional organisations are to be regarded as having a legitimate interest in acting in court disputes involving distance sales.

The Directive is not applicable to:
- agreements relating to financial services;
- agreements concluded by means of automatic vending machines;
- agreements concluded with telecommunications operators through the use of public payphones;
- agreements relating to immovable property, except for rental;
- agreements concluded at an auction.

TRANSITIONAL MEASURES: none.

DIRECTIVE: Directive 92/28/EEC of 31 March 1992.
PUBLICATION: Official Journal No. L113 of 30 April 1992, pp. 0013–0018.
SUMMARY: the advertising of medicinal products for human use.

This Directive prohibits advertising for a medicine for which no licence has been issued to market it according to Community law. Furthermore, this Directive lays down the conditions under which advertising can be done for medicinal products for human use. A distinction is drawn between the advertising of medicines to the general public and advertising directed to professionals in the health sector.

TRANSITIONAL MEASURES: none.

DIRECTIVE: Directive 93/13/EEC of 5 April 1993.

PUBLICATION: Official Journal No. L095 of 21 April 1993, pp. 0029–0034.
SUMMARY: unfair terms in consumer contracts.

This Directive deals with unfair terms in contracts between traders and consumers. The Directive draws a distinction between terms negotiated between the parties and terms not expressly negotiated between the parties. A term which has not been individually negotiated is regarded as unfair if, contrary to the requirement of good faith, it causes a significant imbalance in the rights and obligations arising under the contract to the detriment of the consumer. Unfair terms are not binding on consumers and unclear terms are interpreted in the consumer's favour.
TRANSITIONAL MEASURES: none.

DIRECTIVE: Directive 99/44/EC of 25 May 1999.
PUBLICATION: Official Journal No. L171 of 7 July 1999, pp. 0012–0016.
SUMMARY: certain aspects of the sale of consumer goods and associated guarantees.

This Directive harmonises the rules on consumers' rights where the goods supplied are not in accordance with the contract, states when this is the case and lays down a number of rules with regard to guarantees on goods supplied.
TRANSITIONAL MEASURES: none.

DIRECTIVE: Directive 89/397/EEC of 14 June 1989.
PUBLICATION: Official Journal No. L186 of 30 June 1989, pp. 0023–0026.
SUMMARY: the official control of foodstuffs.

Under this Directive are laid down the general principles for official controls of foodstuffs. The controls relate inter alia to raw materials, semi-finished products, finished products and cleaning and maintenance products that are used in the production of foodstuffs.
TRANSITIONAL MEASURES: none.

DIRECTIVE: Directive 90/219/EEC of 23 April 1990.
PUBLICATION: Official Journal No. L117 of 8 May 1990, pp. 0001–0014.
SUMMARY: the contained use of genetically modified micro-organisms.

This Directive obliges the member states to limit as far as possible the use of genetically modified micro-organisms. Decision 2001/204/EC of 8 March 2001 lays down the criteria for determining what types of genetically modified micro-organisms are safe for human health and the environment. Directive 2001/18/EC of the European Parliament and of the Council of 12 March 2001 governs the deliberate release into the environment of genetically modified organisms.
TRANSITIONAL MEASURES: none.

REGULATION: Regulation (EC) No. 258/97 of 27 January 1997.
PUBLICATION: Official Journal No. L043 of 14 February 1997, pp. 0001–0006.

SUMMARY: novel foods and novel food ingredients.

This Regulation deals with novel foods and novel food ingredients:
- that contain or consist of genetically modified organisms;
- that comprise a primary molecular structure;
- that comprise micro-organisms, fungi or algae;
- that comprise plants or are isolated from plants or animals;
- whose nutritional value, metabolism or level of undesirable substances is significantly changed during the production process.

This Regulation does not apply to food additives, flavourings and extraction solvents.

Under the Regulation, the aforementioned novel foods and food ingredients may not present any danger to consumers, may not deceive the consumer and may not differ from the foods they are intended to replace such that normal consumption thereof would be detrimental to the consumer. This is monitored by making admission to the European market for such products dependent on a European licence, to be applied for from the national authorities of a given member state.

Further, the Regulation lays down specific labelling requirements with regard to novel foods and novel food ingredients.

Directive 87/357/EEC of the Council of 25 June 1987 prohibits articles that are not edible but that, due to their shape, aroma or packaging could easily be confused with foodstuffs.

TRANSITIONAL MEASURES: none.

4.11 Are transitional measures applicable to the European rules on consumer protection and public health?

No.

4.12 Is the European environmental legislation becoming a (r)evolution in durability?

As a result of the economic past of most of the candidate member states, the types of their industries and their state, pollution per inhabitant is greater than in the European Union. Implementation of the European environment rules is a first step toward putting this right.

The EU environmental rules will also be applicable in the new member states. Relaxation of the standards is not permissible. This therefore means that, as of their accession, all the European environmental rules have to be transposed into the national legal systems. This is no easy task, since the European environmental legislation numbers some three hundred legislative instruments. The implementation of some sub-areas is therefore a time-consuming matter and will entail heavy investment, such as in water-purification plants.

Given the financial and practical limitations in the accession countries, a number of transitional periods have been provided for. These transitional rules are limited both in time and in scope, since the intention is to fully implement the "environmental acquis" in the short term. Only that way can disruption to the market be avoided.

An example: the transitional measures applicable to Poland.

- sulphur content of liquid fuel by 2006;

- volatile organic matter from the storage of oil by 2005;

- useful application and recycling of packaging waste by 2007;

- waste dumps by 2010 (by 2009 for the present member states);

- waste transport by 2007;

- treatment of municipal waste water by 2015;

- discharge of hazardous materials into surface water by 2007;

- integrated prevention and anti-pollution measures by 2010 (by 2007 for the present member states);

- protection of the health of individuals who work in a medical context and are exposed to ionising radiation by 2006.

In a number of fields, no extension has been granted. These are environmental rules for which, owing to their special importance, no extension can be tolerated. Thus, there are no transitional measures for the framework directives on water and air, the directives concerning nature protection, access to environmental information and environmental impact reporting.

Furthermore, the EU rules out transitional periods for:

- product-related rules: this concerns inter alia the fact that products that satisfy the legislation of a given member state can freely be marketed in the other member states;

- new plants: in principle these must in all cases fulfil the new rules.

Just as for the other member states, the EU can take action against new member states that fail to meet their obligations. A breach can even be brought before the European Court of Justice.

4.13   Is a new environmental market being created for goods and services in the new member states?

For the accession countries, the investment cost for implementation of the European environmental legislation is estimated by the Commission to be 80 to 110 billion euros. Via programmes such as PHARE and ISPA, the EU has made significant funds available in order to make up the backlog as quickly as possible. A major part of the investment will nonetheless have to be financed by the accession countries themselves.

These extensive investments have brought about an active environmental market. Here, it involves mainly the provision of services and supply of goods to combat pollution, clean technologies and environmental consultancy. Since 1995, this sector has seen annual turnover growth of around 10%. Jobs in the environmental sector are also on the increase. In the next few years, as well, vast investment will be made in order to further implement the European environmental legislation. The environmental market will thus be able to further grow.

A well-organised environmental sector is frequently identified as being one of the central conditions for an efficient and rapid implementation of new rules.

4.14   What risks and opportunities are there in the environmental field if I invest in the candidate member states?

Undertakings from accession countries will have to be sufficiently flexible to adapt to the new standards. In addition to investment in adjustments or the renewal of existing plants, the business culture also has to be incorporated into the change process. This means that, in addition to new or adapted plants and systems, the attitude of business leaders and workforces vis-à-vis the environment will have to adjust to the new context.

Given the scope of the investments, it can be expected that some of these expenses will be recouped from industry. New environment-related taxes and levies for funding implementation of the environment legislation and conducting an adapted environmental policy are not unconscionable.

For instance a Belgian business that wants to take over an existing undertaking in a new member state has to dwell upon the following questions:

*   What transitional period do I have in which to adapt the existing, old-fashioned plant to the requirements of the new legislation? Depending on the accession country in question, a shorter or longer transitional period will be accorded for the adaptation of plants

and production processes to bring them into line with European standards.

- What is the cost price of the requisite investments?

- Can I get subsidies or tax breaks for the investments for bringing the old plant into line with the new standards?

- To what degree am I answerable for the historical liabilities of the undertaking? Lend a thought to the serious financial consequences of a soil clean-up duty further to soil pollution over a good many years;

- What environmentally related levies will be charged on my business activities and do they affect my cost structure?

- Is there an environmental management system present and has this system been adjusted to the undertaking's environmental risks?

- Is environmental awareness embedded into the business culture?

- To what extent does the takeover of the undertaking entail a risk for the reputation of my business? How does the undertaking deal with its neighbours and other relevant societal players?

Taking over an undertaking with outmoded plant can also offer certain benefits. One example from the field of European climate policy is that, for energy-intensive businesses that fall under the European emissions-trading system, the replacement of an outmoded plant by a new, more energy-efficient installation can result in an excess of emission rights. These excess emission rights can then be sold on the European emissions-trading market. With the proceeds from the sale of these emission rights, part of the investment cost can be funded.

The accession of the new member states therefore brings with it a number of environmentally related issues. It is important to timely identify the relevant environmental aspects so that the pertinent risks are covered and the opportunities used to the full.

5 What is the Impact of the Enlargement of the European Union in the Field of Social and Employment Law?

5.1 Is there an "acquis communautaire" in the field of social law?*

A frequently voiced criticism is that there is no European social policy. There do nevertheless exist a number of social law rules which may be regarded as part of the "acquis communautaire". This part of the "acquis" has a great influence on businesses that employ workers in the accession countries, since these employers (or entrepreneurs) will have to examine whether their policy meets the minimum conditions under the European rules. In addition, there are important changes for cross-border work.

5.2 What changes are there in the field of social security law?

Is Regulation No. 1408/71 of the Council of 14 June 1971 on the application of social security schemes to employed persons and their families moving within the Community[1] applicable after 1 May 2004?

As from 1 May 2004, there are changes to the social security position of employees from the European Economic Area (EEA) who are employed on a cross-border basis. The EEA comprises the countries of the European Union, Iceland, Liechtenstein and Norway.

Up until 1 May 2004, the social security position of these workers is governed by bilateral treaties, on the condition that the EU-Regulation No. 1408/71 was not applicable. Where no bilateral treaty is applicable, then the internal, national social security legislation of the countries concerned is applicable.

As from 1 May 2004, Regulation 1408/71 and the Implementing Regulation 574/72 will also be applicable in the new member states. This Regulation coordinates the various national social security schemes in the European Economic Area, without intending to harmonise them. The intention therefore is not to set up a common European social security system. Thus, each of the member states retains competence to determine its own social security

---

* You will find the source references for this chapter on page 125.

scheme. The Regulation is intended only to avoid migrating workers being disadvantaged in relation to employees that have worked in just one member state.

The coordination of the various social security schemes rests on four main principles:

First principle: unity of legislation

The basic principle is that a worker is only subject to the legislation of one member state.

However, there is an exception to this. Someone who is simultaneously an employee in one member state and self-employed in another member state can in some cases be subject at one and the same time to the legislation of both member states.[2]

Second principle: prohibition against discrimination on the basis of nationality

Migrating workers have the same rights and duties as national workers.

Third principle: retention of vested rights

In order not to hinder the free movement of persons, Regulation 1408/71 provides for the retention of vested rights.

Fourth principle: retention of rights being accumulated

The Regulation provides for the "recognition of periods". This means that the insurance, employment or residence periods that are fulfilled under the legislation of one member state can be taken into account in so far as is necessary to be entitled to a benefit or allowance in another member state.

5.3 What social security legislation is a worker subject to?

Work state principle[3]

The general rule is that a worker is only subject to the social security legislation of one single member state, i.e. the member state where he works. This is the "work state principle".

Secondment and simultaneous employment in two or more member states constitute exceptions to the "work state principle", however.

What about secondment?[4]

In the case of secondment, the worker continues to be subject to the social security scheme of the member state of the seconding employer.

Secondment means that a worker is sent by his employer to another member state to work there temporarily. However, throughout the whole period, the worker continues to be linked to the original employer. Consequently, it is necessary that, during the period of secondment, an organic link continues to exist between the seconding undertaking and the seconded worker.

Example: an undertaking established in Latvia sends an employee of French nationality to a German undertaking for four months to install machinery. Provided the organic link between the Latvian employer and the employee continues to exist, he will be able to remain subject to the Latvian social security scheme during his temporary employment in Germany.

What is the situation with simultaneous employment?

The rules applying when a worker works in various member states at the same time are as follows:

- the legislation of the state of residence[5] applies if he carries out part of his activities in the state of residence or if he is linked to various undertakings or employers that have their registered office or place of business on the territory of various member states.

  For example: a Polish employee works for a Belgian undertaking. 70% of his time is spent working in Belgium and 30% in the Netherlands. He lives in the Netherlands. The Polish employee will be subject to the Dutch social security scheme, because he lives and works there.

Or:

- the legislation of the country where the registered office or place of business of the undertaking or employer[6] is located and if the employee does not live on the territory of any of the member states where he works.

  For example: if the Polish employee moves to France, the Belgian social security scheme applies.

5.3.1 What about nationals of third countries?

Since 1 June 2003, non-EEA nationals have also fallen under Regulation 1408/71.[7]

For example: an American works full-time in Spain for a Spanish company and is subject to the Spanish social security scheme. His Spanish employer sends him to a Czech plant for six months. If an organic link continues to exist between the Spanish employer and the American employee, during his employment in the Czech Republic, the employee will continue to be subject to the Spanish social security scheme. (See also the secondment rule above.)

Regulation 1408/71 only applies to foreign employees who are already legally resident in a member state and who meet the other conditions under the Regulation. It therefore is not applicable in a situation which is confined in all respects within a single member state. This is namely the case where the circumstances of a national of a third country relate solely to a third country or a single member state.

The Regulation does not entitle nationals from outside the EEA to reside in or access the labour market of any member state.

We would, however, point out that Denmark has not accepted this Regulation, and therefore it does not apply there.

5.4　What about employment law?

5.4.1　Do employees from the new member states need a work permit?

The "acquis communautaire" gives employees an inalienable right to move house to another member state and work there.

With the exception of Malta and Cyprus, for all the other accession countries there is a general transitional measure as regards the free movement of workers. For two years after accession, the present member states can themselves lay down rules to limit access by workers from the accession countries to their national labour markets. After that period, the European Commission will evaluate the situation. Depending on that evaluation, it will be decided whether or not the "acquis communautaire" in respect of the free movement of workers will be fully implemented.

The transitional period may not extend beyond five years. If the labour market in one of the member states is seriously disrupted, the transitional period can be extended to seven years. No later than 1 May 2011, the labour market will be fully open in all member states.

In principle, the transitional period does not apply to:

- the free movement of workers between the new member states;[8]
- the free provision of services (specific exceptions exist in Austria and Germany); or
- secondments.

5.4.2　Are there restrictions for the employment of EU workers in one of the new member states?

Owing to a fear of an influx of workers, Malta can ask for transitional measures that will remain in force until seven years after accession.

5.4.3 The secondment Directive[9]

Directive 96/71/EC of the European Parliament and of the Council of 16 December 1996 concerning the posting of workers in the framework of the provision of services[10] applies to undertakings that post workers to carry out temporary work in another member state.

The Directive coordinates the laws of the member states. The aim is to lay down minimum protection rules for seconded workers. Employers that second workers to another member state have to take account of the work conditions, work circumstances and social security obligations in force there.

Thus, a foreign employer must take account of the rules in force in the other country in relation to:

- maximum work and minimum rest periods;

- minimum numbers of paid holidays;

- minimum wages, including overtime payments;

- health, safety and hygiene in the workplace;

- equal treatment for men and women;

- the conditions for posting workers, especially by temp agencies;

- protective measures regarding work conditions and circumstances for pregnant women and new mothers, children and young people.

The compulsory provisions regarding minimum protection that apply in the host country do mean that more favourable work conditions and circumstances cannot be accorded.

Nor does the Directive affect national laws on the admission, residence and access to the labour market of workers from third countries.

5.4.4 Are other employment law Directives applicable?

In the following, you will find an overview of the most important other European rules in the field of employment law and the transitional measures accorded to the accession countries.

5.4.5 General Directives

DIRECTIVE: Health and safety at work, Directive 86/188/EEC of 12 May 1986. PUBLICATION: Official Journal No. L137 of 24 May 1986, pp. 0028–0034.

SUMMARY: the protection of workers from the risks related to exposure to noise at work.

This Directive is aimed at protecting workers from the dangers to their health as a result of noise at work. This Directive states that, where the daily personal exposure of a worker to noise is likely to exceed 85 dB or the maximum value of the unweighted instantaneous sound pressure is likely to be greater than 200 Pa, appropriate measures have to be taken to ensure that:

(a) workers and/or their representatives in the undertaking or establishment receive adequate information and, when relevant, training concerning:

— potential risks to their hearing arising from noise exposure,
— the measures taken to reduce the noise nuisance,
— the obligation to comply with protective and preventive measures, in accordance with national legislation,
— the wearing of personal ear protectors and the role of checks on hearing;

(b) workers and/or their representatives in the undertaking or establishment have access to the results of noise assessments and measurements made pursuant to the Directive and can be given explanations of the significance of those results.

TRANSITIONAL MEASURES: Slovenia may delay applying this Directive until 31 December 2005.

DIRECTIVE: Directive 89/391/EEC of 12 June 1989.
PUBLICATION: Official Journal No. L183 of 29 June 1989, pp. 0001–0008.
SUMMARY: the introduction of measures to encourage improvements in the safety and health of workers at work.

This Directive is applicable to all individual or public sectors, except for certain specific public service activities or to certain specific activities in the civil protection services.

The Directive lays down general principles regarding the obligations of employers and employees in the field of the prevention of occupational risks and the protection of health and safety, exclusion of risk and accident factors, information to employees, consultation of employees, training of employees, etc. On the basis of this Directive, subsequently, more detailed directives have been issued. These directives are called individual directives, and a summary of the most important, i.e. those that affect the widest number of sectors, is given below. The other Directives mostly deal with working with particular products.

TRANSITIONAL MEASURES: none.

5.4.6 Particular Directives

DIRECTIVE: First individual directive: Directive 89/654/EEC of 30 November 1989.

PUBLICATION: Official Journal No. L393 of 30 December 1989, pp. 0001–0012.

SUMMARY: the minimum safety and health requirements for the workplace.

This Directive lays down the minimum provisions regarding health and safety in the workplace. The Directive does not apply to:

- means of transport used outside the undertaking and/or the establishment, or workplaces inside means of transport;
- temporary or mobile work sites;
- extractive industries;
- fishing boats;
- fields, woods and other land forming part of an agricultural or forestry undertaking but situated away from the undertaking's buildings.

The Annex to the Directive lays down the minimum requirements. For example:

- emergency routes and exits must remain clear and lead as directly as possible to the open air or to a safe area;
- emergency doors must open outwards;
- if air-conditioning or mechanical ventilation installations are used, they must operate in such a way that workers are not exposed to draughts which cause discomfort;
- windows, skylights and glass partitions should allow excessive effects of sunlight in workplaces to be avoided, having regard to the nature of the work and of the workplace;
- the floors of workplaces must have no dangerous bumps, holes or slopes and must be fixed, stable and not slippery;
- in rest rooms appropriate measures must be introduced for the protection of non-smokers against discomfort caused by tobacco smoke;
- adequate and suitable showers must be provided for workers if required by the nature of the work or for health reasons;
- etc.

TRANSITIONAL MEASURES: Latvia can delay applying this Directive until 31 December 2004.

DIRECTIVE: Second individual directive: Directive 89/655/EEC of 30 November 1989.

PUBLICATION: Official Journal No. L393 of 30 December 1989, pp. 0013–0017.

SUMMARY: minimum safety and health requirements for the use of work equipment by workers at work.

This Directive lays down the minimum health and safety requirements for the use of work equipment by workers. Work equipment is all machinery, apparatus, tools and installations used in the workplace.

The Directive imposes a general requirement on employers to take the necessary measures to ensure that the work equipment made available to workers in the undertaking and/or establishment is suitable for the work to be carried out or properly adapted for that purpose and may be used by workers without impairment to their safety or health. If it is not possible to fully guarantee the health and safety of workers in using work equipment, the employer has to take the appropriate measures to limit the risks to a minimum.

In an annex to the Directive, there is a list of the minimum requirements that work equipment has to fulfil. For example:

- it must be possible to start work equipment only by deliberate action on a control provided for the purpose;
- depending on the hazards the equipment presents and its normal stopping time, work equipment must be fitted with an emergency stop device;
- work equipment must bear the warnings and markings essential to ensure the safety of workers;
- etc.

TRANSITIONAL MEASURES: Latvia can delay applying this Directive until 1 July 2004, Malta until 31 December 2005 and Poland until 31 December 2005.

DIRECTIVE: Third individual directive: Directive 89/656/EEC of 30 November 1989.

PUBLICATION: Official Journal No. L393 of 30 December 1989, pp. 0018–0028.

SUMMARY: the minimum health and safety requirements for the use by workers of personal protective equipment at the workplace.

This Directive lays down the minimum health and safety requirements for the use by workers of personal protective equipment at the workplace. Personal protective equipment is defined as all equipment designed to be worn or held by the worker to protect him against one or more hazards likely to endanger his safety and health at work, and any addition or accessory designed to meet this objective. Under the Directive, personal protective equipment must comply with the relevant Community provisions on design and manufacture with respect to safety and health. In all cases, personal protective equipment must:

- be appropriate for the risks involved, without itself leading to any increased risk;
- correspond to existing conditions at the workplace;
- take account of ergonomic requirements and the worker's state of health;
- fit the wearer correctly after any necessary adjustment.

TRANSITIONAL MEASURES: none.

DIRECTIVE: Fourth individual directive: Directive 90/269/EEC of 29 May 1990.
PUBLICATION: Official Journal No. L156 of 21 June 1990, pp. 0009–0013.
SUMMARY: the minimum health and safety requirements for the manual handling of loads where there is a risk particularly of back injury to workers.

This Directive lays down the minimum health and safety requirements for the manual handling of loads where there is a risk particularly of back injury to workers. Employers must take appropriate organisational measures, or have to use the appropriate means, in particular mechanical equipment, in order to avoid the need for the manual handling of loads by workers. Where this cannot be avoided, the employer must reduce the nuisance as much as possible in accordance with the rules laid down in the Directive.

TRANSITIONAL MEASURES: none.

DIRECTIVE: Fifth individual directive: Directive 90/270/EEC of 29 May 1990.
PUBLICATION: Official Journal No. L156 of 21 June 1990, pp. 00147–00148.
SUMMARY: minimum safety and health requirements for work with display screen equipment.

This Directive lays down minimum safety and health requirements for workers working with display screen equipment. The annex to this Directive lists a number of specific minimum requirements. For example:

- the image on the screen should be stable, with no flickering or other forms of instability;
- the keyboard has to be tiltable and separate from the screen so as to allow the worker to find a comfortable working position avoiding fatigue in the arms or hands;
- etc.

TRANSITIONAL MEASURES: Latvia can delay applying this Directive until 31 December 2004.

DIRECTIVE: Eighth individual directive: Directive 92/57/EEC of 24 June 1992.
PUBLICATION: Official Journal No. L245 of 26 August 1992, pp. 0006–0022.
SUMMARY: minimum safety and health requirements at temporary or mobile construction sites.

This Directive lays down the minimum safety and health requirements at temporary or mobile construction sites. As an annex to this Directive a number of more detailed provisions are laid down. For example:

- during working hours, the temperature must be appropriate for human beings, having regard to the working methods used and the physical demands placed on the workers;
- sliding doors must be fitted with a safety device to prevent them from being derailed and falling over;
- etc.

TRANSITIONAL MEASURES: none.

DIRECTIVE: Ninth individual directive: Directive 92/58/EEC of 24 June 1992.
PUBLICATION: Official Journal No. L245 of 26 August 1992, pp. 0023–0042.
SUMMARY: the minimum requirements for the provision of safety and/or health signs at work.

This Directive lays down the minimum requirements for safety and/or health signs at work. It does not relate to the Community provisions regarding the marketing of hazardous materials and preparations, products and/or apparatus unless those Community provisions expressly refer hereto. Nor is this Directive applicable to signs for road and railway traffic, inland and seagoing shipping or air traffic. As a general rule, the Directive provides that employers must provide safety and/or health signs as laid down in the Directive where hazards cannot be avoided or adequately reduced by techniques for collective protection or measures, methods or procedures used in the organisation of work, or ensure that such signs are in place. More detailed rules are laid down in the annexes to the Directive, although the member states retain a broad freedom to evaluate how signs specifically have to be designed.

TRANSITIONAL MEASURES: none.

DIRECTIVE: Tenth individual directive: Directive 92/85/EEC of 19 October 1992.
PUBLICATION: Official Journal No. L348 of 28 November 1992, pp. 0001–0008.
SUMMARY: the introduction of measures to encourage improvements in the safety and health at work of pregnant workers and workers who have recently given birth or are breastfeeding.

This Directive stipulates that working conditions during such periods must be adapted and rights under employment contracts must be maintained. Dismissal directly or indirectly on grounds of pregnancy is unlawful under the Directive.

TRANSITIONAL MEASURES: none.

DIRECTIVE: Fourteenth individual directive: Directive 98/24/EC of 7 April 1998.

PUBLICATION: Official Journal No. L131 of 5 May 1998, pp. 0011–0023.
SUMMARY: the protection of the health and safety of workers from the risks related to chemical agents at work.
TRANSITIONAL MEASURES: Slovenia may delay applying this Directive until 31 December 2005.

DIRECTIVE: Directive 91/322/EEC of 29 May 1991.
PUBLICATION: Official Journal No. L177 of 5 July 1991, pp. 0022–0024.
SUMMARY: the establishment of indicative limit values by implementing Council Directive 80/1107/EEC on the protection of workers from the risks related to exposure to chemical, physical and biological agents at work.
TRANSITIONAL MEASURES: Slovenia may delay applying this Directive until 31 December 2005.

DIRECTIVE: Directive 2000/39/EC of 8 June 2000.
PUBLICATION: Official Journal No. L142 of 16 June 2000, pp. 0047–0050.
SUMMARY: the establishment of a first list of indicative occupational exposure limit values in implementation of Council Directive 98/24/EC on the protection of the health and safety of workers from the risks related to chemical agents at work.
TRANSITIONAL MEASURES: Slovenia may delay applying this Directive until 31 December 2005.

DIRECTIVE: Directive 91/383/EEC of 25 June 1991.
PUBLICATION: Official Journal No. L206 of 29 July 1991, pp. 0019–0021.
SUMMARY: supplement to the measures to encourage improvements in the safety and health at work of workers with a fixed-duration employment relationship or a temporary employment relationship.

Surveys show that these employment contracts entail extra risk to health and safety and it was therefore felt necessary to introduce European laws in this regard.

The aim of the Directive is to ensure that relevant temporary workers are afforded, as regards safety and health at work, the same level of protection as that of other workers in the user undertaking and/or establishment. Furthermore, such workers must be given the necessary information regarding the need for any special occupational qualifications or skills or special medical surveillance required, as defined in national legislation. In addition, any increased specific risks, as defined in national legislation, that the job may entail must be indicated. If necessary, training has to be provided for temporary workers.
TRANSITIONAL MEASURES: none.

DIRECTIVE: Directive 94/33/EC of 22 June 1994.
PUBLICATION: Official Journal No. L216 of 20 August 1994, pp. 0012–0020.
SUMMARY: the protection of young people at work.

This Directive is applicable to all persons under 18 years of age having an employment contract or an employment relationship. This Directive prohibits the employment of children under 15 years of age and requires the member states to ensure that employers offer young people working conditions that are suited to their age. Furthermore, a number of more specific rules are laid down regarding children that perform in cultural, artistic, sports or advertising activities, work that may not be carried out by young people, working time, night working, rest time, annual rest time and breaks.
TRANSITIONAL MEASURES: none.

DIRECTIVE: Information on working conditions, Directive 91/533/EEC of 14 October 1991.
PUBLICATION: Official Journal No. L288 of 18 October 1991, pp. 0032–0035.
SUMMARY: This Directive lays down an employer's obligation to inform employees of the conditions applicable to the contract or employment relationship under the European rules. The rules under the Directive are minimum rules and are in principle applicable to all agreements, but the member states can exclude from the scope of application of the Directive employment contracts with a total duration not exceeding one month, and/or with a working week not exceeding eight hours and employment contracts of an occasional and/or specific nature.

The employer must inform the employee of the following matters:
- the identities of the parties;
- the place of work;
- the title, grade, nature, category, a brief specification or description of the work;
- the date of commencement of the contract or employment relationship;
- in the case of a temporary contract or employment relationship, the expected duration thereof;
- the amount of paid leave or the procedures for allocating and determining such leave;
- the length of the periods of notice to be observed by the employer and the employee should their contract or employment relationship be terminated or, where this cannot be indicated, the method for determining such periods of notice;
- the initial basic amount, the other component elements and the frequency of payment of the remuneration;
- the length of the employee's normal working day or week;
- where appropriate, the collective agreements that apply.

The foregoing information must be given in the form of a written contract of employment, a letter of engagement or one or more other written documents. These documents have to be made available to the employee no later than two months after the commencement of work. If this deadline is not adhered to, the employer has to give a signed, written statement.

As already stated above under the freedom of movement for workers, an employee has to be able to present the foregoing documents upon his arrival in another member state in which he is going to take up a working position. In this case, the documents must at least contain the following information, unless the work will last for no longer than one month:
- the duration of the employment abroad;
- the currency to be used for the payment of remuneration;
- where appropriate, the benefits in cash or kind attendant on the employment abroad;
- where appropriate, the conditions governing the employee's repatriation.

Finally, the Directive states that any changes to the details in the contract or employment relationship have to be notified to the employee in writing.
TRANSITIONAL MEASURES: none.

DIRECTIVE: Collective redundancies, Directive 98/59/EC of 20 July 1998.
PUBLICATION: Official Journal No. L225 of 12 August 1998, pp. 0016–0021.
SUMMARY: this directive governs approximation of the laws of the member states relating to collective redundancies.

This Directive does not apply to:
- collective redundancies effected under contracts of employment concluded for limited periods of time or for specific tasks except where such redundancies take place prior to the date of expiry or the completion of such contracts;
- workers employed by public administrative bodies;
- the crews of seagoing vessels.

The Directive states that in the case of collective redundancies, the workers' representatives first have to be consulted with a view to reaching an agreement. These consultations must, at least, cover ways and means of avoiding collective redundancies or reducing the number of workers affected, and of mitigating the consequences by recourse to accompanying social measures aimed at redeploying or retraining workers made redundant. The Directive goes on to stipulate what information the employer has to give to the employees and the procedure the employer has to follow. The Directive lays down only minimum provisions. The member states can make provision for more favourable rules for the benefit of employees.
TRANSITIONAL MEASURES: none.

DIRECTIVE: Protection of workers in the case of the insolvency of the employer, Council Directive 80/987/EEC of 20 October 1980.
PUBLICATION: Official Journal No. L283 of 28 October 1980, pp. 0023–0027.
SUMMARY: this Directive governs the approximation of the laws of the member states relating to the protection of employees in the event of the insolvency of their employer.

This Directive governs the creation of guarantee institutions to guarantee workers' pay as well as the principle that workers must not undergo any disadvantage owing to failure by the employer to pay social security contributions.

TRANSITIONAL MEASURES: none.

DIRECTIVE: Anti-discrimination, Directive 76/207/EEC of 9 February 1976.
PUBLICATION: Official Journal No. L039 of 14 February 1976, pp. 0040–0042.
SUMMARY: This Directive has laid down the principle of equal treatment for men and women as regards access to employment, vocational training and promotion, and working conditions.

The member states can however exclude certain occupational activities for which sex is a determining factor for the exercise thereof from application of the Directive.

This Directive deals with access to the employment market. On 19 December 1978, a directive was passed that lays down the principle that discrimination on the basis of sex is to be eliminated from the national social security schemes of the member states. The Directive is applicable to the working population as to workers who have temporarily interrupted their work, job-seekers, retired persons and disabled workers.

The next directive on equal treatment of men and women is that of 11 December 1986 on application of the principle of equal treatment for self-employed men and women, including the agricultural sector, and the protection of mothers. This Directive states that the constitution of a company between spouses may not be more difficult than the constitution of a company amongst third parties. The Directive goes on to state that co-worker spouses have to be able to get a social security status, in particular in respect of interruption of work for pregnancy or giving birth.

For the sake of completeness we would also mention:

- Council Directive 86/378/EEC on the implementation of the principle of equal treatment for men and women in occupational social security schemes;
- Council Directive 96/34/EC of 3 June 1996 on the framework agreement on parental leave concluded by UNICE, CEEP and the ETUC;
- Council Directive 97/80/EC of 15 December 1997 on the burden of proof in cases of discrimination based on sex.

TRANSITIONAL MEASURES: none.

DIRECTIVE: Anti-discrimination, Directive 2000/43/EC of 29 June 2000.
PUBLICATION: Official Journal No. L180 of 19 July 2000, pp. 0022–0026.
SUMMARY: This Council Directive of 29 June 2000 governs implementation of the principle of equal treatment between persons irrespective of racial or ethnic origin. This equal treatment also covers equal treatment on the labour market and with regard to social security protection.

TRANSITIONAL MEASURES: none.

DIRECTIVE: Working time, Directive 93/104/EC of 23 November 1993, Directive 2000/34/EC of 22 June 2000.

PUBLICATION: Official Journal No. L307 of 13 December 1993, pp. 0018–0024; Official Journal No. L195 of 1 August 2000, pp. 0041–0045.

SUMMARY: In 1993, Council Directive 93/104/EC of 23 November 1993 was adopted concerning certain aspects of the organisation of working time.

This Directive was amended by Directive 2000/34/EC of 22 June 2000.

The Directive applies to all business sectors apart from transport, work activities at sea and the activities of trainee doctors.

The Directive provides that the member states have to take measures necessary to ensure that:

- every worker is entitled to a minimum daily rest period of 11 consecutive hours per 24-hour period;
- per each seven-day period, every worker is entitled to a minimum uninterrupted rest period of 24 hours plus the 11 hours' daily rest;
- in keeping with the need to protect the safety and health of workers:
  — the period of weekly working time is limited by means of laws, regulations or administrative provisions or by collective agreements or agreements between the two sides of the industry;
  — the average working time for each seven-day period, including overtime, does not exceed 48 hours;
  — every worker is entitled to paid annual leave of at least four weeks in accordance with the conditions for entitlement to, and granting of, such leave laid down by national legislation and/or practice.

Furthermore, other rules are laid down regarding night working, team work and work rosters.

TRANSITIONAL MEASURES: Malta can delay applying this Directive until 31 July 2004. Existing collective agreements that provide for working time that exceeds the Directive's limits remain in force until 31 December 2004.

Source references for Chapter 5

1. Official Journal No. L149 of 5 July 1971, pp. 0002–0050.
2. Article 14C of EU Regulation 1408/71 in conjunction with annex 7.
3. Article 13 of EU Regulation 1408/71.
4. Articles 14(1)(a), 14(1)(b) and 17 of EU Regulation 1408/71.
5. Article 14(2)(b)(i) of EU Regulation 1408/71.
6. Article 14(2)(b)(ii) of EU Regulation 1408/71.
7. Official Journal No. L124 of 20 May 2003, pp. 0001–0023.
8. http://europa.eu.int/comm/enlargement/negotiations/treaty_of_accession_2003/index.htm.
9. Official Journal No. L018 of 21 January 1997, pp. 0001–0006.
10. Official Journal No. L018 of 21 January 1997, pp. 0001–0006.

6 What is the Impact of the Enlargement of the European Union in the Field of Indirect Taxation?

6.1 What changes will there be in the field of indirect taxation when goods are shipped from a current EU member state to one of the new member states?*

Upon enlargement of the European Union, the new member states will accede to the internal market and the principle of the free movement of goods will apply with all member states. The European rules on VAT, customs and excise will become applicable upon enlargement. This will have a major impact on businesses in the new member states and their business partners in the current European Union.

Prior to 1 May 2004, the words import and export are still used to describe cross-border movements of goods between the European Union and the accession countries. As from 1 May 2004, in most cases, these will be intra-Community transactions: intra-Community supplies and acquisitions.

Before 1 May 2004, under customs arrangements, VAT registration in the accession countries could usually be avoided. As from 1 May 2004, these customs arrangements disappeared for Community goods. The question arises whether VAT registration in the new member states can still be avoided then. The simplification measures for, amongst other things, triangular transactions, consignment stocks and contract work, laid down by the Sixth VAT Directive, the VAT Committee or local VAT laws or local administrative arrangements, are only able partially to replace the benefit of customs arrangements.

It falls to each of the accession countries to further develop these simplification measures. Businesses will more often than they currently do have to be in possession of a VAT number in the new member states where a simplification measure does not exist.

---

* You will find the source references for this chapter on page 175.

After enlargement, of the European Union, the administrative procedures for intra-Community transactions come into force.

The impact of enlargement of the European Union on VAT and customs procedures for goods traffic between the European Union and the new member states can be illustrated using the example of Table 6.1.

Table 6.1   Example showing the impact of a supply of goods (before and after 1 May 2004).

Administrative procedures	Transaction before 1 May 2004	Transaction as from 1 May 2004
Transaction: Sale of goods shipped from a current member state (e.g. the UK) to a new member state, transport for the account of the supplier		
Documents to be issued by the supplier	Invoice for export without VAT Reason for exemption of export	Invoice for intra-Community supply without VAT mentioning the reason for exemption (in a case of distance selling: invoice subject to the VAT of the current member state where shipments starts from or VAT of one of the 10 member states)
Onus of proof for exemption from VAT by supplier	Export document All other supporting documents showing the goods have left the current member state (e.g. the UK)	Mention of the valid VAT numbers of both parties on the invoice All other supporting documents showing the goods have left the current member state
Declaration by supplier	Export declaration VAT return	VAT return EC sales list Intrastat return
Documents to be received by the customer	Import document Invoice from the supplier	Invoice from the supplier
Declarations by the customer	Import declaration VAT return	VAT return Listing of intra-Community acquisitions performed (if required by the new member state in question)
Statistical obligations	None – contained in customs documents for export and import	Intrastat return by supplier and customer

Even for domestic transactions, businesses that are VAT-registered in the new member states may, as from 1 May 2004, have a number of additional new administrative obligations, such as submission of a (summary) annual return or an annual sales listing.

6.2 What changes are there in the field of VAT in the accession countries?

The "acquis communautaire" also determines the VAT legislation in the accession countries. The Sixth VAT Directive[1] underlies all VAT legislation in the current member states of the European Union. Together with the rest of the European rules on VAT, this will have to be transposed as from 1 May 2004 into the national legislation of the new member states.

Thus, the European VAT principles will also become applicable in those member states. The VAT treatment of a given transaction will then be determined by a combination of the following factors:

- Are the parties liable for VAT?

- Does the transaction qualify as one of the four taxable transactions: a supply of goods, supply of a service, an import or an intra-Community acquisition?

- What is the place of the transaction?

- When does the transaction take place?

- What is the taxable basis for the transaction?

- What is the VAT rate for the transaction?

- Is any exemption from VAT applicable?

- Who is the party liable to pay the VAT?

- Is there a right to deduct VAT?

- What are the administrative obligations are there in this connection?

In the following, you will find an overview of the "acquis communautaire" for VAT.

6.2.1 Overview of the "acquis communautaire": VAT (selected titles)

What follows is a summary of the VAT Directives. We also indicate the transitional measures that have been granted to the new member states.

DIRECTIVE: First Council Directive 67/227/EEC of 11 April 1967 on the harmonisation of legislation of member states concerning turnover taxes. Amended on several occasions.

PUBLICATION: Official Journal No. L71 of 14 April 1967, pp. 1301–1303. For a consolidated version, see http://europa.eu.int/eur-lex/en/lif/reg/en_register_093010.html.

SUMMARY:

- By 1 January 1972, each member state replaces its turnover tax scheme with the common VAT scheme, but without harmonisation of rates and exemptions.
- The principle of this common scheme is neutrality: within each member state, similar goods and services are taxed in the same way, regardless of the length of the production and distribution chain.
- The structure of the common VAT scheme and the manner in which it is applied will be laid down in a second directive.
- In a second stage and on a proposal from the Commission, the Council must, before 1 January 1969, lay down the measures for fiscal controls at the internal borders within the Community.

DIRECTIVE: Sixth Council Directive 77/388/EEC of 17 May 1977 on the harmonisation of the laws of the member states relating to turnover taxes – Common system of value added tax: uniform basis of assessment. Amended on several occasions.

PUBLICATION: Official Journal No. L145 of 13 June 1977, pp. 0001–0040. For a consolidated version, see http://europa.eu.int/eur-lex/en/lif/reg/en_register_093010.html.

SUMMARY:

- VAT is due on the supply of goods or services effected for consideration within the territory of the country by a taxable person and on the importation of goods.
- Taxable persons are persons who independently carry out in any place any of the following economic activities, whatever the purpose or results of that activity: all activities of producers, traders and persons supplying services including mining and agricultural activities and activities of the professions, or their equivalents.
- Exclusion of a number of national territories from the scope of application of the directives.
- As from 1 January 1993, the terms "import" and "export" are abolished for all supplies that are carried out between member states and these terms are restricted to trade with third countries. In this manner, the intra-Community sale and purchase of goods is treated in the same way as sales and purchases within the member states.
- Transitional arrangements for taxation, intended for intra-Community trade without border controls, for a limited period (from 1 January 1993 till 31 December 1996) and in derogation from the "origin principle" (tax levied in the member state where the supplier is established) on goods supplied and services provided.
- For such transactions, tax has to be charged in accordance with the rate and conditions in the member state of destination of the goods and

services provided, within the limits of the approximation of the rates that are laid down in the relevant directives:
— the standard rate of VAT has to be at least 15% in all member states by December 2005;
— one or two reduced rates are permitted with a minimum of 5% for products intended for social or cultural purposes (annex H, whose working scope is investigated every two years by the Council).

- The transitional arrangements are replaced by a definitive arrangement for the levying of tax on trade between member states, which in principle is based on taxation in the member state of origin of the goods supplied or services provided. If the Council does not lay down the necessary provisions for bringing into force and the functioning of the definitive arrangement (see below), the provisional arrangement is automatically extended until such date as the definitive arrangement comes into effect or for as long as the Council has not taken any decision regarding the definitive arrangement.
- Simplification of the taxation procedures, both for taxable persons and for the relevant national authorities:
  — for transactions that are carried out with third countries and relate to goods qualifying as Community goods;
  — for intra-Community trade in products for which excise duties are due;
  — for the provision of services and supplies of goods that are taxable within a member state if the trader is not established on that country's territory;
  — for transition from the provisions that applied up until 31 December 1992 to those that came into force on 1 January 1993.
- Exemption from tax for certain transactions within a member state, upon exportation outside the Community and upon importation.
- Right of deduction: scope of application and rules governing the right to deduct.
- Special rules applicable to used goods, works of art, antiques and collectors' items.
- Special rules applicable to gold.
- Special rules applicable to labour-intensive services.
- European rules on VAT registration for businesses not established in a member state – principle of direct registration for businesses established in the European Union.
- Special rules for services supplied by electronic means.
- European rules on the content of invoices, who has to issue an invoice (the supplier), who can issue an invoice (outsourcing, self-billing), electronic invoicing, the obligation to keep records for purchase and sales invoices issued on paper or electronically.

- Under certain conditions, the member states can apply derogations in order to simplify collection of VAT or to prevent certain forms of fraud and tax-evasion.
- Constitution of a consultative VAT Committee.

TRANSITIONAL MEASURES

Cyprus

Turnover threshold for VAT exempt small businesses is 15 600 euros.

- By way of derogation from Article 12(3)(a) of Directive 77/388/EEC, Cyprus may maintain an exemption with refund of tax paid at the preceding stage on the supply of pharmaceuticals and foodstuffs for human consumption, with the exception of ice cream, ice lollies, frozen yoghurt, water ice and similar products and savoury food products (potato crisps/sticks, puffs and similar products packaged for human consumption without further preparation), until 31 December 2007. By way of derogation from Article 12(3)(a) of Directive 77/388/EEC, Cyprus may maintain a reduced rate of value added tax of not less than 5% on the supply of restaurant services until 31 December 2007 or until the end of the transitional period referred to in Article 28*l* of the Directive, whichever is the earlier.
- Without prejudice to the procedure set out in Article 27 of Directive 77/388/EEC, Cyprus may continue to apply a simplified procedure on value added tax for the application of a cash accounting scheme and on the value of supplies between connected persons until one year after the date of accession.
- For the purposes of applying Article 28(3)(b) of Directive 77/388/EEC, Cyprus may exempt from value added tax the supply of building land referred to in point 16 of Annex F of the Directive until 31 December 2007. Such an exemption shall not have any effect on own resources for which the basis of assessment will have to be re-established in accordance with Council Regulation (EEC, Euratom) No 1553/89 on the definitive uniform arrangements for the collection of own resources accruing from value added tax (OJ L 155, 7.6.1989, p. 9). Regulation as amended by Regulation (EC, Euratom) No. 1026/1999 (OJ L 126, 20.5.1999, p. 1).
- For the purposes of applying Article 28(3)(b) of Directive 77/388/EEC, Cyprus may maintain an exemption from value added tax on international transport of passengers, referred to in point 17 of Annex F to the Directive, until the condition set out in Article 28(4) of the Directive is fulfilled or for as long as the same exemption is applied by any of the present member states, whichever is the earlier.

Estonia

Turnover threshold for VAT exempt small businesses is 16 000 euros.

- By way of derogation from Article 12(3)(a) of Directive 77/388/EEC, Estonia may maintain a reduced rate of value added tax of not less than 5% on the supply of heating sold to natural persons, housing associations, apartment associations, churches, congregations, and institutions or bodies financed from the state, rural municipality or city budget, as well as on the supply of peat, fuel briquettes, coal and firewood to natural persons, until 30 June 2007.
- For the purposes of applying Article 28(3)(b) of Directive 77/388/EEC, Estonia may maintain an exemption from value added tax on international transport of passengers, referred to in point 17 of Annex F to the Directive, until the condition set out in Article 28(4) of the Directive is fulfilled or for as long as the same exemption is applied by any of the present member states, whichever is the earlier.

Hungary

Turnover threshold for VAT-exempt small businesses is 35 000 euros.

- By way of derogation from Article 12(3)(a) of Directive 77/388/EEC, Hungary may maintain:
  - (i) a reduced rate of value added tax of no less than 12% on the supply of coal, coal-brick and coke, firewood and charcoal, and on the supply of district heating services until 31 December 2007, and
  - (ii) a reduced rate of value added tax of no less than 12% on the supply of restaurant services and of foodstuffs sold on similar premises until 31 December 2007 or until the end of the transitional period referred to in Article 28*l* of the Directive, whichever is the earlier,
- Without prejudice to a formal decision to be adopted according to the procedure set out in Article 12(3)(b) of Directive 77/388/EEC, Hungary may maintain a reduced rate of value added tax of not less than 5% on the supply of natural gas and electricity until one year after the date of accession.
- For the purposes of applying Article 28(3)(b) of Directive 77/388/EEC, Hungary may maintain an exemption from value added tax on international transport of passengers, referred to in point 17 of Annex F to the Directive, until the condition set out in Article 28(4) of the Directive is fulfilled or for as long as the same exemption is applied by any of the present member states, whichever is the earlier.

Latvia

Turnover threshold for VAT exempt small businesses is 17 200 euros.

- By way of derogation from Article 12(3)(a) of Directive 77/388/EEC, Latvia may maintain an exemption from value added tax on the supply of heating sold to households until 31 December 2004.

- Without prejudice to the procedure set out in Article 27 of Directive 77/388/EEC, Latvia may continue to apply a simplified procedure for charging value added tax on timber transactions until one year after the date of accession.
- For the purposes of applying Article 28(3)(b) of Directive 77/388/EEC, Latvia may maintain an exemption from value added tax on services supplied by authors, artists and performers, referred to in point 2 of Annex F of the Directive, until the condition set out in Article 28(4) of the Directive is fulfilled or so long as the same exemptions are applied by any of the present member states, whichever is the earlier.
- For the purposes of applying Article 28(3)(b) of Directive 77/388/EEC, Latvia may also maintain an exemption from value added tax on international transport of passengers referred to in point 17 of Annex F of the Directive, until the condition set out in Article 28(4) of the Directive is fulfilled or so long as the same exemptions are applied by any of the present member states, whichever is the earlier.

Lithuania

Turnover threshold for VAT-exempt small businesses is 29 000 euros.

- For the purposes of applying Article 28(3)(b) of Directive 77/388/EEC, Lithuania may maintain an exemption from value added tax on international transport of passengers, referred to in point 17 of Annex F to the Directive, until the condition set out in Article 28(4) of the Directive is fulfilled or for as long as the same exemption is applied by any of the present member states, whichever is the earlier.

Malta

The turnover threshold for VAT-exempt small businesses is 37 000 euros for undertakings whose activities comprise just the supply of goods, 24 300 euros for undertakings whose activities comprise just the provision of services with a low value-added and 14 600 for all other cases.

- For the purposes of applying Article 28(3)(b) of Directive 77/388/EEC, Malta may maintain the following exemptions:
  - (a) from value added tax with credit on inland passenger transport, international passenger transport and domestic inter-island sea passenger transport, referred to in point 17 of Annex F to the Directive, until the condition set out in Article 28(4) of the Directive is fulfilled or for as long as the same exemption is applied by any of the present member states, whichever is the earlier,
  - (b) from value added tax without credit for input VAT on the supply of water by public authorities, referred to in point 12 of Annex F to the Directive, until the condition set out in Article 28(4) of the Directive is fulfilled or for as long as the same exemption is applied by any of the present member states, whichever is the earlier,

(c) from value added tax without credit for input VAT on the supply of buildings and building land, referred to in point 16 of Annex F to the Directive, until the condition set out in Article 28(4) of the Directive is fulfilled or for as long as the same exemption is applied by any of the present member states, whichever is the earlier.

(d) from value added tax with credit on foodstuffs and pharmaceuticals until 1 January 2010. If after such transitional period any member state qualities for similar exemptions in terms of article 28(1), Malta may request an extension of the transitional period beyond 2010. Certain confectionery items and medical accessories do not quality for the same exemption.

Poland

Turnover threshold for VAT-exempt small businesses is 10 000 euros.

- By way of derogation from Article 12(3)(a) of Directive 77/388/EEC, Poland may (i) apply an exemption with refund of tax paid at the preceding stage on the supply of certain books and specialist periodicals, until 31 December 2007, and (ii) maintain a reduced rate of value added tax of not less than 7% on the supply of restaurant services until 31 December 2007 or until the end of the transitional period referred to in Article 28*l* of the Directive, whichever is the earlier.

- By way of derogation from Article 12(3)(a) of Directive 77/388/EEC, Poland may maintain

  (i) a reduced rate of value added tax of no less than 3% on foodstuffs (including beverages but excluding alcoholic beverages) for human and animal consumption; live animals, seeds, plants and ingredients normally intended for use in preparation of foodstuffs; products normally intended to be used to supplement or substitute foodstuffs; and on the supply of goods and services of a kind normally intended for use in agricultural production, but excluding capital goods such as machinery or buildings, referred to in points 1 and 10 of Annex H to the Directive, until 30 April 2008, and

  (ii) a reduced rate of value added tax of no less than 7% on the supply of services, not provided as part of a social policy, for construction, renovation and alteration of housing, excluding building materials, and on the supply before first occupation of residential buildings or parts of residential buildings as referred to in Article 4(3)(a) of the Directive until 31 December 2007.

- For the purposes of applying Article 28(3)(b) of Directive 77/388/EEC, Poland may maintain an exemption from value added tax on international transport of passengers referred to in point 17 of Annex F to the Directive, until the condition set out in Article 28(4) of the Directive is fulfilled or for as long as the same exemption is applied by any of the present member states, whichever is the earlier.

Slovakia

Turnover threshold for VAT-exempt small businesses is 35 000 euros. Currently, the turnover threshold is SKK 1.5 million (approximately EUR 37,300).

- By way of derogation from Article 12(3)(a) of Directive 77/388/EEC, Slovakia may maintain
  - (a) a reduced rate of value added tax of not less than 5% on the supply of heat energy used by private households and small entrepreneurs who are not registered for VAT for heating and the production of hot water, excluding raw materials used to generate heat energy, until 31 December 2008, and
  - (b) a reduced rate of value added tax of not less than 5% on the supply of construction work for residential housing not provided as part of a social policy, and excluding building materials until 31 December 2007.
- Without prejudice to a formal decision to be adopted according to the procedure set out in Article 12(3)(b) of Directive 77/388/EEC, Slovakia may maintain a reduced rate of value added tax of not less than 5% on the supply of natural gas and electricity until one year after the date of accession. Currently, there is a single VAT rate of 19% in Slovakia and no reduced rate application.
- For the purposes of applying Article 28(3)(b) of Directive 77/388/EEC, Slovakia may maintain an exemption from value added tax on international transport of passengers, referred to in point 17 of Annex F to the Directive, until the condition set out in Article 28(4) of the Directive is fulfilled or for as long as the same exemption is applied by any of the present member states, whichever is the earlier.

Slovenia

Turnover threshold for VAT-exempt small businesses is 25 000 euros.

- By way of derogation from Article 12(3)(a) of Directive 77/388/EEC, Slovenia may maintain
  - (i) a reduced rate of value added tax of not less than 8.5% on the preparation of meals until 31 December 2007 or until the end of the transitional period referred to in Article 28*l* of the Directive, whichever is the earlier, and
  - (ii) a reduced rate of value added tax of not less than 5% on the supply of construction, renovation and maintenance work for residential housing not provided as part of a social policy, and excluding building materials until 31 December 2007.
- For the purposes of applying Article 28(3)(b) of Directive 77/388/EEC, Slovenia may maintain an exemption from value added tax on international transport of passengers, referred to in point 17 of Annex F to

the Directive, until the condition set out in Article 28(4) of the Directive is fulfilled or for as long as the same exemption is applied by any of the present member states, whichever is the earlier.

Czech Republic

Turnover threshold for VAT exempt small businesses is 35 000 euros.

- By way of derogation from Article 12(3)(a) of Directive 77/388/EEC, the Czech Republic may maintain a reduced rate of value added tax of not less than 5% until 31 December 2007 on (a) the supply of heat energy used by households and small entrepreneurs who are not registered for VAT for heating and the production of hot water, excluding raw materials used to generate heat energy, and (b) on the supply of construction work for residential housing not provided as part of a social policy, and excluding building materials.
- For the purposes of applying Article 28(3)(b) of Directive 77/388/EEC, the Czech Republic may maintain an exemption from value added tax on international transport of passengers, referred to in point 17 of Annex F to the Directive, until the condition set out in Article 28(4) of the Directive is fulfilled or for as long as the same exemption is applied by any of the present member states, whichever is the earlier.

DIRECTIVE: Eighth Directive 79/1072/EEC of the Council of 6 December 1979 on the harmonization of the laws of the member states relating to turnover taxes – arrangements for the refund of VAT to taxable persons not established in the territory of the country.

PUBLICATION: Official Journal No. L331 of 27 December 1979, pp. 0011–0019.

SUMMARY:

- This Directive relates to taxable persons that are not established in the relevant country but in another member state. Taxable persons are regarded as being those persons defined as such in Council Directive 77/388/EEC.
- A taxable person falls within the scope of application of the Directive if, over a period of more than three months and less than one calendar year or for a period of less than three months where the period concerned is the remainder of the calendar year:
  — he has had in that country neither the seat of his economic activity nor a fixed establishment from which business transactions are effected,
  — nor, if no such seat or fixed establishment exists, his domicile or normal place of residence,
  — he has supplied no goods or services deemed to have been supplied in that country, with the exception of:

- o transport services and services ancillary thereto,
- o services provided in cases where tax is payable solely by the person to whom they are supplied.
- The member states refund the taxable person:
  — any value added tax charged in respect of services or movable property supplied to him by other taxable persons,
  — any value added tax charged in respect of the importation of goods into the country that are used for the purposes of the economic activities or the provision of services for which the recipient is taxed.
- Conditions for making an application for refund.
- The right to a refund of tax is assessed according to Directive 77/388/EEC.
- Supplies of exempted goods or goods that can be exempted on the basis of the aforementioned directive are not eligible for refund. Exempted are the supply of goods dispatched or transported by or on behalf of a purchaser not established within the territory of the country, with the exception of goods transported by the purchaser himself for the equipping, fuelling and provisioning of any means of transport for private use.
- The treatment of taxable persons that are not established on the territory of the Community is governed by the Thirteenth VAT Directive, 86/560/EEC of the Council.[2]

TRANSITIONAL MEASURES: none.

DIRECTIVE: Thirteenth Council Directive 86/560/EEC of 17 November 1986 on the harmonisation of the laws of the member states relating to turnover taxes – arrangements for the refund of value added tax to taxable persons not established in Community territory.

PUBLICATION: Official Journal No. L326 of 21 November 1986, pp. 0040–0041.

SUMMARY:

- A taxable person not established in the territory of the Community is regarded as being any person that, over a period to be determined by the member states, has not had a trading address or permanent place of residence in any member state and that has not supplied any goods or services in that member state, with the exception of transport service or services on which only tax has to be paid by the recipient.
- In general, the member states will refund any form of VAT that a taxable person not established in the territory of the Community has paid on goods or services that a taxable person has supplied on the territory of the Community. This refund can be made dependent on equal treatment by the third country (reciprocity).
- The refund has to be applied for by the taxable person not established in the territory of the Community. The member states determine the

practical arrangements for applying for such refunds, such as time limits, minimum amounts, etc. They may also require the appointment of a fiscal representative. They have to take the measures necessary to prevent fraud.

* Refunds may not be made under more favourable conditions than refunds to taxable persons established in the EEC.
* The expenditure that is eligible for refund is fixed by the national provisions of the member states on VAT deduction. However, certain expenditure may be ruled out or certain conditions imposed.

6.3 Does this mean that the VAT rules are identical in all the member states?

The "acquis communautaire" in the field of VAT comprises Directives for the most part.

These Directives give a wide room for choice to the member states in implementing the European VAT rules into their own legislation. As a result, there is no total harmonisation of the VAT rules in the European Union. It is on these points of difference that local transposition has to be examined.

In Table 6.2, we give a non-exhaustive overview of the most important options that the new member states have in transposing the Sixth Directive, 77/388/EEC, into their own legal systems and that are of importance to business.

6.4 What changes are there for sales of goods?

As from 1 May 2004, a large number of transactions will be treated differently for customs and VAT purposes. Two instances exemplify this.

Example 1: Sale of goods from Hungary to an undertaking in the Netherlands, with transportation on behalf of the supplier

* Transaction prior to 1 May 2004

    — The Hungarian business issues an invoice for exportation without charging VAT and has an export document drawn up. It reports the export in its VAT return. For carriage of the goods from Hungary's border with the EU to the Netherlands, the Hungarian business has to go through the requisite customs formalities (or have them gone through).

Table 6.2 Most important options within the sixth VAT directive.

Feature	Option possibilities	Sixth Directive
Taxability	Possibility of subjecting certain immovable property transactions to VAT	Article 4
Taxability	VAT Grouping	Article 4
Taxability	Transfers of a totality of assets or a line of business	Article 5
VAT rate	Reduced VAT rates	Article 12 and Annex H
Deduction (how arising and manner of exercise)	Conditions for refunds of VAT	Articles 17 and 18 & 8th and 13th Refund Directive
Review of deduction	Recovery of VAT on lost receivables (doubtful debts)	Article 20
Payment of VAT liability	Extension of the possibility of reverse charge	Article 21
Obligations	Obligations regarding invoicing and documentation	Article 22 as amended by the Invoicing Directive 2001/115/EC
Obligations	Details and intervals for the VAT returns to be submitted	Article 22
Obligations	Reverse charge for import VAT	Article 23
Simplification measures	VAT registration for consignation stock Chain sales	
Administrative obligations	Simplified administrative obligations for small and medium-sized enterprises	

— The Dutch undertaking has an import document drawn up for importation of the goods. It pays the VAT on the import, either in cash at the border or via its VAT return (reverse charge). On the basis of the import declaration, it can deduct this VAT in its VAT return (provided it has a full right of deduction).

• Transaction as from 1 May 2004

— The Hungarian undertaking issues an invoice for the intra-Community supply of goods without charging VAT, but mentions the VAT numbers of both parties. The Hungarian undertaking will have to retain the necessary documents to be able to defend applying the exemption.

The Hungarian undertaking reports the intra-Community supply in its VAT return, intra-Community Sales Listing (EC Sales List) and Intrastat return.

— The Dutch undertaking reports the intra-Community acquisition in its VAT return and Intrastat return. In the VAT return, it reports the VAT due (reverse charge). If it has a due and proper invoice and a full right of deduction, it can deduct the VAT in the same VAT return (no cash to pay).

Example 2: Contract work: goods that are in free circulation are sent from Belgium by a Belgian undertaking to Slovenia, are processed there by a contract worker and subsequently sent back to Belgium

- Transaction prior to 1 May 2004

    — In Belgium, the undertaking will export its goods under an outward processing license.

    — In Slovenia, the contract worker will import the goods under an inward processing license, process them (without adding any goods) and re-export them without VAT or customs duties being due.

    — Finally, the Belgian undertaking imports the worked-on goods into Belgium and only pays import duties and import VAT on the added value (by means of the import declaration).

    — The Belgian undertaking pays the VAT on import either in cash at the border or via its VAT return (reverse charge). On the basis of the import declaration, it can deduct this VAT in its VAT return (if it has a full right of deduction).

- Transaction as from 1 May 2004

    — The Belgian undertaking, the owner of the goods, transports its goods outside Belgium to Slovenia, within the European Union.

    — Since the goods are sent to Slovenia and, after being processed returned to Belgium, the Belgian undertaking will not have to register for VAT purposes in Slovenia. It will have to keep a register of non-transfers in Belgium to record the dispatch of the goods. The goods shipment will also have to be recorded in its Intrastat return.

    — The Slovenian undertaking in its turn will keep a register of received goods, recording the arrival and dispatch of the goods. It also has to record the arrival of the goods in its Intrastat return.

    — The Slovenian undertaking can invoice its services free from VAT to the Belgian VAT number of its customer. The invoice has to mention two VAT numbers. It also has to record the departure of the goods in its Intrastat return.

— The Belgian undertaking registers return of its goods in its register of non-transfers. It also records this in its Intrastat. It reports the Belgian VAT that is due on the processing services performed in Slovenia in its Belgian VAT return. If it has a right of deduction (which will normally be the case), it can fully deduct the VAT.

6.5   What changes are there for the provision of services?

The difference between supplies of goods and provision of services is essential for VAT purposes. Depending on how the supply is classified, the rules will change for determining the place, the time and the VAT due, the applicable rate, the right of deduction, any exemptions and even the party liable to pay the VAT.

It is also of importance for the details to be included on the invoice.

For the provision of services provided as from 1 May 2004 there will also be a change in the rules. Two instances exemplify this.

Example 1: A UK company provides legal and other advice to a Czech local authority

• Transaction prior to 1 May 2004

— The UK company issues an invoice without charging UK VAT and reports this invoice in its UK VAT return.

— The Czech local authority will as a rule not submit any VAT return and, if it does in fact have to submit a VAT return, will not effect any reverse charge.

• Transaction as from 1 May 2004

— The UK company has to verify whether the Czech local authority is vatable and whether it has a VAT number.

— If the Czech local authority is a taxable person due to its activities, then the UK company should not charge UK VAT. The invoice must bear both the VAT number of the UK business and that of the Czech local authority.

— The UK undertaking reports this invoice in its UK VAT return.

— The Czech authority reports the invoice in its Czech VAT return. It has to pay Czech VAT. This is done by reporting the Czech VAT due in its VAT return. If the Czech authority is entitled to VAT deduction, it will recover the VAT in the same VAT return (reverse charge of the VAT).

— If, the Czech authority is acting in its capacity as an authority and therefore has no VAT number, then the UK company must charge 17.5% UK VAT on its services. It reports this in its UK VAT return.

— For the Czech local authority, the UK VAT will be an additional cost.

Transaction 2: A Belgian undertaking receives an invoice from a Polish carrier for the transportation of goods from Poland to Belgium

• Transaction prior to 1 May 2004

— The Polish carrier issues an invoice without charging VAT.

— The price of the transport has to be included in the taxable basis of the goods upon importation. The Belgian undertaking has to pay the VAT upon importation (unless it has a special permit allowing it to delay payment or reverse-charge the import VAT).

— On the basis of the import document, the Belgian undertaking can deduct the VAT upon importation.

— The invoice from the Polish carrier is reported along with the other purchases in the Belgian VAT return.

• Transaction as from 1 May 2004

— The Polish carrier issues an invoice without VAT. It has to mention its own VAT number and the Belgian VAT number of the customer.

— The invoice from the Polish carrier has to be reported in the Belgian VAT return. The Belgian undertaking has to calculate the VAT due and report this in its VAT return (reverse charge). The Belgian undertaking can deduct this VAT provided it has a due and proper invoice and a right of deduction.

6.6 Is the case law from the Court of Justice also applicable in the new member states?

The case law of the European Court of Justice is an indispensable source for correctly interpreting and applying the European VAT rules.

In Table 6.3, we cite a selection of important judgments that will also be applicable in the new member states as from 1 May 2004:[3]

Table 6.3 A selection of the most important judgments by the European Court of Justice.

Case	Date	European Court Reports	Issue	Parties	Directive	Articles
168/84	4 Jul. 85	1985, 2251	Definition of a fixed establishment	Günther Berkholz v. Finanzamt Hamburg-Mitte-Altstadt	Dir. 77/388/EEC	3, 9(1), 15(8)
268/83	14 Feb. 85	1985, 655	Definition of "taxable person"	D. A. Rompelman and E. A. Rompelman-Van Deelen, Amsterdam v. Minister of Finance	Dir. 77/388/EEC	4(1)
C-16/00	27 Sep. 01	2001, I-06663	Tax liability and exemption for interference by a holding company in the management of its subsidiaries	Cibo Participations SA v. Directeur régional des impôts du Nord-Pas de Calais	Dir. 77/388/EEC	4(1) and (2), 13B(d), 17(2)(a) and (5)
C-190/95	17 Jul. 97	1997, I-04383	Leasing company for private cars – place from which service provider carries on business – fixed establishment and the place of the service	Aro Lease BV v. Inspecteur van de Belastingdienst Grote Ondenemingen te Amsterdam	Dir. 77/388/EEC	9(1)
C-131/91	9 Jul. 92	1992, I-04513	Minimum taxable amount for taxing used cars	"K" F114 Line Air Service Europe BV v. Eulaerts N.V. and the Belgian State	Dir. 77/388/EEC	11
C-288/94	25 Oct. 96	1996, I-05311	Taxable amount	Argos Distributors Limited v. Commissioners of Customs & Excise	Dir. 77/388/EEC	11A(1)(a)
C-184/00	22 Nov. 01	2001, I-09115	Taxable amount – subsidies bearing a direct relation to price	Office des Produits Wallons ASBL v. Belgian State	Dir. 77/388/EEC	11A(1)(a)

(cont.)

Table 6.3   (*Cont.*)

Case	Date	European Court Reports	Issue	Parties	Directive	Articles
C-409/98 and C-108/99	9 Oct. 01	2001, I-07175	Exemption for lease of immovable property	Commissioners of Customs & Excise v. Mirror Group plc and Cantor Fitzgerald International		
C-235/00	13 Dec. 01	2001, I-10237	Exempting transactions – dealings in securities – brokerage – provision of a so-called call-centre service	Commissioners of Customs & Excise v. CSC Financial Services Limited	Dir. 77/388/EEC	13B(b)(5)
8/81	19 Jan. 82	1982, 53	Direct applicability of directives – including in the field of VAT	Ursula Becker v. Finanzamt Münster-Innenstadt	Dir. 77/388/EEC	13B, 13C
C-37/95	15 Jan. 98	1998, I-00001	Right of deduction – investment costs	Belgian State v. Ghent Coal Terminal NV	Dir. 77/388/EEC	17, 20(3)
C-155-01	11 Sep. 03	2003, 0000	Right of deduction – exclusions provided for under national legislation (in Austria) at the time Directive came into force	Cookies World Vertriebsge-sellschaft mbH iL v. Finanzlandesdi-rektion für Tirol	Dir. 77/388/EEC	17(6) and (7)

6.7   Are the VAT rates being harmonised?

Upon accession by the new member states, the provisions of the Sixth Directive on VAT rates will also be applicable. The Sixth Directive does not lay down any fixed rates for the whole EU. It merely stipulates that member states must apply a minimum rate of 5% on goods or services mentioned in annex H of the Sixth Directive and a minimum standard rate of 15%.

Change to the VAT rate on telecommunications services in the Czech Republic

• Transaction prior to 1 May 2004

Table 6.4   VAT rates applicable as per 1 May 2004.

VAT rates	Cyprus CY	Czech Republic CZ	Estonia EE	Hungary HU	Latvia LV	Lithuania LT	Malta MT	Poland PL	Slovakia SK	Slovenia SI
Standard VAT rate	15	22	18	25	18	18	18	22	19	20
Reduced VAT rate	5	5	5	15/5	9	9/5	5	7/3	None	8.5

> A Czech individual receives periodic statements for telephone connection and calls. 5% VAT is charged on it.

- Transaction as from 1 May 2004
  A Czech individual receives periodic statements for telephone connection and calls. 22% VAT is charged on it.

An example of the impact of the Sixth VAT Directive can be found in the Czech Republic. There, it is no longer possible to apply the reduced rate of 5% for telecommunications services.[4] For individuals, and also for undertakings with a limited right of deduction and a high telecommunications bill, an increase in this cost of 17% can quickly take a fair bite out of the budget. The Czech Republic increased the VAT rate for telecommunication services as from 1 January 2004 to 22%. As from 1 May 2004 a standard rate of 19% applies.

Table 6.4 gives an overview expected to be applicable as per 1 May 2004 (status mid-February 2004):

6.8   Will there be a greater or lesser right to deduct VAT in the accession countries?

Regarding the right of deduction, the accession countries had a number of "conservative" measures that limited the right for undertakings to deduct VAT. These restrictions have been (and had to be) abolished as of 1 May 2004. This means that VAT not yet deducted can in principle be reclaimed.

This new legislation, together with the abolition of the internal borders, will have a major impact on the budgets of the new member states.

Member states may not introduce any new deduction restrictions.[6]

6.9 How far on are the new member states with the implementation of the Sixth VAT Directive? a stock-take.[7]

Table 6.5 European case law on the deduction of VAT.

Case	Date	European Court Reports	Issue	Parties	Directive
C-37/95	15 Jan. 98	1998, I-00001	Right of deduction – investment costs	Belgian State v. Ghent Coal Terminal NV	Dir. 77/388/EEC
C-317/94	24 Oct. 96	1996, I-05339	Money-back and discount coupons – taxable basis	Elida Gibbs Ltd. v. Commissioners of Customs & Excise	Dir. 77/388/EEC
C-48/97	27 Apr. 99	1999, I-02323	Sales promotion campaign – goods handed over in exchange for coupons – supply for consideration – price reductions and rebates	Kuwait Petroleum Ltd. v. Commissioners of Customs & Excise	Dir. 77/388/EEC
C-142/99	14 Nov. 00	2000, I-09567	Deduction of input tax – undertaking that is only taxable for part of its transactions – pro rata deduction	Floridienne SA and Berginvest SA v. Belgian State	Dir. 77/388/EEC
C-16/00	27 Sep. 01	2001, I-06663	Involvement of a holding company in the management of its subsidiaries	Cibo Participations SA v. Directeur régional des impôts du Nord-Pas de Calais	Dir. 77/388/EEC

Table 6.6 VAT conformity in the 10 new EU member states (status May 2004).

Situation after accession to the EU	Cyprus	Czech Republic	Estonia	Hungary	Latvia	Lithuania	Malta	Poland	Slovakia	Slovenia
Has a new EU VAT Law been adopted?	Yes	Yes	Yes	Yes	Yes	Yes	Yes	Yes	Yes	Yes
VAT registration Threshold for distance selling in local currency. (VAT registration is also an option)	CY pounds 20 000	As yet unknown	EEK 550 000	As yet unknown	LVL 24 000	LTL 100 000	Will be calculated on the basis of the exchange rate on 1 January of the relevant year (EUR 35 000 in Maltese pounds)	As yet unknown	SKK 1 500 000	As yet unknown

(cont.)

Table 6.6 *(cont.)*

Situation after accession to the EU	Cyprus	Czech Republic	Estonia	Hungary	Latvia	Lithuania	Malta	Poland	Slovakia	Slovenia
Equivalent in EUR (Art. 28(b)(B) 6th Directive): EUR 35 000	EUR 34 220		EUR 35 151.41		EUR 36 952	EUR 29000			EUR 37,300	
VAT responsible representative required for non-EU undertakings?	Yes/No[b]	No	No	No	No	Yes	No[a]	Yes	Not at the moment	Yes, in certain cases
In a case of direct VAT registration of EU undertakings: will all correspondence can be received by a local representative be sent to the relevant undertaking or can it be received by a representative?	Yes	No data available	Can be received by a local representative	No, only if the representative acts as a VAT representative	Yes	Probably, but not certain	Possible at the moment; no indications that this will change	Yes, on basis of notarial agreement	Yes, based on the power of attorney	Yes/No[c]
In a case of direct VAT registration of EU undertakings: can a representative also sign documents on behalf of the undertaking under a power of attorney?	Yes	Probably, but this is not certain	No[d]	Yes	Yes	Yes	Yes	No	Yes	Generally yes, but sometimes the responsible person within the undertaking is obliged to sign
Does a bank guarantee or other guarantee have to be put up before VAT registration? By EU undertakings?	No	No	No	No	No	Yes[e]	No	No	No	No
Does a bank guarantee or other guarantee have to be put up before VAT registration? By non-EU undertakings?	No	No	No	No	No	No	No	No	No	No

Table 6.6 (cont.)

Situation after accession to the EU	Cyprus	Czech Republic	Estonia	Hungary	Latvia	Lithuania	Malta	Poland	Slovakia	Slovenia
VAT registration: do the authorities accept documents (e.g. articles of association) in a foreign language or does everything have to be translated?	Documents are accepted in English or Greek	The documents have to be translated	Documents are accepted in English. Authories can ask for a translation	The documents have to be translated	The documents have to be translated	The documents have to be translated	No	The documents have to be translated	The documents have to be translated	The documents have to be translated
VAT registration: do documents in general have to be validated by a notary public before they are submitted to the authorities?	No	No	No	Yes	Yes	Yes	No, copies are sufficient	No, copies are sufficient [f]	Yes, the memorandum and the power of attorney (if applicable) articles of association	Only where translation is compulsory
How long does it take for a VAT number to be issued?	Less than 1 week	1 week	3 working days	1 or 2 days	According to the law 15 working days, in practice 10 working days	15 working days	3 to 5 days	1 month	1 month	Less than 1 week
VAT returns										
What taxable periods will be deployed?	Quarterly [h]	Month or quarter	1 month. Filing for several months possible, upon the permission of the Tax Authorities	Year, quarter and month [g]	1 month, 3 months and 6 months	1 month and 6 months	3 months in principle. Under certain conditions 1 month or per year	1 month; quarterly for smaller taxable persons with turnover of up to EUR 800 000 inc. VAT (22%)	Month or quarter. Under the current and also the draft new VAT legislation, filing on quarterly basis is possible for entities with turnover lower than SKK 10 million per calendar year (approximately EUR 250 000).	1 month, 3 months and 6 months

(cont.)

Table 6.6 (cont.)

Situation after accession to the EU	Cyprus	Czech Republic	Estonia	Hungary	Latvia	Lithuania	Malta	Poland	Slovakia	Slovenia
Will use now or in future be made of an annual or other summary declaration?	No	No	No	No	Yes	Yes	No	No	No	No
How will the electronic submission of VAT returns be organised?	Unknown	Authorised persons can submit returns electronically, but rare; future situation unknown	At the moment possible via internet with authentication procedure (passwords); rules for future not yet known	At the moment only possible for certain large taxable persons on individual basis[j]	Probably an agreement has to be signed with the authorities[i]	Will be possible; no draft rules available	Probably submission via internet coupled to electronic payment[k]	At the moment no suitable VAT provisions available	Will be possible; further details not known	Rules not yet publicly announced
Are there fines for late registration? (VAT is payable but is only reported at a later stage when there is a VAT number)	Yes, plus interest	Yes, fine of 10% in supplies reported too late	Yes, plus interest will be due	Yes, fine of up to 50% plus interest	No[l]	Yes, plus interest	Yes, fine for late registration and interest[n]	No, no fines if VAT due is paid	Yes, plus interest	Yes, plus interest
Payment and refunds										
Is it possible to pay VAT via a foreign bank account	Yes	Yes	Yes	Yes	Yes	Yes	Yes	Yes	Yes	Yes
Is it possible to receive a refund of the balance of the VAT return in a foreign bank account? (Bank charges are of course borne by the recipient)	No, cheques are used	No	Possible at the moment[o]	No	Yes	Yes	No	No	Yes	Yes
VAT audits										
How often are undertakings audited by the authorities on average?	No frequently planned visits	In theory, once every 3 years, but some are superficial and some never take place	Once every 2 years	Once every 2 years; always in case of VAT refund of more than HUF 500 000 1+/_ EUR 1988	Officially once every 3 years, going back over 3 years, but can also be once a year	At least once every 5 years[p]	Not often. Particular events can lead to VAT audits	Once every 3 years	Particular events can lead to VAT audits, such as VAT refund positions[q]	Once every 10 years

Table 6.6 (cont.)

Situation after accession to the EU	Cyprus	Czech Republic	Estonia	Hungary	Latvia	Lithuania	Malta	Poland	Slovakia	Slovenia
Expected situation after accession to the EU										
How long beforehand are VAT audits generally announced?	Several weeks	Can even be only 3 days, but can be negotiated	7 days, but negotiation is possible	1 day to 2 weeks	3 days to 6 months – depends	No specific deadline for announcement of start of VAT audit. In some cases VAT audit is started immediately	1 week, but can be negotiated	Generally no prior announcement	1 to 2 weeks, but negotiable	Generally a few days beforehand or not at all
Format EU VAT number	CY 999999999L	C2 99999999 C2 999999999 C2 9999999999	EE 999999999	Hu 99999999	LV 99999999999	LT 999999999 LT 999999999999	MT 999999999	PL 9999999999	SK 999999999 SK 9999999999 SK 99999999999	SI 999999999
Are there any logical checks with regard to the VAT number?	No	Yes	Yes	N/A	N/A	Yes	Yes	No	Yes	Yes
If so, please specify?	N/A	For individuals 1234567890 will represent their birth number	Not known	N/A	N/A	Current VAT number: first 7 digits – company's registration number; The eighth digit – "1".	Logical checks are not public	N/A	Website of Tax Directorate – www.drsr.sk	The prefix SI- and 8-digit numbers
Will a European VAT ID number be introduced for intra-Community transactions in addition to the current tax ID number?	No	No	No	Yes	No	No	No	Yes	No	No

(cont.)

Table 6.6 (cont.)

Situation after accession to the EU	Cyprus	Czech Republic	Estonia	Hungary	Latvia	Lithuania	Malta	Poland	Slovakia	Slovenia
If so, please specify format of the European VAT ID number and whether this will be granted automatically?	N/A	Draft legislation suggests only one VAT ID number for both local and intra-Community supplies, see above the new format	N/A	It has already been given to companies active in foreign trade with current EU member states. Can be requested after 15 August 2003. The last 3 digits of the current tax ID are removed, and the HU prefix is added (e.g. HU 9999 9999)		N/A	N/A	According to the current knowledge the new VAT number will be the present VAT number with a country prefix PL	N/A	We believe that the only number that will be used in Slovenia is the above described

[a] Not legally compulsory, but the authorities can designate a VAT responsible representative. The taxable person can appoint its own VAT responsible representative, but this must be acceptable to the authorities.
[b] Such an undertaking can either designate a VAT responsible representative or produce a bank guarantee to the VAT authorities.
[c] Under the automated processing system of the tax authorities, VAT forms are sent directly to the undertaking; other correspondence can be sent to another address.
[d] This can only be organised by means of VAT representation.
[e] If direct registration becomes possible, a guarantee may be required. In certain cases, a guarantee is asked for in any event from businesses.
[f] The tax office does sometimes, say, ask that the Polish consulate confirm that the documents produced by the foreign entity are fully in conformity with the legislation of the country of issue.
[g] In certain cases, it is possible for VAT returns to be submitted more frequently: on a monthly basis and twice a month instead of quarterly and monthly.
[h] Monthly or yearly can also be allowed where the undertaking is in a net refund position.
[i] But the paper version has to be submitted in all events.
[j] No idea how this will be organised when the possibility will be open to all taxable persons.
[k] On the VAT return that is sent to the taxable person, an access code will be given. [l] It is possible to submit a VAT return prior to registration.
[m] Probably, it will be so that a part of the input VAT cannot be refunded.
[n] Late registration is more than 30 days after the start of activities.
[o] The taxable person does have to present a bank guarantee. This probably will not change after accession.
[p] This depends on the undertaking. Several times a year if the undertaking applies for a VAT refund.
[q] This depends on the sorts of entities or the amounts to be paid.
[r] At the present time, no permission is required by the tax authorities.
[s] At the present time, no permission is required by the tax authorities.

6.10 What checklist can you use in order to prepare your business?

Table 6.7 Company details for the questionnaire.

Name
Address
VAT numbers
Contact person
Short description of business activities

THE TEN COUNTRIES THAT ACCEDED TO THE EUROPEAN UNION ON 1 MAY 2004 ARE:
CYPRUS, CZECH REPUBLIC, ESTONIA, HUNGARY, LATVIA, LITHUANIA, MALTA, POLAND, SLOVAKIA, SLOVENIA

DOES YOUR COMPANY HAVE IN ANY OF THE ACCESSION COUNTRIES:

Suppliers?	Group companies?
Customers?	Subsidiaries?
Agents?	Parent companies?
Undisclosed commission agents?	Branches?
Distributors?	Production units?
Warehouses?	Contract workers?

Call-off or consignment stock?

Other?

Does your company anticipate doing business or extending its activities in the near future in one or more of the accession countries?

Does your company have a particular structure in mind for this and what logistical concept is it going to use (drop shipments, central warehousing, etc.)?

Has your company assessed the impact of enlargement of the EU on the VAT treatment of the transactions with your business partners in the accession countries, from and in the current EU member states or any other country?

TAX LIABILITY
Has your company checked whether, in the accession countries after enlargement of the EU:

— it will need to have additional registrations for VAT purposes?

— it will still need existing VAT numbers?

— it can limit the obligations that VAT registration entails?

Do your business partners in the accession countries have:

(*cont.*)

Table 6.7 (*cont.*)

— a tax ID number and/or a VAT number? If so, do you have this information?

— a special VAT status (public authorities, small undertakings)?

— Has your company already determined what the VAT treatment of your transactions is after enlargement of the EU?

— Has your company also mapped out the ERP/ICT impact thereof?

GOODS AND SERVICES
Give a short description of the most important goods and services that your company buys and sells in the accession countries.

Has there been an analysis of the goods and services whose VAT treatment significantly differs from that within the EU?

IS YOUR BUSINESS CATERING FOR POSSIBLE CHANGES IN THE VAT TREATMENT OF THE FOLLOWING SERVICES?

Agency fees	Advertising
Commissions	Royalties
Consultancy fees	Management services
Services supplied electronically	Telecommunications
Hire of movable property	Supply of staff
Licences	Transport services

Is your business involved in cross-border transactions involving excisable goods?

Has your business identified the VAT treatment of transactions involving goods that can no longer benefit from a customs arrangement after enlargement of the European Union?

RATES
If your business trades in the accession countries, it is prepared for possible changes to VAT rates in those countries? For instance, have your price-lists and catalogues been adjusted?

If your business does not trade in but with the accession countries, is it prepared for the possible abolition of zero rates or exemptions in those countries?

DEDUCTION OF VAT
Is your business examining whether, following enlargement, it will be able to exercise a full, immediate right to deduct and reclaim VAT in the accession countries for the following costs:

Major investments for which only part of the VAT could be immediately deducted (such as a factory or office building)?

Marketing activities such as lotteries, competitions, sponsoring, trade gifts, savings campaigns, money-off coupons, warranties and goods and services provided free of charge?

VAT incurred locally for which you did not previously claim a refund (on the basis of the 13th Directive in a current member state)?

Table 6.7 (*cont.*)

INVOICING
If you have automated invoicing, have you already scheduled the necessary resources and time for examining the VAT treatment of transactions with and in the accession countries and making any necessary adjustments as from EU enlargement?

Is your business prepared for possible changes to the rules in the accession countries regarding obligatory invoice details and the like?

Do you have the information you need from your business partners in the accession countries (such as VAT numbers) in order to issue due and proper invoices?

Is your business looking into the possibility of electronically issuing and storing sales invoices in the accession countries where this is not yet allowed?

Is your business looking into the possibility of outsourcing invoicing for transactions with or in accession countries where this is not yet allowed?

Is your business looking into doing self-billing for transactions with or in accession countries where this is not yet allowed?

Has your business mapped out the ERP/ICT impact of this (master records, tax codes and tables, reporting, etc.)?

BOOKKEEPING, RECORDS STORAGE AND OTHER FORMALITIES
If your VAT bookkeeping is automated, have you already scheduled the necessary resources and time for verifying and potentially adapting the VAT treatment of transactions with and in the accession countries as from the EU enlargement?

If your business is required to submit returns in one of the accession countries, is it prepared for possible changes to VAT returns (a new format, additional information, supplementary returns)?

Does your accounting system store sufficient information for keeping the necessary ledgers, registers, completing VAT returns, listings of intra-Community supplies and/or acquisitions, listing of services received (required by Hungary), and/or Intrastat returns?

Does your accounting system allow the necessary information easily to be processed for keeping ledgers and registers and submitting VAT returns, listings and Intrastat returns?

Can your accounting system automatically generate Intrastat returns for the arrival or dispatch of goods from or to the accession countries as of enlargement of the EU?

Has your company worked out the necessary procedures internally or with your transport firms for collating the necessary documentation for proof of intra-Community movements of goods between the present and the future member states?

(*cont.*)

Table 6.7 (*cont.*)

OTHER POINTS TO NOTE

Is your staff adequately prepared for the consequences of enlargement of the EU?

Are your business partners adequately prepared for the consequences of enlargement of the EU?

Is someone else (or are you yourself) paying attention to the changes in the field of, say, direct taxes, customs and excise, logistics, ICT, competition law, employment law, environmental law, packaging or other legal rules specific to your sector?

6.11 What changes are there in the field of VAT obligations?

The enlargement of the European Union will entail extra administrative obligations.

In the VAT system of the European Union, companies that are taxable persons act as "tax collectors" for the state. The undertaking receives the VAT from its customers. It pays the VAT on its purchases that, apart from a number of restrictions, it can deduct from the VAT on its turnover. The balance can be an amount to be paid to the state or to be received back from the state.

The tax authorities have to be able to audit the undertaking (the taxable person). In order to enable this, an extensive reporting obligation is imposed. This could encompass inter alia:

- issuing invoices with compulsory statements[8] for supplies that are made;

- issuing a credit note with compulsory statements for corrections;[9]

- keeping purchase and sales ledgers, a day book of receipts or a centralisation book, a returns register and a table of capital goods;

- compulsory sequential numbering and entries;

- the periods for keeping records and the related documentation (for instance an order form);

- intra-Community returns: the EC Sales List and the EC Acquisition list (the latter is optional – a member state can impose this obligation);

- registers of non-transfers.

Here, mention must also be made of the Intrastat obligations for intra-Community movements of goods. We would refer in this regard to the following regulations:

- Council Regulation (EEC) No. 3330/91 of 7 November 1991 on the statistics relating to the trading of goods between member states;

- Commission Regulation (EC) No. 1901/2000 of 7 September 2000 laying down certain provisions for the implementation of Council Regulation (EEC) No. 3330/91 of the Council of 7 November 1991 on the statistics relating to the trading of goods between member states.

For undertakings, it is of crucial importance that they adhere to these formalities in order to avoid administrative and sometimes criminal penalties and liability for interest.

In a number of cases, failure to comply will also jeopardise the right of deduction. The tax authorities can sometimes also go so far as to reject the VAT bookkeeping and levy an assessment *ex officio*.

6.12 What about the issuance of invoices?

The cases for which an invoice (or a document taking the place of an invoice) has to be issued or made available by a taxable person are:[10]

- supplies of goods and services where the customer is a VAT taxable person or a non-taxable legal person;

- supplies of goods subject to the rules on distance selling;

- exempted intra-Community supplies of new means of transport;

- where, prior to the supply of goods, a payment is received in whole or in part; and

- where prior to performance of a service, a payment made by a taxable person or a non-taxable legal person is received in whole or in part.

However, member states can require issuance of an invoice for other than the goods or services referred to in the foregoing, that are supplied or provided on their territory by a supplier established in their member state. If they do so, they can impose less stringent obligations regarding the invoice.[11]

Under certain circumstances, member states may release taxable persons from the obligation to issue an invoice where the supply takes place in their member state:[12]

- for certain supplies of goods and services with or without a right of deduction according to Article 13 (exemption without right of deduction) of the Sixth Directive;

- Article 28(2)(a) of the Sixth Directive (exemption with right of deduction and greatly reduced rates that were in force on 1 January 1991 and that the member states may maintain); and

- Article 28(3)(b) of the Sixth Directive (exemptions without right of deduction that member states can maintain under the so-called stand-still clause).

The VAT legislation may not lay down any specific requirements as to the language in which an invoice is drawn up. The VAT authorities may require the invoices drawn up in another language than an official national language should be translated if necessary for control purposes. That only applies to invoices for supplies of goods and services that take place on the territory of the auditing authority. This is also applicable to purchase invoices that are received by VAT taxable persons established in the member state of the auditing authority.

Invoices can be issued or made available by the supplier, the customer (self-billing) or by a third party (outsourcing). The ultimate responsibility for invoicing lies with the supplier of the goods or services.

Self-billing is permitted where:

- there is agreement between the parties to apply the system;

- furthermore, each invoice is accepted by the supplier/service provider.

In cases where the customer is liable for the VAT and there is no invoice, a member state can require him to draw up a document himself. This may, for example, be the case with an intra-Community acquisition or the receipt of services such as royalties, data processing, professional advice (so called 9 (2)(e) services) from a service provider not established in that member state.[13]

Possession of a due and proper invoice is in principle essential for the right to deduct input VAT.

6.13 Can I invoice electronically?[14]

Invoices can be issued on paper or electronically.

Sending invoices or making them available electronically is subject to a number of conditions:

- it must be accepted by the customer; and

- authenticity of the origin and the integrity of the content of the invoice must be guaranteed.

This can be done in three ways:

(1) Use of an advanced electronic signature that:

- is uniquely linked to the signatory;

- enables identification of the signatory;

- is created with means that the signatory is able to keep under his exclusive control;

- is bound to the data in such a way that any subsequent change to the data can be traced.

The member states can require that the advanced electronic signature is based on a qualified certificate and is produced by secure means for the creation of signatures.

At this time, only Germany, Greece, Portugal and Spain lay down this obligation.[15] For the accession countries Cyprus, the Czech Republic, Lithuania, Slovakia and Slovenia will require a qualified certificate produced by a secure means.

(2) The use of EDI (Electronic Data Interchange), where the agreement between the parties provides for procedures that guarantee authenticity of the origin, integrity and content of the data.[16]

(3) Use of any other electronic means subject to acceptance by the member states concerned.

The member states can impose other, additional conditions where electronic invoices are issued from a country outside the EU. For instance, where a service or supply is effected by a taxable person not established in the European Union, and the place of the service or supply is located in their member state.

In the case of cross-border invoices,[17] it is important to know the rules for issuing compliant invoices. And also the recipient of the invoice has an interest in the invoice being in conformity in order not to endanger his right of deduction and to avoid supplementary levies of VAT, fines and interest and potential joint and several liability.[18]

6.14 Will I be able to store my records electronically?[19]

Every undertaking that is a taxable person has to store copies of:

- the invoices issued by itself, its customers, in its name and for its account by a third party; and

- all invoices received by it itself.

An undertaking that is a taxable person may itself select the storage place. However, it has to be able to make the stored invoices and data available to the competent authorities on request without unnecessary delay.

The member states can, nonetheless, oblige taxable persons established on their territory:

* to notify them of the storage place where this is situated outside their territory;

* to store invoices issued by them, by their customers or in their name and for their account by third parties as well as invoices received by them on their territory. This is the case where storage is not done electronically that guarantees full on-line access to the relevant data.

Authenticity of the origin and integrity of the content of these invoices, and their readability, must be guaranteed throughout the entire storage period. The details on the invoice may not be altered and must remain legible throughout this period. The member states determine how long taxable persons have to store invoices for goods or services that are supplied or provided on their territory. For purchase invoices, the record-keeping period is fixed by the member state where the undertaking (taxable person) is established.

In order to ensure that the conditions are complied with, the member states can stipulate that invoices have to be stored in the original form in which they were sent out. They can also require that, if the invoices are stored electronically, the data that guarantee the origin and integrity of their content are also stored.

Member states can prohibit storage of invoices in a country with which no mutual assistance treaty has been concluded.[20] The member states can also impose a storage obligation for invoices received by non-taxable persons.

An example: an undertaking stores its electronic invoices centrally. However, it makes supplies in the United Kingdom and Germany. For the supplies in the United Kingdom, the invoices have to be stored for six years, and for the supplies in Germany 10 years. If it is hard to differentiate between the various types of invoices, the undertaking will have to store everything for 10 years.[21]

6.15 What impact does the altered legislation in the field of VAT have on my bookkeeping system and/or my ERP system?

Undertakings that have automated their processes, such as logistics, invoicing, reporting and payments, have to examine whether they are sufficiently prepared for the coming changes. Given the complexity of the current ERP systems, this is not a job to be underestimated.

Many businesses nowadays use an ERP[22] system that electronically records most movements within an undertaking in an integrated manner and links them together (even with third parties).

For instance, the ERP system plays an important role in each component of the sales process:

- offers to the customer;

- acceptance of the offer by the customer;

- entering the order into the system;

- manufacture in production, verification of the stock and, if necessary, ordering of goods;

- entry into stock upon finishing of production or arrival of the order;

- reporting of purchase invoices for production or arrival of the order;

- result from stock and supply;

- invoicing of the supply and reporting in the bookkeeping;

- internal reporting;

- preparation of periodic (VAT) returns and listings;

- receipt of payment of the invoice.

In this whole process, from the offer to the customer (in Belgium, for example, it is compulsory to mention the VAT number on all documents that relate to the economic activity of taxpayers) through issuance of the invoice (minimum requirements regarding statements) to drawing up the listings (having possession, of the necessary details of how they are prepared), the VAT legislation intervenes at each stage.

Given the enormous impact of the VAT legislation on the administration, risk-management and cashflow of an undertaking, for each transaction in the business process, the impact of enlargement of the Union on 1 May 2004 has to be determined.

There follow a few points to note.

Master data

These are basic data that are stored in the system and are permanently consulted and used when a process (administrative, logistical, financial, etc.) arises within the undertaking. They are extremely important for fulfilling various obligations incumbent on an undertaking such as drawing up correct invoices or collating the many reports. Where automatic entries are booked that directly affect the tax position (VAT rate, VAT treatment, etc.), these data become all the more important.

Customers' and suppliers' data and information about the product or service supplied will have to be adjusted or expanded upon in order to be able to issue invoices and provide for completion of VAT returns, Intrastat declarations, quarterly intra-Community declarations, etc. all without any problem after 1 May 2004, even if your undertaking is not itself active in the accession countries.

Tax codes

New codes will have to be created and old codes will ultimately have to be deactivated, after a thorough analysis of the company's activities.

New codes are needed inter alia in order to be able to:

- provide for completion of the VAT returns, which will be wholly or partially changed;

- report certain dealings that will be given differing VAT treatment (exports to the EU will normally become intra-Community supplies);

- report changed reasons for VAT exemptions or other specific, compulsory statements on invoices.

It is important to take account of the fact that, after 1 May 2004, improvements can occur for transactions for which the taxable event took place before 1 May 2004, as a result of which it can be appropriate to retain its old tax codes.

Automatic book entries (updating the tax-decision matrices)

Depending on a number of parameters such as ship to, ship from and the product or service supplied, automatic allocation of the tax code is possible, as is even automatic entry into the (accounting) system.

Given that on 1 May 2004 a new term, "intra-Community" (additional to national supplies and exports and imports) has been added to the provisions on, say, the place of supply of goods in the accession countries, it goes without saying that the necessary adjustments need to be made here. Conversely, this applies for undertakings in the current EU countries that carry on trade in or with the accession countries.

More particularly, the necessary parameters will have to be fixed so that the automatic VAT treatment and the subsequent book entry, calculation of the tax (as the case may be) and reporting all run correctly.

We would point out that certain entries will have to be activated at the same time, whereby account will have to be taken of possible corrections as from 1 May 2004 of transactions that took place prior to accession.

Reporting obligations

New or changed obligations regarding inter alia:

- EC sales lists;
- listings of intra-Community acquisitions effected (this is an option);
- listing of services received (this is an option);
- Intrastat returns;
- VAT returns and intervals at which they have to be submitted;
- an annual sales listing of vatable customers (an option);
- and others.

For this, functions within the bookkeeping or ERP system either have to be activated or programmed, or more likely a combination of the two.

Invoice and related formats

The formats that steer the statements on an invoice or a related document (for instance a transfer document for transfers) and the processes that lie behind this have to be adjusted in order to cater for the new situation. At the same time, it has to still be possible to print off old invoices as copies.

Ledgers

As a result of the many adjustments referred to in the foregoing, the break-down of the ledgers may well have to be adapted.

6.16 What changes are there in the field of customs?

As from 1 May 2004, the new member states will form part of the European Union, which is also a customs union. This customs union has two specific features that will have a direct impact on the new member states. There is a customs union based on the principle of uniform application of one and the same customs legislation, whereby uniform levy of duties (the so-called common customs tariff) lies at the core. Upon importing goods, wherever in the customs union, the same import duties will therefore be charged. In addition, the term "free movement of goods" lies at the basis of a customs union. The status of these goods is designated by the term "Community goods". With these Community goods, all duties, such as import duties and import VAT, are fully settled and they can be carried freely throughout the whole customs union. This measure does of course also apply for goods that are produced within free circulation.

As a result of enlargement of the European Union, all goods that were already in free circulation can be freely transported. There will no longer be any customs formalities at the border, with the exception of shipments of non-Community goods. These are goods coming from outside the EU, which are still under customs control.

6.17 What regulations are applicable in the field of customs?

All regulations that at the present time are applicable in the field of customs are as from 1 May 2004 directly applicable in the new member states. The basic Community customs legislation is contained in the following regulations:

- Council Regulation (EEC) No. 2913/92 of 12 October 1992 establishing the Community Customs Code;
- Commission Regulation (EEC) No. 2454/93 of 2 July 1993 laying down provisions for the implementation of Council Regulation (EEC) No. 2913/92 establishing the Community Customs Code.

6.18 Are there transitional measures in the field of customs?

Apart from some transitional measures the customs legislation has become applicable in its entirety on 1 May 2004.

General

There are a number of specific transitional arrangements for the movement of goods that are placed under customs control from the EU to one of the accession Member States or vice versa. These arrangements are included in the appendix to the act of accession of the individual country concerned. On 10 December 2003, the EU Commission published an information document with a summary of these transitional arrangements (TAXUD/763/2003/Final-EN).

In essence, these arrangements boil down to the following principles:

— Goods coming from the EU or from one of the accession Member States that are under customs control after 1 May 2004 in either an accession country or in one of the 15 old Member States can be brought in free circulation without any charge of import duty. A T2, T2L, T2LF (proof of origin) or an EUR 1 (preferential proof of origin) will have to be submitted (or a document of equal status – see information document) for EU goods. Import VAT is due, but can normally be deducted by businesses that are entitled to VAT deduction.

— Customs licences for processing activities (inward processing, outward processing, treatment under customs control) continue under the old conditions until a maximum of 1 year after accession, or earlier where the licence expires before this one-year period.

— Any clearance after processing under the arrangements mentioned above from a customs warehouse or from the temporary importation arrangement takes place according to the rules of the Community Customs Code (duty to be charged to the EU; in the case of inward processing, the accession Member State in question has to refund the import duties).

— Customs warehouse licences in the accession countries will expire on 1 May 2004 and have to be renewed under the conditions of the Community Customs Code.

— Remaining customs arrangements which do not fit in with the arrangements within the Community Customs Code will expire, for example, the customs-free zones in Hungary and the free zones in the Czech Republic. This also applies to local arrangements for the postponed/delayed payment of duties.

For a more comprehensive and detailed explanation we refer to the information document mentioned above.

Hungary

31987 R 2658: Council Regulation (EEC) No. 2658/87 of 23 July 1987 on the tariff and statistical nomenclature and on the Common Customs Tariff (OJ L 256, 7.9.1987, p. 1), as last amended by: 32002 R 0969: Commission Regulation (EC) No. 969/2002 of 6.6.2002 (OJ L 149, 7.6.2002, p. 20).

(a) By way of derogation from Article 5(1) of Regulation (EEC) No. 2658/87, Hungary may until the end of the third year following the date of accession or until 31 December 2007, whichever is the earlier, open a yearly tariff quota for aluminium, not alloyed (CN Code 7601 10 00), in accordance with the following schedule:

- a quota of a maximum of 110 000 tonnes, at a rate of 2% *ad valorem*, or one third of the prevailing EU duty, whichever is the higher, during the first year;

- a quota of a maximum of 70 000 tonnes, at a rate of 4% *ad valorem*, or two thirds of the prevailing EU duty, whichever is the higher, during the second year;

- a quota of a maximum of 20 000 tonnes, at a rate of 4% *ad valorem*, or two thirds of the prevailing EU duty, whichever is the higher, during the third year; provided that the goods in question:

- are released for free circulation in the territory of Hungary and are consumed there or undergo processing conferring Community origin there, and

- remain under customs supervision pursuant to the relevant Community provisions on end-use as laid down in Articles 21 and 82 of Council Regulation (EEC) No. 2913/92 establishing the Community Customs Code (OJ L 302, 19.10.1992, p. 1). Regulation as last amended by Regulation (EC) No. 2700/2000 of the European Parliament and of the Council (OJ L 311, 12.12.2000, p. 17).

(b) The provisions laid down above shall be applicable only if a licence issued by the relevant Hungarian authorities stating that the goods in question fall within the scope of the provisions laid down above is submitted in support of the declaration of entry for release for free circulation.

(c) The Commission and the competent Hungarian authorities shall take whatever measures are needed to ensure that the final consumption of the product in question, or the processing by which it acquires Community origin, takes place in the territory of Hungary.

Malta

31987 R 2658: Council Regulation (EEC) No. 2658/87 of 23 July 1987 on the tariff and statistical nomenclature and on the Common Customs Tariff (OJ L 256, 7.9.1987, p. 1), as last amended by: 32002 R 0969: Commission Regulation (EC) No. 969/2002 of 6.6.2002 (OJ L 149, 7.6.2002, p. 20).

(a) By way of derogation from Article 5(1) of Regulation (EEC) No. 2658/87, Malta may until the end of the fifth year following the date of accession or until 31 December 2008, whichever is the earlier, open yearly tariff quotas for woven fabrics of combed wool or of combed fine animal hair (CN Code 5112 11 10), denim (CN Code 5209 42 00), woven fabrics of artificial filament yarn (CN Code 5408 22 10) and other made-up clothing accessories (CN Code 6217 10 00), in accordance with the following schedule:

- a zero rate of duty during the first and second years;

- one-third of the prevailing EU duty *ad valorem* during the third and fourth years;

- two-thirds of the prevailing EU duty *ad valorem* during the fifth year;
  for the following volumes:

  — for CN Code 5112 11 10: a maximum of 20 000 square metres per year;

  — for CN Code 5209 42 00: a maximum of 1 200 000 square metres per year;

  — for CN Code 5408 22 10: a maximum of 110 000 square metres per year;

  — for CN Code 6217 10 00: a maximum of 5000 kilos per year, provided that the goods in question:

    ○ are used in the territory of Malta for the production of men's and boys' outerwear (not knitted or crocheted), and

    ○ remain under customs supervision pursuant to the relevant Community provisions on end-use as laid down in Articles 21 and 82 of Council Regulation (EEC) No. 2913/92 establishing the Community Customs Code (OJ L 302, 19.10.1992, p. 1). Regulation as last amended by Regulation (EC) No. 2700/2000 of the European Parliament and of the Council (OJ L 311, 12.12.2000, p. 17).

(b) The provisions laid down above shall be applicable only if a licence issued by the relevant Maltese authorities stating that the goods in question fall within the scope of the provisions laid down above is submitted in support of the declaration of entry for release for free circulation.

(c) The Commission and the competent Maltese authorities shall take whatever measures are needed to ensure that the goods in question are used

for the production of men's and boys' outerwear (not knitted or cro-
cheted) in the territory of Malta.

6.19 Will the new transit system (NCTS) also be applicable for shipments to the new member states?

The NCTS (New Computerised Transit System), for the electronic processing
of transit shipments, will also have to be used in the new member states as
from 1 May 2004 (for those enterprises that use simplified arrangements for
community transport).

6.20 What changes are there in the field of excise duties?

The excise rules in the European Union will have to be implemented into
the national laws of the accession countries. The regulations, directives and
decisions in this regard are given in Table 6.8.

Goods subject to Community excise duties are:

*   mineral oils,

*   alcoholic drinks, and

*   manufactured tobacco.

These products will therefore also be subject to excise duties in the new
member states as of 1 May 2004 as from the time of production or importation
from outside the EU. The excise duties that will be charged at the time the
new goods are declared for use in the new member states are in some cases
still below the minimum EU tariffs, by way of transition. These differences will
probably give rise to intensive trade with individuals on the traditional access
routes along the frontiers of the new member states.

As from 1 May 2004, if undertakings wish to avoid excise duties being due
in the country of departure and in the country of destination, they will have
to take the necessary measures to ship such products under suspension of
excise duties.

The shipment should therefore best be sent under cover of an AAD (or Administrative Accompanying Document) to an authorised warehouse keeper
(or registered trader). Just as used to be the case for shipments under a
customs-suspension regime, a guarantee will have to be put up and special measures will have to be taken so that the shipments are regularly
verified.

Table 6.8   Overview of EU excise legislation.

Regulations

31/96	10 Jan. 1996	Commission Regulation (EC) No. 31/96 of 10 January 1996 on the excise duty exemption certificate
3199/93	22 Nov. 1993	Commission Regulation (EC) No. 3199/93 of 22 November 1993 on the mutual recognition of procedures for the complete denaturing of alcohol for the purposes of exemption from excise duty
3649/92	17 Dec. 1992	Commission Regulation (EEC) No. 3649/92 of 17 December 1992 on a simplified accompanying document for the intra-Community movement of products subject to excise duty which have been released for consumption in the member state of dispatch
2719/92	11 Sep. 1992	Commission Regulation (EEC) No. 2719/92 of 11 September 1992 on the accompanying administrative document for the movement under duty-suspension arrangements of products subject to excise duty

Directives

95/59	27 Nov. 1995	Council Directive 95/59/EC of 27 November 1995 on taxes other than turnover taxes which affect the consumption of manufactured tobacco
95/60	27 Nov. 1995	Council Directive 95/60/EC of 27 November 1995 on fiscal marking of gas oils and kerosene
94/74	22 Dec. 1994	Council Directive 94/74/EC of 22 December 1994 amending Directive 92/12/EEC on the general arrangements for products subject to excise duty and on the holding, movement and monitoring of such products, Directive 92/81/EEC on the harmonization of the structures of excise duties on mineral oils and Directive 92/82/EEC on the approximation of the rates of excise duties on mineral oils
92/84	19 Oct. 1992	Council Directive 92/84/EEC of 19 October 1992 on the approximation of the rates of excise duty on alcohol and alcoholic beverages
92/83	19 Oct. 1992	Council Directive 92/83/EEC of 19 October 1992 on the harmonisation of the structures of excise duties on alcohol and alcoholic beverages
92/82	19 Oct. 1992	Council Directive 92/82/EEC of 19 October 1992 on the approximation of the rates of excise duties on mineral oils
92/81	19 Oct. 1992	Council Directive 92/81/EEC of 19 October 1992 on the harmonisation of the structures of excise duties on mineral oils
92/80	19 Oct. 1992	Council Directive 92/80/EEC of 19 October 1992 on the approximation of taxes on manufactured tobacco other than cigarettes
92/79	19 Oct. 1992	Council Directive 92/79/EEC of 19 October 1992 on the approximation of taxes on cigarettes

Table 6.8 (*cont.*)

92/12	25 Feb. 1992	Council Directive 92/12/EEC of 25 February 1992 on the general arrangements for products subject to excise duty and on the holding, movement and monitoring of such products
Decisions		
2001/224	12 Mar. 2001	2001/224/EC: Council Decision of 12 March 2001 concerning reduced rates of excise duty and exemptions from such duty on certain mineral oils when used for specific purposes
2000/446	17 Jul. 2000	2000/446/EC: Council Decision of 17 July 2000 authorising Italy to apply reductions in excise duties on certain mineral oils used for specific purposes, in accordance with the procedure provided for in Article 8(4) of Directive 92/81/EEC
2000/434	29 Jun. 2000	2000/434/EC: Council Decision of 29 June 2000 authorising the United Kingdom of Great Britain and Northern Ireland to apply a reduced rate of excise duty to certain mineral oils, when used for specific purposes, in accordance with the procedure provided for in Article 8(4) of Directive 92/81/EEC
99/880	17 Dec. 1999	1999/880/EC: Council Decision of 17 December 1999 authorising member states to apply and to continue to apply to certain mineral oils, when used for specific purposes, existing reduced rates of excise duty or exemptions from excise duty, in accordance with the procedure provided for in Directive 92/81/EEC
97/425	30 Jun. 1997	97/425/EC: Council Decision of 30 June 1997 authorising member states to apply and to continue to apply to certain mineral oils, when used for specific purposes, existing reduced rates of excise duty or exemptions from excise duty, in accordance with the procedure provided for in Directive 92/81/EEC

Correct completion of procedures and formalities for entry and storage of excise goods in tax warehouses and return of copy 3 from AADs from the new member states is of crucial importance in this, so as to avoid excise duties nonetheless being levied in the member state of departure of the excise goods and high fines also being imposed. In that framework, any irregularity in the transport process (theft, loss of excise goods, return of excise goods) will have to be closely monitored and registered in order to avoid risks.

For particular goods flows, such as sales via the internet or distance sales of such goods, administratively/logistically coherent processes will also have to be set up within this new legal framework.

In addition, sight should not be lost of the fact that each member state (including the new ones) is able to levy excise duties on other products apart from those that are already defined as Community goods. It is all too possible that, for instance, colour television sets are subject to excise duties in a new member state and that, under national rules, they have to be declared, the excise duties thereon paid, they can be shipped under suspension, in certain cases exempted, etc. This is a daily occurrence in Poland for certain electronics products.

6.21   Are there transitional measures for excise duties?[23]

General

Also for this matter, a couple of general rules apply (for details we refer to the same information document as mentioned in paragraph 18):

—   Excisable goods that are transported under customs control to or from the new Member States before 1 May 2004: where these goods are cleared after 1 May, the excise duty on importation is due in the Member State where the importation takes place.

—   Excisable goods that are exported from the EU (under a combination of an AAD and an export document) to an accession Member State before 1 May 2004 can be delivered after 1 May 2004 under cover of that AAD, which has to be adapted to the procedures laid down.

Cyprus

31992 L 0081: Council Directive 92/81/EEC of 19 October 1992 on the harmonisation of the structures of excise duties on mineral oils (OJ L 316, 31.10.1992, p. 12), as last amended by: 31994 L 0074: Council Directive 94/74/EC of 22.12.1994 (OJ L 365, 31.12.1994, p. 46).

Without prejudice to a formal decision to be adopted according to the procedure set out in Article 8(4) of Directive 92/81/EEC, Cyprus may apply an exemption from excise duties on mineral oils used for the production of cement until one year after the date of accession. Without prejudice to a formal decision to be adopted according to the procedure set out in Article 8(4) of Directive 92/81/EEC, Cyprus may also apply an exemption from additional excise duties on all types of fuel used for local passenger transport until one year after the date of accession.

Hungary

31992 L 0081: Council Directive 92/81/EEC of 19 October 1992 on the harmonisation of the structures of excise duties on mineral oils (OJ L 316, 31.10.1992, p. 12), as last amended by: 31994 L 0074: Council Directive 94/74/EC of 22.12.1994 (OJ L 365, 31.12.1994, p. 46).

Without prejudice to a formal decision to be adopted according to the procedure set out in Article 8(4) of Directive 92/81/EEC, Cyprus may apply an exemption from excise duties on mineral oils used for the production of cement until one year after the date of accession. Without prejudice to a formal decision to be adopted according to the procedure set out in Article 8(4) of Directive 92/81/EEC, Cyprus may also apply an exemption from additional excise duties on all types of fuel used for local passenger transport until one year after the date of accession.

Latvia

31992 L 0079: Council Directive 92/79/EEC of 19 October 1992 on the approximation of taxes on cigarettes (OJ L 316, 31.10.1992, p. 8) as last amended by: 32002 L 0010: Council Directive 2002/10/EC of 12.2.2002 (OJ L 46, 16.2.2002, p. 26).

By way of derogation from Article 2(1) of Directive 92/79/EEC, Latvia may postpone the application of the overall minimum excise duty on the retail selling price (inclusive of all taxes) for cigarettes of the price category most in demand until 31 December 2009, provided that during this period Latvia gradually adjusts its excise duty rates towards the overall minimum excise duty provided for in the Directive.

Without prejudice to Article 8 of Council Directive 92/12/EEC of 25 February 1992 on the general arrangements for products subject to excise duty and on the holding, movement and monitoring of such products ((OJ L 76, 23.3.1992, p. 1). Directive as last amended by Directive 2000/47/EC (OJ L 193, 29.7.2000, p. 73)), and having informed the Commission, member states may, as long as the above derogation applies, maintain the same quantitative limits for cigarettes which may be brought into their territories from Latvia without further excise duty payment as those applied to imports from third countries. Member states making use of this possibility may carry out the necessary checks provided that these checks do not affect the proper functioning of the internal market.

Lithuania

31992 L 0079: Council Directive 92/79/EEC of 19 October 1992 on the approximation of taxes on cigarettes (OJ L 316, 31.10.1992, p. 8) as last amended by: 32002 L 0010: Council Directive 2002/10/EC of 12.2.2002 (OJ L 46, 16.2.2002, p. 26).

By way of derogation from Article 2(1) of Directive 92/79/EEC, Lithuania may postpone the application of the overall minimum excise duty on the retail selling price (inclusive of all taxes) for cigarettes of the price category most in demand until 31 December 2009, provided that during this period Lithuania gradually adjusts its excise duty rates towards the overall minimum excise duty provided for in the Directive.

Without prejudice to Article 8 of Council Directive 92/12/EEC on the general arrangements for products subject to excise duty and on the holding, movement and monitoring of such products ((OJ L 76, 23.3.1992, p. 1). Directive as last amended by Directive 2000/47/EC (OJ L 193, 29.7.2000, p. 73)), and having informed the Commission, member states may, as long as the above derogation applies, maintain the same quantitative limits for cigarettes which may be brought into their territories from Lithuania without further excise duty payment as those applied to imports from third countries. Member states making use of this possibility may carry out the necessary checks provided that these checks do not affect the proper functioning of the internal market.

Poland

31992 L 0079: Council Directive 92/79/EEC of 19 October 1992 on the approximation of taxes on cigarettes (OJ L 316, 31.10.1992, p. 8) as last amended by: 32002 L 0010: Council Directive 2002/10/EC of 12.2.2002 (OJ L 46, 16.2.2002, p. 26).

By way of derogation from Article 2(1) of Directive 92/79/EEC, Poland may postpone the application of the overall minimum excise duty on the retail selling price (inclusive of all taxes) for cigarettes of the price category most in demand until 31 December 2008, provided that during this period Poland gradually adjusts its excise duty rates towards the overall minimum excise duty provided for in the Directive.

Without prejudice to Article 8 of Council Directive 92/12/EEC on the general arrangements for products subject to excise duty and on the holding, movement and monitoring of such products ((OJ L 76, 23.3.1992, p. 1). Directive as last amended by Directive 2000/47/EC (OJ L 193, 29.7.2000, p. 73)), and having informed the Commission, member states may, as long as the above derogation applies, maintain the same quantitative limits for cigarettes which may be brought into their territories from Poland without further excise duty payment as those applied to imports from third countries. Member states making use of this possibility may carry out the necessary checks provided that these checks do not affect the proper functioning of the internal market.

31992 L 0081: Council Directive 92/81/EEC of 19 October 1992 on the harmonisation of the structures of excise duties on mineral oils (OJ L 316, 31.10.1992, p. 12), as last amended by: 31994 L 0074: Council Directive 94/74/EC of 22.12.1994 (OJ L 365, 31.12.1994, p. 46).

Without prejudice either to a formal decision to be adopted according to the procedure set out in Article 8(4) of Directive 92/81/EEC, or to an assessment of this measure under Article 87 of the EC Treaty, Poland may maintain a reduced rate of excise duty on petrol manufactured with anhydrous alcohol, gas oil with a low sulphur content and petrol containing ethyl butyl alcohol ether until one year after the date of accession.

Slovakia

31992 L 0079: Council Directive 92/79/EEC of 19 October 1992 on the approximation of taxes on cigarettes (OJ L 316, 31.10.1992, p. 8) as last amended by: 32002 L 0010: Council Directive 2002/10/EC of 12.2.2002 (OJ L 46, 16.2.2002, p. 26).

By way of derogation from Article 2(1) of Directive 92/79/EEC, Slovakia may postpone the application of the overall minimum excise duty on the retail selling price (inclusive of all taxes) for cigarettes of the price category most in demand until 31 December 2008, provided that during this period Slovakia gradually adjusts its excise duty rates towards the overall minimum excise duty provided for in the Directive.

Without prejudice to Article 8 of Council Directive 92/12/EEC on the general arrangements for products subject to excise duty and on the holding, movement and monitoring of such products ((OJ L 76, 23.3.1992, p. 1). Directive as last amended by Directive 2000/47/EC (OJ L 193, 29.7.2000, p. 73)), and having informed the Commission, member states may, as long as the above derogation applies, maintain the same quantitative limits for cigarettes which may be brought into their territories from Slovakia without further excise duty payment as those applied to imports from third countries. Member states making use of this possibility may carry out the necessary checks provided that these checks do not affect the proper functioning of the internal market.

Slovenia

31992 L 0079: Council Directive 92/79/EEC of 19 October 1992 on the approximation of taxes on cigarettes (OJ L 316, 31.10.1992, p. 8), as last amended by: 32002 L 0010: Council Directive 2002/10/EC of 12.2.2002 (OJ L 46, 16.2.2002, p. 26).

By way of derogation from Article 2(1) of Directive 92/79/EEC, Slovenia may postpone the application of the overall minimum excise duty of EUR 60 and EUR 64 per 1000 cigarettes for cigarettes of the price category most in demand until 31 December 2007, provided that during this period Slovenia gradually adjusts its excise duty rates towards the overall minimum excise duty provided for in the Directive.

Without prejudice to Article 8 of Council Directive 92/12/EEC on the general arrangements for products subject to excise duty and on the holding, movement and monitoring of such products ((OJ L 76, 23.3.1992, p. 1). Directive as last amended by Directive 2000/47/EC (OJ L 193, 29.7.2000, p. 73)), and having informed the Commission, member states may, as long as the above derogation applies, maintain the same quantitative limits for cigarettes which may be brought into their territories from Slovenia without further excise duty payment as those applied with regard to imports from third countries. Member states making use of this possibility may carry out the necessary checks provided that these checks do not affect the proper functioning of the internal market.

Czech Republic

31992 L 0079: Council Directive 92/79/EEC of 19 October 1992 on the approximation of taxes on cigarettes (OJ L 316, 31.10.1992, p. 8), as last amended by: 32002 L 0010: Council Directive 2002/10/EC of 12.2.2002 (OJ L 46, 16.2.2002, p. 26).

By way of derogation from Article 2(1) of Directive 92/79/EEC, the Czech Republic may postpone the application of the overall minimum excise duty equivalent to 57% of the retail selling price (inclusive of all taxes) and a minimum of EUR 60 per 1000 cigarettes for cigarettes of the price category most in demand until 31 December 2006, provided that during this period the Czech Republic gradually adjusts its excise duty rates towards the overall minimum excise duty provided for in the Directive. The Czech Republic may also postpone the application of the overall minimum excise duty of EUR 64 on the retail selling price (inclusive of all taxes) for cigarettes of the price category most in demand until 31 December 2007, provided that during this period the Czech Republic gradually adjusts its excise duty rates towards the overall minimum excise duty provided for in the Directive.

Without prejudice to Article 8 of Council Directive 92/12/EEC on the general arrangements for products subject to excise duty and on the holding, movement and monitoring of such products ((OJ L 76, 23.3.1992, p. 1). Directive as last amended by Directive 2000/47/EC (OJ L 193, 29.7.2000, p. 73)), and having informed the Commission, member states may, as long as either of the above derogations applies, maintain the same quantitative limits for cigarettes which may be brought into their territories from the Czech Republic without further excise duty payment as those applied to imports from third countries. Member states making use of this possibility may carry out the necessary checks provided that these checks do not affect the proper functioning of the internal market.

31992 L 0080: Council Directive 92/80/EEC of 19 October 1992 on the approximation of taxes on manufactured tobacco other than cigarettes (OJ L 316, 31.10.1992, p. 10), as last amended by: 32002 L 0010: Council Directive 2002/10/EC of 12.2.2002 (OJ L 46, 16.2.2002, p. 26).

By way of derogation from Article 3(1) of Directive 92/80/EEC, the Czech Republic may postpone the application of the overall minimum excise duties levied on tobacco products other than cigarettes until 31 December 2006.

Without prejudice to Article 8 of Council Directive 92/12/EEC on the general arrangements for products subject to excise duty and on the holding, movement and monitoring of such products ((OJ L 76, 23.3. 1992, p. 1). Directive as last amended by Directive 2000/47/EC (OJ L 193, 29.7.2000, p. 73)), and having informed the Commission, member states may, as long as the above derogation applies, maintain the same quantitative limits for tobacco products other than cigarettes which may be brought into their territories from the Czech Republic without further excise duty payment as those applied to imports from third countries. Member states making use of this possibility may carry out the necessary checks provided that these checks do not affect the proper functioning of the internal market.

Source references for Chapter 6

1. Sixth Directive No. 77/388/EEC of 17 May 1977 on the harmonisation of the laws of the member states relating to turnover taxes – Common system of value added tax: uniform basis of assessment.
2. For further information on the refund of VAT, see also the book, *VAT Refunds to Foreign Businesses by European Countries, 2003 Update,* from PricewaterhouseCoopers: http://www.globalvatonline.pwcglobal.com.
3. See I. Lejeune, *BTW-zakboekje,* Belgium, Kluwer, 2004.
4. A. Turczynowicz, *VAT in Central and Eastern Europe,* London, Tolley, 2002, no. 4.3, versus Annex H to the Sixth Directive.
5. See, for instance, E.C.J. C-305/97 of 5 October 1999 (Royscot Leasing Ltd., Allied Domecq plc, T. C. Harrison Group Ltd. v. Commissioners of Customs); E.C.J.

C-177/99 and C-181/99 of 19 September 2000 (Ampafrance SA v. Directeur des services fiscaux de Maine-et-Loire, Sanofi Winthrop SA v. Directeur des services fiscaux deVal-de-Marne); E.C.J., C-155-01 from 11 September 2003 (Cookies World Vertriebsgesellschaft mbH iL v. Finanzlandesdirektion für Tirol).

6. Based on a Circular Questionnaire within the PricewaterhouseCoopers network of mid-February 2004. For further update, see http://www.globalvatonline.com.

7. See also in this connection the new Article 22(3)(b), para. 1, of the Sixth Directive as introduced by Council Directive 2001/115/EC of 20 December 2001 amending Directive 77/388/EEC with a view to simplifying, modernising and harmonising the conditions laid down for invoicing in respect of value added tax. Comes into force on 1 January 2004 for the 15 member states and, logically, on 1 May 2004 for the 10 accession countries.

8. See also in this connection the new Article 22(3)(b), para. 1, of the Sixth Directive as introduced by Council Directive 2001/115/EC of 20 December 2001 amending Directive 77/388/EEC with a view to simplifying, modernising and harmonising the conditions laid down for invoicing in respect of value added tax. Comes into force on 1 January 2004 for the 15 member states and, logically, on 1 May 2004 for the 10 accession countries.

9. Article 22(3)(a) = Article 28H of Directive 77/388/EEC as incorporated by Article 1(22) of Directive 91/960/EEC, Council Directive 2001/115/EC of 20 December 2001 amending Directive 77/388/EEC with a view to simplifying, modernising and harmonising the conditions laid down for invoicing in respect of value added tax. Comes into force on 1 January 2004 for the 15 member states and, logically, on 1 May 2004 for the 10 accession countries.

10. Article 22(3)(a) = Article 28H of Directive 77/388/EEC as incorporated by Article 1(22) of Directive 91/960/EEC, fourth subparagraph, of the Sixth Directive/Article 2(2) of the Invoicing Directive.

11. Article 22(3)(a) = Article 28H of Directive 77/388/EEC as incorporated by Article 1(22) of Directive 91/960/EEC, fourth subparagraph, of the Sixth Directive/Article 2(2) of the Invoicing Directive.

12. Article 28H of Directive 77/388/EEC as incorporated by Article 1(22) of Directive 91/960/EEC.

13. Council Directive 2001/115/EC of 20 December 2001 amending Directive 77/388/EEC with a view to simplifying, modernising and harmonising the conditions laid down for invoicing in respect of value added tax. Comes into force on 1 January 2004 for the 15 member states and, logically, on 1 May 2004 for the 10 accession countries.

14. Based on http://www.globalvatonline.com.

15. In this connection, see Commission Recommendation 94/820/EC of 19 October 1994 on the legal aspects of EDI.

16. This arises where the place of supply of goods or a service is located outside the supplier's country of establishment.

17. See I. Lejeune, A. Smits, J. Cambien, M. Joostens, P. Van Eecke, *E-Invoicing and E-Archiving*, Belgium, PricewaterhouseCoopers Tax Consultants cbvba, 2003.

18. See Article 2(2) of Council Directive 2001/115/EC of 20 December 2001 amending Directive 77/388/EEC with a view to simplifying, modernising and harmonising the conditions laid down for invoicing in respect of value added tax. Comes into force on 1 January 2004 for the 15 member states and, logically, on 1 May 2004 for the 10 accession countries.

19. See Directives 76/308/EEC and 77/799/EEC and Regulation (EEC) No. 218/92.
20. See "Storage Period", p. 214, I. Lejeune, A. Smits, J. Cambien, M. Joostens, P. Van Eecke, *E-Invoicing and E-Archiving*, PricewaterhouseCoopers Tax Consultants cbvba, 2003.
21. Enterprise Resource Planning
22. The Treaty of Accession 2003,
   http://europa.eu.int/comm/enlargement/negotiations/treaty_of_accession_2003/index.htm.

7 What is the Impact of the Enlargement of the European Union in the Field of Direct Taxes?

7.1 What is the impact of accession?*

The fiscal impact of accession of the candidate member states to the EU is not just limited to VAT or other indirect taxes but also affects direct taxes, particularly encompassing personal and corporate income taxes. In this chapter we discuss just corporate income tax (corporation tax).

The consequences of accession for corporate income tax certainly should not be underestimated. Proper preparation for EU enlargement is therefore an absolute necessity for every business.

As from 1 May 2004, businesses active in the new EU member states will have to take account of the fact that EU rules and case law will affect daily business reality.

By contrast with indirect taxation, the harmonisation of corporate income tax is not yet even at the nursery stage. However, there are already a number of European Directives:

- the Parent–Subsidiary Directive;
- the Merger Directive;
- the Directive concerning mutual assistance by the competent authorities of the member states in the field of direct and indirect taxation;
- the Interest and Royalties Directive.

In relation to transfer prices, the Arbitration Convention is also relevant, but as it is not within the scope of this book we shall not delve further into it.

We also discuss the most relevant EU case law on corporate income tax.

A number of recent developments in the field of EU fiscal policy are also of importance:

---

* You will find the source references for this chapter on page 198.

- the EU Code of Conduct and EU position regarding harmful tax competition; and

- the EU position regarding (prohibited) state aids.

Finally we also explain the European Company, fiscal unity, tax-friendly planning of intra-group financing activities and tax-friendly planning for intellectual property.

7.2   What can a taxpayer do if an EU directive has not been transposed into the national laws of one of the new member states?

The new member states have to integrate a number of directives on corporate income tax into their local laws. If they fail to do so, then taxpayers in the new member states can invoke these directives before the courts.

Correct transposition of these directives offers taxpayers greater legal certainty and flexibility to develop their activities within the EU to the optimum.

The dates by which the directives have to be transposed into internal law are fixed separately for each country.

7.3   Is the Parent–Subsidiary Directive applicable?[1]

The Parent–Subsidiary Directive is the one that has best been naturalised into the local legislation of the current EU member states. The Directive states that profit distributions or dividends within the EU have to be paid out as neutrally as possible.

In practice, this translates into an exemption from withholdings at source on dividends from EU subsidiaries. Each member state is free to decide how large the exemption is. Thus, for dividend distributions within the EU, there is a zero rate where the EU shareholder possesses at least 25% of the share capital for at least two years. Member states can shorten this period.

An EU shareholder can usually claim a participation exemption or a tax credit in order to avoid economic double taxation. Otherwise, the same profit is taxed twice, once in the hands of the subsidiary and once in the hands of the parent.

This participation exemption is normally linked to a taxation condition. The profit that is used to distribute the dividend has to have been subjected to "normal" taxation in the hands of the subsidiary before the parent can apply for a participation exemption for the dividend received. In some local tax laws, this condition is deemed to be fulfilled where the subsidiary has its tax residence in the EU (regardless of its actual tax rate).

The candidate member states have to adapt their local tax laws to the provisions of the Parent–Subsidiary Directive. In the Czech Republic, Estonia, Hungary, Latvia and Slovakia, this has already been done for withholdings at source on dividend distributions. Hungary has already progressed furthest as regards the participation exemption.

Furthermore, the candidate member states also have to follow EU case law. In some member states, there was only an exemption from withholdings at source if at the time of the dividend distribution the EU parent had at least a 25% stake in the share capital for the minimum holding period. However, the Parent–Subsidiary Directive states that an *intention* to maintain the shareholding for the minimum period is sufficient to be exempted from a retention at source. Denmark and Belgium have accordingly had to amend their legislation under pressure from the EU judgment in the case of *Denkavit*.[2]

The participation exemption is also an area in which the European Court of Justice or a national court can oblige a member state to bring its legislation into line with the Parent–Subsidiary Directive.

Correct transposition of the provisions of the Parent–Subsidiary Directive is designed to enable a tax-friendly dividend policy within the EU. This is supposed to promote investments in the EU's candidate member states.

At the moment, there is a proposal to adjust the Parent–Subsidiary Directive:

- reduction of the minimum threshold for shareholdings from 25% to 10%;

- adaptation of the annex with qualifying bodies;

- application of the Directive to qualifying share interests that are accredited to a permanent establishment established in an EU member state;

- adapted rules for tax-transparent entities and where in a given EU member state the set-off method instead of the exemption method is deployed for dividends.

7.4 Is the Merger Directive[4] applicable as from 1 May 2004?

The Directive on mergers, divisions and the contribution of assets provides for common tax rules for reorganisations at both national and European levels. This Directive seeks to eliminate the tax hurdles to the freedom of establishment for undertakings.

Local tax legislation has to enable reorganisations in a tax neutral manner. This means that latent capital gains on the assets involved in the reorganisation are regarded as unrealised as a result of the reorganisation.

Many member states have only partially implemented the Merger Directive into their local legislation. This means that it could be necessary to invoke direct application of the Directive before the courts.

An exception to this "inertia" rule is the exemption from capital taxes (registration duties) where a qualifying minimum share package is contributed to an EU company. In most EU countries, a proportional capital tax is due on the market value of a contribution in kind to the capital of the company receiving the contribution.

Under certain conditions, most member states apply a zero rate, so that an exchange of shares is a tax-friendly technique for setting up an EU holding structure. The majority of the accession countries do not yet have any capital taxes for the contribution of shares. They will have to bring their internal conditions for exemption into line with the Merger Directive.

At the present time, only Cyprus, Hungary, Latvia, Lithuania, Malta, Poland and Slovakia have taken legislative steps to implement the Directive.

7.5 Is the Directive concerning mutual assistance by the competent authorities of the member states in the field of direct and indirect taxation[5] applicable as of 1 May 2004?

Yes, the Directive concerning mutual assistance by the competent authorities of the member states is intended to:

- combat international tax fraud and tax-evasion;
- reinforce cooperation between the member states' tax authorities;
- facilitate the exchange of information that is relevant for evidencing taxes on income and wealth.

The competent authorities of the member states provide each other with all information that is relevant for correct assessment of tax liabilities as regards personal income tax, wealth tax and VAT.

7.6 Is the Interest and Royalties Directive[6] applicable as from 1 May 2004?

The Interest and Royalties Directive abolishes tax on payments of interest and royalties between associated undertakings from different member states.

Two EU undertakings are associated where one of them directly holds at least 25% of the capital in the other or where a third EU undertaking holds at least 25% of each of the other two undertakings. By contrast with the Parent–Subsidiary Directive, this Directive is also applicable to sister companies, where there is a common EU parent.

The member states may also apply the Directive where the shareholding involved is less than 25%. The member states may also replace the criterion of a shareholding of at least 25% in the capital by possession of at least 25% of the voting rights.

This EU Directive only came into force on 1 January 2004 and is designed to make interest and royalty payments within the EU more tax-friendly. In member states that currently have no general exemption from withholdings at source on interest or royalties, businesses have to rely on double taxation treaties in order to claim an exemption from or reduction in local withholding taxes. However, there are few double taxation treaties that provide for an exemption from withholdings at source on interest payments. Moreover, the formalities that have to be gone through in order to be able to enjoy treaty protection are more stringent and time-consuming than exemptions under municipal law.

The timing of approval of the Interest and Royalties Directive is opportune given the imminent EU enlargement. However, there is a good chance that some of the new member states will get eight years in which to implement the Directive, predominantly for budgetary reasons. Moreover, Greece, Portugal and Spain have already been granted transitional rules. Hungary, on the other hand, is anticipating a zero withholding on interest and royalties as from 2004.

7.7 What EU case law on direct taxation is also applicable to the new EU countries on 1 May 2004?

The candidate member states also have to take account of EU case law. In the following, we give an overview of the most important EU court judgments with a direct impact on corporate income tax.

The recent Kobler decision[7] shows that the EU's case law is also relevant for both the current and the candidate member states, for the court held that a member state has to compensate its inhabitants where a local court fails to apply European law correctly.

DATE: 28 January 1986.
CASE: C-270/83.
BREACH OF: Freedom of establishment.

PARTIES: European Court – France.
BRIEF STATEMENT OF THE FACTS AND POSITION OF THE COURT OF JUSTICE:
  Avoir fiscal (tax credit) may not be limited to French inhabitants.

Facts: In order to avoid double taxation, French law accorded a tax credit (a so-called "*avoir fiscal*") where an insurance company having its registered office or a subsidiary in France received a dividend. French agencies or branches of insurance companies having their registered offices in another EU member state were excluded from the credit, however.

The court held that this internal French rule was a travesty of the freedom of movement and found against the French State.

DATE: 13 July 1993.
CASE: C-330/91.
BREACH OF: Freedom of establishment.
PARTIES: European Court – UK – re: Commerzbank.
BRIEF STATEMENT OF THE FACTS AND POSITION OF THE COURT OF JUS-
  TICE: Refund supplements may not be only for inhabitants of the United
  Kingdom.

Facts: A German company, Commerzbank AG, had, via its London branch, granted various loans to borrowers in the USA. On the interest it received, the branch had paid tax in the UK and applied for and received a refund of a certain portion of the British tax from the Inland Revenue. In addition, the branch claimed a so-called refund supplement, i.e. interest on the initially overpaid tax for the period the Inland Revenue had been in possession of the funds. However, the Revenue rejected the application on the technical ground that only companies tax-resident in the UK (and hence not mere branches in the UK) could benefit from these refund supplements.

The court found against the UK for a breach of the freedom of establishment.

DATE: 15 May 1997.
CASE: C-250/95.
BREACH OF: Freedom of establishment.
PARTIES: European Court – Luxembourg – re: Futura Participations.
BRIEF STATEMENT OF THE FACTS AND POSITION OF THE COURT OF JUSTICE:
  Set-off of tax losses may not be linked to the condition that books of account
  be kept in Luxembourg.

Facts: Futura Participations SA was tax-resident in France and had a branch in Luxembourg. In accordance with the French–Luxembourg double taxation treaty, its results that are allocable to the Luxembourg branch are taxable there. Under internal Luxembourg legislation, residents of Luxembourg can offset carryover losses with book profits if due and proper books of account are present. Non-residents, on the other hand, have to apply a pro rata rule where they do not have due and proper books of account. However, if they wish to offset carryover losses with subsequent profits, it has to be shown that the loss results from books of account that have been kept in Luxembourg.

Futura Participations initially had no regular bookkeeping in Luxembourg – a pro rata rule was conversely applied in order to determine the Luxembourg result – but in a later accounting period it wished to offset a carryover loss (calculated on a pro rata basis). The Luxembourg tax authorities rejected this on the ground that no bookkeeping was present in Luxembourg for the year of the loss.

The court found against Luxembourg because it utterly ignored the presence of books of account in a country other than Luxembourg (here, France).

DATE: 17 July 1997.
CASE: C-28/95.
BREACH OF: Freedom of establishment.
PARTIES: European Court – The Netherlands – re: Leur-Bloem.
BRIEF STATEMENT OF THE FACTS AND POSITION OF THE COURT OF JUSTICE:
   A tax-neutral share exchange may not be refused despite local legislation transposing the Merger Directive.

Facts: Mr Leur-Bloem, the sole shareholder and manager of two Dutch companies, was intending to buy a third company, albeit not for cash but for an exchange of shares in the existing companies. Mr Leur-Bloem tried to convince the Dutch tax authorities that this was a "share exchange", as a result of which he would be able to benefit from tax-neutrality in the Netherlands. The Dutch exemption rules invoked by Mr Leur-Bloem were introduced into Dutch law as a transposition of the Merger Directive. The Dutch tax authorities refused to share this viewpoint since, in its view, the EU Directive could not be invoked for a purely Dutch transaction.

The court ruled here that the tax treatment of purely domestic cases had to be in line with EU directives where a rule of common law was invoked whose aim was the transposition of an EU directive. Hence, in the present case, the provisions of the Merger Directive were violated.

DATE: 16 January 1998.
CASE: C-264/96.
BREACH OF: Freedom of establishment.
PARTIES: European Court – UK – re: ICI.
BRIEF STATEMENT OF THE FACTS AND POSITION OF THE COURT OF JUSTICE:
   Set-off of losses for a consortium has to be permitted even where there is a majority of non-UK subsidiaries.

Facts: Two English companies, A (49%) and B (51%), together formed a consortium and thus each held shares in a holding company, C. The holding company, C, just held shares in 23 subsidiaries, four of which were in the UK. One of these British companies sustained severe losses and A wanted to deduct them to the extent of 49%. The Inland Revenue rejected the claim because, from a technical tax viewpoint, C could not be labelled a holding company because 19 of the 23 subsidiaries were tax-resident outside the UK.

The court regarded this as being contrary to the freedom of establishment.

DATE: 21 September 1999.
CASE: C-307/97.
BREACH OF: Freedom of establishment.
PARTIES: European Court – Germany – re: Saint Gobain.
BRIEF STATEMENT OF THE FACTS AND POSITION OF THE COURT OF JUSTICE: Participation exemption may not be restricted and only allowed for German companies.

Facts: A German permanent establishment of a French company directly received dividends from an American company. In addition, the permanent establishment also received dividends (from Italy, Austria and Switzerland) via two German intermediate companies. Given the fiscal unity rules in Germany, the latter dividends were directly accredited to the German permanent establishment. To avoid double taxation, the German permanent establishment wished to exempt the American and Swiss dividends from German corporate income tax. The German tax authorities refused, since only German companies can invoke this exemption.

Here, too, the court held that this rule was a breach of the freedom of establishment.

DATE: 26 October 1999.
CASE: C-294/97.
BREACH OF: Freedom of services.
PARTIES: European Court – Germany – re: Eurowings.
BRIEF STATEMENT OF THE FACTS AND POSITION OF THE COURT OF JUSTICE: Only lease of economic chattel from German lessor not in tax base for trade tax.

Facts: In Germany there is a special municipal tax on businesses, called *Gewerbesteuer*, which is separate from regular corporate income tax. The tax base for this trade tax comprises half of the lease price for economic chattels, except if the lease price itself is subject to trade tax in the hands of the lessor. The measure is intended to avoid double taxation. However, no such tax exists outside Germany. In practice this exception thus means that leases from foreign companies are always taxable under the trade tax provisions and there is thus discrimination in relation to leases from domestic companies, which are generally exempted.

The court thus held that the German tax ran counter to the European rules on the freedom to provide services.

DATE: 6 June 2000.
CASE: C-35/98.
BREACH OF: Free movement of capital.
PARTIES: European Court – The Netherlands – re: Verkooijen.
BRIEF STATEMENT OF THE FACTS AND POSITION OF THE COURT OF JUSTICE: Refusal of participation exemption because distributing company did not have tax residence in the Netherlands.

Facts: Mr Verkooijen, resident in the Netherlands, was employed as an employee with the Dutch subsidiary of a Belgian stock market-listed company. Within the context of an employee savings plan, Verkooijen held shares in the Belgian parent. When the Belgian parent distributed a dividend, Verkooijen reported this in his Dutch return, but the participation exemption was refused because the company declaring the dividend did not have tax residence in the Netherlands.

The court held that this rule was contrary to the free movement of capital.

DATE: 14 December 2000.
CASE: C-141/99.
BREACH OF: Freedom of establishment.
PARTIES: European Court – Belgium – re: Amid.
BRIEF STATEMENT OF THE FACTS AND POSITION OF THE COURT OF JUSTICE: Belgian tax losses are forfeit as a result of compulsory set-off against exempted profit of permanent establishment in treaty country.

Facts: A Belgian company, Amid, had a permanent establishment in Luxembourg. In book year 1981, Amid suffered a loss in Belgium, but made a profit in Luxembourg. In 1982, both Belgium and Luxembourg made a profit. In the Belgian corporate income tax return for 1982, Amid set off the carryover Belgian losses against the Belgian profits for that year. The Belgian tax authorities required that the Belgian losses be set off against the profits from Luxembourg (which were exempted under the Belgian–Luxembourg double taxation treaty).

The European court ruled that Belgium had thereby breached the right to freedom of establishment.

DATE: 12 December 2002.
CASE: C-324/00.
BREACH OF: Freedom of establishment.
PARTIES: European Court – Germany – re: Lankhorst.
BRIEF STATEMENT OF THE FACTS AND POSITION OF THE COURT OF JUSTICE:

Deductible interest only not reclassified as a taxable dividend where lender is German resident.

Facts: A Dutch company, Lankhorst-Hohorst BV, granted a loan to a German company, Lankhorst-Hohorst GmbH. The German tax authorities regarded the GmbH, however, as undercapitalised and therefore viewed the interest paid to the BV as a distribution of profits. Under the then German tax law, the "interest" was subjected to a 30% tax on dividends.

In argument before the Court of Justice, it found that reclassification would not have been possible had the lender been tax-resident in Germany. The court thus came to the conclusion that this was a breach of the freedom of establishment.

DATE: 18 September 2003.
CASE: C-168/01.
BREACH OF: Freedom of establishment.
PARTIES: European Court – The Netherlands – re: Bosal.
BRIEF STATEMENT OF THE FACTS AND POSITION OF THE COURT OF JUSTICE:
   Only expenses relating to Dutch holdings are tax-deductible.

Facts: Bosal Holding BV was a Dutch holding company and wished to deduct the expenses with regard to the financing of its holding in foreign subsidiaries from its taxable result. The Dutch tax legislation did not, however, allow tax-deduction of expenses relating to holdings outside the Netherlands.

The European Court of Justice held this to be contrary to the right to freedom of establishment.

7.8   Is the EU Code of Conduct and the EU position regarding harmful tax competition also applicable in the new EU countries on 1 May 2004?

The EU Code of Conduct is a purely political undertaking and relates to harmful tax measures that significantly influence or are significantly likely to influence the location of economic activities in the EU. This also covers official practice by the member states.

A measure is fiscally harmful if it results in a level of taxation that is considerably lower than is normally applicable in the member state in question.

This EU analysis resulted in the so-called Primarolo Report,[8] a list of 66 tax measures in various member states with so-called harmful features. They were subdivided into six categories:

- financial services and group financing;

- (re)insurance and captive insurance;

- intra-group services;

- holding companies;

- offshore and exempted regimes; and

- a residual category.

The accession countries also have to examine to what extent some components of their tax legislation can be hallmarked as "harmful". If they can, then they will certainly have to make adjustments, otherwise the European Commission will most assuredly do it for them.

In particular, the corporate income tax regimes in Estonia, the Hungarian HOC regime (see below) and certain tax rules in Latvia and Malta will be scrutinised in minute detail.

7.9 Can the European Union take action against state aids in the new member states as from 1 May 2004?

The European Code of Conduct refers expressly to state aid rules. The Code of Conduct protects tax revenues. The Code of Conduct is not Community law. The rules on state aids, however, are formulated as regulations. They therefore take legal precedence.

Moreover, many writers suggest that most measures on the Primarolo list can be classified as state aids.

In the accession countries, too, state aids will no longer be permitted as from 1 May 2004. In this connection, questions may be raised about so-called "tax holidays" that apply in Poland. Those benefiting from these pay no tax for a certain period. However, it is currently hard to assess whether undertakings that benefit from proscribed state aids will have to pay them back.

7.10 Will the European Company exist in all member states as from 8 October 2004?

As from 8 October 2004, the European Company, or Societas Europaea[9] (SE) will exist as a legal form of doing business. Companies established in more than one member state of the European Union can be brought together under one single legal structure. The European Company is then governed by one system of rules regarding how it functions and the disclosure of information.

This is supposed greatly to reduce the burden of officialdom under the traditional member state-by-member state approach. The European Commission reckons that business can thus save approximately 30 billion euros. This figure applies only to the 15 countries that were member states before 1 May 2004.

The European Company is also intended to facilitate access by SMEs to the European market.

The company's registered office and principal management have to be established in the same member state. The company law of that member state will then apply to the European Company.

However, the tax rules have not been harmonised. This means that the company will have to take account of as many tax regimes as there are member states in which it is active. In principle, a European Company is subject to corporate income tax in the member state where its registered office is established. However, this does not rule out its activities in other member states also being liable to taxation. As can be seen from the case law cited above, this can lead to a lot of controversy. The lack of any harmonised tax legislation limits the benefits of a European Company.

The Regulation will come directly into force in the new member states. The question is to what degree their local tax rules are ready and suited to offer (new) investors practical and practicable solutions.

7.11   Will there be a fiscal unity regime as from 1 May 2004?

The tax regimes of the present member states are currently far from harmonised. Fiscal unity means that the individual tax results from group companies can be offset against one another. Only the net result (loss or profit) is looked at to avoid tax being paid at a group level.

Most regimes are restricted to national tax unity. This means that only group companies and/or branches within a given state's national boundaries can participate in fiscal unity vis-à-vis that state. Schemes for cross-border fiscal unity are at present more the exception within the EU than the rule. Only Denmark has cross-border fiscal unity.

From Table 7.1, it can be seen that Italy, Greece and Belgium have no fiscal unity. However, the European Commission emphasises the need for introducing a system of fiscal unity for domestic companies and establishments that are resident in the EU.

Of the accession countries, only Cyprus, Latvia, Poland and Slovenia already have a form of fiscal unity in their local tax laws.

Table 7.1 Fiscal unity regime.

Country	Does local legislation provide for fiscal unity?	
	Yes	No
Current EU member states		
Austria	×	
Belgium		×
Denmark	×	
Germany	×	
Greece		×
Finland	×	
France	×	
Ireland	×	
Italy		×
Luxembourg	×	
Portugal	×	
Spain	×	
Sweden	×	
The Netherlands	×	
The United Kingdom	×	
Candidate EU member states		
Cyprus	×	
The Czech Republic		×
Estonia		×
Hungary		×
Latvia	×	
Lithuania		×
Malta		×[a]
Poland	×	
Slovakia		×
Slovenia	×	

[a] Under certain conditions, the set-off of losses is possible between group companies.

7.12 Can you plan intra-group financing activities in a tax-friendly manner?

An undertaking needs funds to be able to provide its business activities with the necessary financial oxygen. Financing can assume a variety of forms. Classic examples outlined in the following paragraphs.

7.12.1 Self-financing by forming reserves of profits

Instead of distributing an annual dividend, an undertaking can deploy its book profits within its business, for instance in order to meet cashflow requirements or finance investments. A book profit does not have to be applied to the same purpose every year. For the sake of completeness we would point out that, when opting for a dividend policy, application of the Parent–Subsidiary Directive in the national legislation of the new member states allows tax-friendly declaration of dividends and thus, in a certain sense, promotes financing within a group.

7.12.2   External debt financing

The group can also attract the necessary financial means externally, for instance from a bank. The drawback of this choice is that the interest owed leaves the group in favour of the third-party bank. The interest payments are possibly tax-deductible in the hands of the various debtors, but account has to be taken of the potentially pernicious effect of local thin-capitalisation rules. These have the consequence that deductible interest is reclassified as a non-deductible distribution of profit for local tax purposes. In addition, account also has to be taken of European case law.

7.12.3   Internal debt financing

The group can use its own funds to finance shortfalls amongst group members. This can result in a good many tax benefits. Thus, interest is probably tax-deductible in the hands of the borrower group members. For this, the requisite documentation has to be available in order to underpin the business nature of the expenses. Furthermore, the documentation also has to demonstrate that the rate of interest is in conformity with the market conditions. In the case of internal debt financing, the tax authorities in the debtor's country will carefully scrutinise the acceptability of tax-driven profit shifts between group companies in various jurisdictions. It is not ruled out that the aim might be to link the tax-deductibility of interest in one country with a high effective tax rate to the tax liability of the same interest in a country with a lower effective tax rate. Moreover, many member states lay down documentation requirements with regard to internal transfer prices.

Even where interest is tax-deductible, account has to be taken of possible negative effects of local thin-capitalisation rules.

Internal group financing also has the advantage that the interest payments remain within the group. In addition, such tax planning enables optimisations, including in the context of enlargement. Good planning for the financing structure can also avoid local withholding taxes on the interest payments within the company group. In this event, in the country of the beneficiary there is no need for a tax credit for foreign withholding tax in order to avoid or minimise double taxation (see also section 7.6).

In addition, the new member states offer a number of interesting possibilities for intra-group financing vehicles. The tax rules under which the beneficiary of the interest falls for a large part determine the tax effectiveness of a financing structure. In the European Union, there are numerous tax-friendly financing structures, such as the use of a Belgian coordination centre, use of Dutch concern financing and the use of a Luxembourg financing branch.

After enlargement of the European Union, other alternatives will probably be added, such as the Hungarian company that, as from 1 January 2006, will generally enjoy an effective tax rate of 8% or less for interest and royalty income (see below).

However, the European Commission has to either allow these financing alternatives or ask the member states to change their local legislation. For example, at Europe's request, the tax regime of Belgium coordination centres will in principle change from a limited cost-plus basis to a full cost-plus basis. Currently the Belgian government is also reviewing other alternatives to allow beneficial taxation to keep or attract foreign investors.

Nonetheless, there are a number of examples where member states do not need to abolish their tax-favourable rules. Thus Ireland retains its generalised 12.5% rate of corporation tax for trading activities (strictly viewed), so long as it does not apply to all companies with tax residence in the country. Passive activities are taxed at 25%. The previous 10% rate was only reserved for a select group of companies.

7.13 Is tax-friendly planning possible for intellectual property?

Just as financing structures can be organised in a tax-friendly manner, the same goes for intellectual property. A group company can register the intellectual property and then issue licences to the other group companies, which pay royalties in exchange.

Our earlier remarks on price-setting in conformity with market conditions for the tax-deductibility of interest payments also apply here. Moreover, the company that is the legal owner of the intellectual property has to have adequate substance. Under certain conditions, royalty payments within the European Union are free from local withholdings. In this regard we refer to section 7.6.

Hungary, for example, is a tax-friendly country for companies with intellectual property. The Hungarian legislation provides for a special tax regime for so-called "Hungarian Offshore Companies" (or HOCs). Under certain conditions, these companies benefit from an effective tax rate of 3% for 2003 (4% for 2004 and 2005). However, not all Hungarian companies can qualify as HOCs. Thus, as from 1 January 2006, corporate income tax is at the rate of 16% for all companies with tax residence in Hungary. For companies with interest and royalty income, this is reduced to an effective rate of 8%. In other words, Hungary is an interesting country where one is dealing with intellectual property. Furthermore, Hungary has plans for further reducing corporate income tax, possibly to 12% in 2006[10].

7.14   List of comparisons for corporate income tax in the new member states[11]

In the following, the corporate income tax of each accession member state is compared:

- the most important main features of corporate income tax;

- the corporate income tax rates;

- the current situation regarding implementation of the Parent–Subsidiary and Merger Directives;

- the existence of tax-favourable regimes;

- the existence of banking secrecy.

COUNTRY: Cyprus.
MAIN POINTS: Low rate of corporate income tax, favourable tax treaties with Russia and central and eastern Europe, favourable treatment of dividends and interest, no thin-capitalisation rules.
CORPORATE INCOME TAX RATE: 10%. However, 15% for financial year 2004 in same cases.
HAVE THE PARENT–SUBSIDIARY AND MERGER DIRECTIVES BEEN IMPLEMENTED? Yes.
ARE THERE TAX HOLIDAYS (TEMPORARY NON-TAXED PERIODS) OR OTHER FAVOURABLE SCHEMES? No.
IS THERE BANKING SECRECY? Yes.

COUNTRY: Czech Republic.
MAIN POINTS: Possibility for foreign investors to be given investment stimuli, such as a tax holiday of up to 10 years. Expected transposition of the Parent–Subsidiary Directive into Czech legislation – consequence: possibility of dividend withholding tax.

CORPORATE INCOME TAX RATE: The current rate of corporate income tax is 28%; in 2005 the rate will amount to 26%; and as from 2006 24%.

HAVE THE PARENT–SUBSIDIARY AND MERGER DIRECTIVES BEEN IMPLE-MENTED? Implementation of the Parent–Subsidiary Directive is planned (the government is currently working on the relevant statutory amendments).

ARE THERE TAX HOLIDAYS (TEMPORARY NON-TAXED PERIODS) OR OTHER FAVOURABLE SCHEMES? Yes, investment stimuli are available for greenfield and brownfield investments. A few examples of such stimuli are reductions in corporate income tax, financial support for the creation of jobs/training, etc.

IS THERE BANKING SECRECY? Yes, but banks have to provide certain information when asked by the tax authorities.

COUNTRY: Estonia.

MAIN POINTS: Corporate income tax is only due in the event of actual or undisclosed profit distributions. No thin-capitalisation rules.

CORPORATE INCOME TAX RATE: Undistributed profits are exempt from tax; profit distributions are subject to 26% effective corporate income tax. Tax is payable monthly. There is no annual tax return. In 2005, the tax rate will amount to 24%; in 2006 22%; and as from 2007 20%.

HAVE THE PARENT–SUBSIDIARY AND MERGER DIRECTIVES BEEN IMPLE-MENTED? No (unclear when they will be).

ARE THERE TAX HOLIDAYS (TEMPORARY NON-TAXED PERIODS) OR OTHER FAVOURABLE SCHEMES? Yes, the scheme that applies to undistributed profits (0%) regardless of whether they are invested or just put to reserves.

IS THERE BANKING SECRECY? No.

COUNTRY: Hungary.

MAIN POINTS: Thin-capitalisation rules, low taxation of interest and royalty income.

CORPORATE INCOME TAX RATE: 16%. In 2005 the rate will amount to 14%; and as from 2006 12%.

HAVE THE PARENT–SUBSIDIARY AND MERGER DIRECTIVES BEEN IMPLE-MENTED? Yes, they come into force as of accession.

ARE THERE TAX HOLIDAYS (TEMPORARY NON-TAXED PERIODS) OR OTHER FAVOURABLE SCHEMES? The benefits of the offshore scheme (HOCs) will remain in place for existing offshore companies until 2005. There is also a favourable scheme for interest and royalty income. (50% base exemption.)

IS THERE BANKING SECRECY? Yes.

COUNTRY: Latvia.

MAIN POINTS: Exemption for dividends received, low tax rate, possible group taxation.

CORPORATE INCOME TAX RATE: 15%.

HAVE THE PARENT–SUBSIDIARY AND MERGER DIRECTIVES BEEN IMPLE-
MENTED? They will soon be implemented.

ARE THERE TAX HOLIDAYS (TEMPORARY NON-TAXED PERIODS) OR OTHER
FAVOURABLE SCHEMES? Yes, these schemes (free ports and industry zones)
will be changed or abolished. It does appear that benefits for certain zones
(liepaja/rezekne) are accorded until 31 December 2017. Tax holiday companies will continue to exist until 31 December 2005.

IS THERE BANKING SECRECY? No.

COUNTRY: Lithuania.

MAIN POINTS: Dividends received exempted, low rate of tax, group taxation
is not possible.

CORPORATE INCOME TAX RATE: 15%.

HAVE THE PARENT–SUBSIDIARY AND MERGER DIRECTIVES BEEN IMPLE-
MENTED? According to Government Decision 43 of 15 January 2001 on
the status regarding taxation, EU Directives 90/434 and 90/435 will be
transposed into national legislation and completed no later than the time
of accession.

ARE THERE TAX HOLIDAYS (TEMPORARY NON-TAXED PERIODS) OR OTHER
FAVOURABLE SCHEMES? Abolished in 2002 (existing holidays remain valid
until 31 December 2003). It is not clear whether the free economic zones
are to be abolished.

IS THERE BANKING SECRECY? Yes.

COUNTRY: Malta.

MAIN POINTS: No thin-capitalisation rules or withholding taxes, good
treaty network, there are favourable tax schemes (for both operating
companies and international holding companies that are established in
Malta).

CORPORATE INCOME TAX RATE: 35%.

HAVE THE PARENT–SUBSIDIARY AND MERGER DIRECTIVES BEEN IMPLE-
MENTED? Will be implemented.

ARE THERE TAX HOLIDAYS (TEMPORARY NON-TAXED PERIODS) OR OTHER
FAVOURABLE SCHEMES? Yes, there are tax breaks for production activities,
including low rates and investment deductions. There are special tax rules
for international activities by businesses in foreign hands (refund/credit) in
cases of profit distribution, with the consequence of a possible effective
minimum rate of 4.17% or a zero rate.

IS THERE BANKING SECRECY? Yes, subject to exceptions.

COUNTRY: Poland.
MAIN POINTS: Thin-capitalisation rules, capital gains subject to corporate income tax at standard rate, no separate rate for capital gains. Law on financial support for investments by the state.
CORPORATE INCOME TAX RATE: 19%.
HAVE THE PARENT–SUBSIDIARY AND MERGER DIRECTIVES BEEN IMPLE-MENTED? At present there is no information about whether this will change in the next few years.
ARE THERE TAX HOLIDAYS (TEMPORARY NON-TAXED PERIODS) OR OTHER FAVOURABLE SCHEMES? Will be implemented at the time of accession. There are tax breaks for special economic zones that can result in a tax holiday. This legislation has meanwhile been adjusted in line with EU legislation. For new investors, application of these schemes will still be possible.
IS THERE BANKING SECRECY? Yes.

COUNTRY: Slovakia.
MAIN POINTS: No thin-capitalisation rules and no dividend tax.
CORPORATE INCOME TAX RATE: 25%.
HAVE THE PARENT–SUBSIDIARY AND MERGER DIRECTIVES BEEN IMPLE-MENTED? Yes.
ARE THERE TAX HOLIDAYS (TEMPORARY NON-TAXED PERIODS) OR OTHER FAVOURABLE SCHEMES? On the proviso that certain conditions are ful-filled, it is possible to get a tax credit of 100% from the government for a period of up to 10 years. This will continue to be possible after accession, provided the specific transitional conditions are met.
IS THERE BANKING SECRECY? Yes.

COUNTRY: Slovenia.
MAIN POINTS: No thin-capitalisation rules. Slovenian legislation is undergo-ing change – new laws on personal income tax and corporate income tax are expected in 2004.
CORPORATE INCOME TAX RATE: 25%.
HAVE THE PARENT–SUBSIDIARY AND MERGER DIRECTIVES BEEN IMPLE-MENTED? Not yet.
ARE THERE TAX HOLIDAYS (TEMPORARY NON-TAXED PERIODS) OR OTHER FAVOURABLE SCHEMES? No.
IS THERE BANKING SECRECY? No.

For comparison, we also add in Table 7.2 the general rates of corporate in-come tax in the current EU member states as at 1 January 2003.

Table 7.2 EU rates of corporate income tax as at 1 January 2004.

Nature of tax	Sweden	Finland	UK	Denmark	Luxembourg	Portugal[12]	Belgium
Federal	28%	29%[14]	30%	30%	22%	25%	33%
Regional	n/a	n/a	n/a	n/a	n/a	n/a	n/a
Municipal	n/a	n/a	n/a	n/a	7.5%	10%	n/a
Other	n/a	n/a	n/a	n/a	4%	n/a	3%
Total	**28%**	**29%**	**30%**	**30%**	**30.38%**	**27.5%**	**33.99%**

Nature of tax	Austria	Netherlands	Spain	France	Greece	Italy	Germany
Federal	34%[13]	34.5%	35%	33.33%	33%	33%	25%
Regional	n/a	n/a	n/a	n/a	n/a	4.25%	n/a
Municipal	n/a	n/a	n/a	n/a	n/a	n/a	0–24.5%
Other	n/a	n/a	n/a	3% 3.3%	3%	n/a	n/a
Total	**34%**	**34.5%**	**35%**	**34.32–35.42%**	**38%**	**37.5%**	**33.07–40.86%**

In Ireland, on 1 January 2004, the following rates applied:

•   25% for passive income;

•   12.5% for trade income;

•   10% in accordance with a transitional regime.

Source references for Chapter 7

1. Directive 90/435/EEC of 23 July 1990 on the common system of taxation applicable in the case of parent companies and subsidiaries of different member states.
2. Denkavit judgment of 17 October 1996 by the European Court of Justice.
3. Directive 2003/123/EC of 22 December 2003 amending Directive 90/435/EEC on the common system of taxation applicable in the case of parent companies and subsidiaries of different member states.
4. Directive 90/434/EEC of 23 July 1990 on the common system of taxation applicable to mergers, divisions, transfers of assets and exchanges of shares concerning companies of different member states.
5. Directive 77/799/EEC of 19 December 1977 concerning mutual assistance by the competent authorities of the member states in the field of direct and indirect taxation (consolidated version).
6. Directive 2003/49/EC of 3 June 2003 on a common system of taxation applicable to interest and royalty payments made between associated companies of different member states.
7. Gerhard Kobler v. Republic of Austria, C-224/01.
8. http://europa.eu.int/comm/taxation_customs/french/taxation/law/primarolo/primarolo_en.pdf.
9. Regulation 2157/2001 of 8 October 2001 on the statute for a European company.

10. See I. Verlinden, A. Smits, B. Lieben, Intellectual Property Rights from a Transfer Pricing Perspective, Belgium, PricewaterhouseCoopers Tax Consultants cbvba, 2004.
11. This comparative list is the result of a telephone questionnaire within the PricewaterhouseCoopers network and shows the status of the legislation around mid-2003.
12. As from 2006, reduction is planned to 20% for the federal corporate tax rate.
13. As from 2005, 20% corporate income tax rate.
14. Likely to decrease to 26% as from 2005.

Appendix

Standard Complaint form

COMPLAINT (1)
TO THE COMMISSION OF THE EUROPEAN
COMMUNITIES CONCERNING FAILURE
TO COMPLY WITH
COMMUNITY LAW

1. Surname and forename of complainant:

2. Where appropriate, represented by:

3. Nationality:

4. Address or registered office (2):

5. Telephone/fax/e-mail address:

6. Field and place(s) of activity:

---

(1) You are not obliged to use this form. You may also submit a complaint by ordinary letter, but it is in your interest to include as much relevant information as possible. You can send this form by ordinary mail to the following address:

Commission of the European Communities
(Attn: Secretary-General)
Rue de la Loi/Wetstraat 200
B-1049 Brussels

You may also hand in the form at any of the Commission's representative offices in the Member States. The form is accessible on the European Union's Internet server:
http://europa.eu.int/comm/sg/lexcomm. To be admissible, your complaint has to relate to an infringement of Community law by a Member State.
(2) You should inform the Commission of any change of address and any event likely to affect the handling of your complaint.

7. Member State or public body alleged by the complainant not to have complied with Community law:

8. Fullest possible account of facts giving rise to complaint:

9. As far as possible, specify the provisions of Community law (Treaties, Regulations, Directives, Decisions, etc.) which the complainant considers to have been infringed by the Member State concerned:

10. Where appropriate, mention the involvement of a Community funding scheme (with references if possible) from which the Member State concerned benefits or stands to benefit, in relation to the facts giving rise to the complaint:

11. Details of any approaches already made to the Commission's services (if possible, attach copies of correspondence):

12. Details of any approaches already made to other Community bodies or authorities (e.g. European Parliament Committee on Petitions, European Ombudsman). If possible, give the reference assigned to the complainant's approach by the body concerned:

13. Approaches already made to national authorities, whether central, regional or local (if possible, attach copies of correspondence):

    13.1. Administrative approaches (e.g. complaint to the relevant national administrative authorities, whether central, regional or local, and/or to a national or regional ombudsman):

    13.2. Recourse to national courts or other procedures (e.g. arbitration or conciliation). (State whether there has already been a decision or award and attach a copy if appropriate):

14. Specify any documents or evidence which may be submitted in support of the complaint, including the national measures concerned (attach copies):

15. Confidentiality (tick one box) (1):

    ☐   "I authorise the Commission to disclose my identity in its contacts with the authorities of the Member State against which the complaint is made."

◻ "I request the Commission not to disclose my identity in its contacts with the authorities of the Member State against which the complaint is made."

16. Place, date and signature of complainant/representative:

(*Explanatory note to appear on back of complaint form*)

Each Member State is responsible for the implementation of Community law (adoption of implementing measures before a specified deadline, conformity and correct application) within its own legal system. Under the Treaties, the Commission of the European Communities is responsible for ensuring that Community law is correctly applied. Consequently, where a Member State fails to comply with Community law, the Commission has powers of its own (action for non-compliance) to try to bring the infringement to an end and, if necessary, may refer the case to the Court of Justice of the European Communities. The Commission takes whatever action it deems appropriate in response to either a complaint or indications of infringements which it detects itself.

Non-compliance means failure by a Member State to fulfil its obligations under Community law, whether by action or by omission. The term State is taken to mean the Member State which infringes Community law, irrespective of the authority – central, regional or local – to which the non-compliance is attributable.

Anyone may lodge a complaint with the Commission against a Member State about any measure (law, regulation or administrative action) or practice which they consider incompatible with a provision or a principle of Community law. Complainants do not have to demonstrate a formal interest in bringing proceedings. Neither do they have to prove that they are principally and directly concerned by the infringement complained of. To be admissible, a complaint has to relate to an infringement of Community law by a Member State. It should be borne in mind that the Commission's services may decide whether or not further action should be taken on a complaint in the light of the rules and priorities laid down by the Commission for opening and pursuing infringement procedures.

Anyone who considers a measure (law, regulation or administrative action) or administrative practice to be incompatible with Community law is invited, before or at the same time as lodging a complaint with the Commission, to

---

(1) Please note that the disclosure of your identity by the Commission's services may, in some cases, be indispensable to the handling of the complaint.

seek redress from the national administrative or judicial authorities (including the national or regional ombudsman and/or arbitration and conciliation procedures available). The Commission advises the prior use of such national means of redress, whether administrative, judicial or other, before lodging a complaint with the Commission, because of the advantages they may offer for complainants.

By using the means of redress available at national level, complainants should, as a rule, be able to assert their rights more directly and more personally (e.g. a court order to an administrative body, repeal of a national decision and/or damages) than they would following an infringement procedure successfully brought by the Commission which may take some time. Indeed, before referring a case to the Court of Justice, the Commission is obliged to hold a series of contacts with the Member State concerned to try to terminate the infringement.

Furthermore, any finding of an infringement by the Court of Justice has no impact on the rights of the complainant, since it does not serve to resolve individual cases. It merely obliges the Member State to comply with Community law. More specifically, any individual claims for damages would have to be brought by complainants before the national courts.

The following administrative guarantees exist for the benefit of the complainant:

(a) Once it has been registered with the Commission's Secretariat-General, any complaint found admissible will be assigned an official reference number. An acknowledgment bearing the reference number, which should be quoted in any correspondence, will immediately be sent to the complainant. However, the assignment of an official reference number to a complaint does not necessarily mean that an infringement procedure will be opened against the Member State in question.

(b) Where the Commission's services make representations to the authorities of the Member State against which the complaint has been made, they will abide by the choice made by the complainant in Section 15 of this form.

(c) The Commission will endeavour to take a decision on the substance (either to open infringement proceedings or to close the case) within twelve months of registration of the complaint with its Secretariat-General.

(d) The complainant will be notified in advance by the relevant department if it plans to propose that the Commission close the case. The Commission's services will keep the complainant informed of the course of any infringement procedure.

PricewaterhouseCoopers EU enlargement contact details

AUTHORS

Ine Lejeune
Partner, Leader EU Accession team
Tel: +32 (0) 9 268 93 00
E-mail: ine.lejeune@pwc.be

Walter Van Denberghe
Senior Manager, Indirect Tax department
Tel: + 32 (0) 2 710 93 52
E-mail walter.van.denberghe@pwc.be

CONTRIBUTORS

Kurt De Haen
Director, Corporate Tax department
Tel: +32 (0) 2 710 93 54
E-mail: kurt.de.haen@pwc.be

Dirk Aerts
Director, Indirect Tax department
Tel: +32 (0) 3 259 32 14
E-mail: dirk.aerts@pwc.be

Steve Cosyn
Senior Consultant, Indirect Tax department
Tel: +420 2 5115 2668
E-mail: steve.cosyn@pwc.be

Daniel Evrard
Partner, Global Risk Management Services
Tel: +32 (0)2 710 72 00
E-mail: daniel.evrard@pwc.be

Luc Wittebolle
Manager, Global Risk Management Services
Tel: +32 (0)3 259 31 96
E-mail: luc.wittebolle@pwc.be

Yvette De smedt
Legal Counsel, HR Law
Tel: +32 (0)3 259 31 57
E-mail: yvette.de.smedt@pwc.be

Bart Lieben
Legal Counsel, Company & Contract Law
Tel: +32 (0)3 259 31 35.
E-mail: bart.lieben@pwc.be

EU ACCESSION CORE TEAM

Antoni Turczynowicz

Tel: +420 251 151 111

E-mail: antoni.turczynowicz@cz.pwc.com

Monika Diekert

Tel: +49 30 26 360

E-mail: monika.diekert@de.pwc.com

ACCESSION COUNTRY CONTACTS

Bulgaria Georgy Sarakostov

Tel: +359 2 91003

E-mail: georgy.sarakostov@bu.pwc.com

Cyprus Panikos N. Tsiailis

Tel: +357 22555000

E-mail: panikos.n.tsiailis@cy.pwc.com

Czech Republic Ian Glogoski

Tel: +420 251 151 111

E-mail: ian.glogoski@cz.pwc.com

Estonia Aare Kurist

Tel: +372 614 1800

E-mail: aare.kurist@ee.pwc.com

Hungary Tamás Lőcsei

Tel: +36 1 461 9358

E-mail: tamas.locsei@hu.pwc.com

Latvia Zlata Elksnina

Tel: +371 709 4400

E-mail: zlata.elksnina@lv.pwc.com

Cameron Greaves

Tel: +371 709 4400

E-mail: cameron.greaves@lv.pwc.com

Lithuania Gintaras Balcius

Tel: +370 5 239 2300

E-mail: gintaras.balcius@lt.pwc.com

Malta David Ferry

Tel: +356 2124 7000

E-mail: david.ferry@mt.pwc.com

Poland Miroslaw Barszcz

Tel: +48 22 523 4000

E-mail: miroslaw.barszcz@pl.pwc.com

Romania Andrew Begg

Tel: +40 21 202 8500

E-mail: andrew.begg@ro.pwc.com

Slovakia Tadeja Brencic

Tel: +386 1 475 0166

E-mail: tadeja.brencic@si.pwc.com

Slovenia Andreja Skofic

Tel: +386 1 475 0100

E-mail: andreja.skofic@si.pwc.com

Index

Index compiled by Annette Musker